TRIAL
of the
CENTURY
YOU BE THE JUROR

AN INTERACTIVE TRIAL GUIDE

ROBERT J. WALTON

WITH F. LaGARD SMITH

Marcon³
LIMITED

Trial of the Century

©1994 by Robert J. Walton

Published by Marcon³ Limited
770-101 Wooten Road
Colorado Springs, CO 80915

Cover design and Typeset by Multnomah Graphics, Portland, Oregon

Cover Photo © ALLSPORT USA/Gary Newkirk, 1994

Printed in the United States of America

ISBN # 1-886547-00-9

Library of Congress # 94-73459

94 95 96 97 98 99 00 01 02 03 -- 10 9 8 7 6 5 4 3 2 1

Contents

Appendices

With Gratitude

I needed a chapter; I settled for this brief page. There are literally dozens of people to whom I am indebted for their support on this project.

First, I wish to thank my wonderful family, the Waltons. Over the years, they have endured far too many cancelled trips and second-hand cars while I have busily pursued a unique and demanding legal career. A special thanks to my lovely wife, Rene, who has made it all work.

There is one person without whom this book would never have been possible. For your vision, energy, and commitment to this project, thank you, Joseph Finney. Nor could I possibly overlook your assistant, Debbie Henderson.

I also want to thank numerous friends who, in one way or another, assisted in the completion of this book. Thank you, Don and Terry Goldblum, Tom and Michele Ogdon, Harry and Joan McCarthy, and Patsy Bakunin. Thank you, also, Don Johnson and Al Gonzales, Jim Connard, Charlie Knight, Joan and Robert Jones, Robert Brodt, Jim Eveld, Ruben Carbajal, Gaeton Fonzi, and Robert Beard. And thank you, Myra Harris and your research paralegal, Scott Stern. To all of you, and so many more who provided insight and inspiration, God bless!

Special appreciation goes to Robert and Susan Taylor of the Taylor Resource Center in Colorado Springs, and to Carol Chase and Tammy Ditmore for their assistance in the editing process.

Finally, I want to especially thank F. LaGard Smith and Harry Caldwell, professors of law at Pepperdine University School of Law, whose contributions significantly enhanced this book.

—Robert J. Walton

1

Murder, Mystery, and Intrigue—You Must Decide

An Interactive Trial Guide

*It's the greatest murder trial of the century—
about every two years another one of 'em comes along.*

—Frances Noyes Hart
The Bellamy Trial (1928)

It is being called the trial of the century. The case of *The People of the State of California v. Orenthal James Simpson, aka O.J. Simpson* has mesmerized a global audience of countless millions who watch in disbelief as the man they affectionately know simply as "O.J." plays in the most important game of his life. But this is not just another game. A defeat on the gridiron of America's criminal justice system could mean that there will never be another season for O.J. This is the big one, and, for O.J., the trial of his life.

You'd have to be living on another planet not to know that O.J. Simpson—football legend, superstar actor, and popular media personality—faces charges of First Degree Murder in the brutal slaying of his ex-wife, Nicole Brown Simpson, and Nicole's friend, Ronald Lyle Goldman. The discovery of their slashed and bloodied bodies outside Nicole's westside Los Angeles condominium on June 12, 1994, initiated a police investigation which quickly focused on O.J. and eventually led to his arrest.

In the absence of eyewitnesses, what was it that pointed the finger of suspicion at O.J.? Was it the physical evidence gathered by police at the crime scene itself and later at O.J.'s Brentwood estate? (There was early talk of bloody gloves, hair, and footprints.) Was it the fact that O.J. was strangely late meeting his limo for a flight to Chicago that night? Or was it, perhaps, something he might have said to police during a three-hour interrogation after his return to L.A. the following morning?

Everybody knows there has to be a motive. No one brutally kills a fellow human being without having at least what they themselves believe to be an awfully good reason for it. Enter, stage left, what may be the most damning evidence of all—and that which most shocked O.J.'s admirers. The evidence? A history of spousal abuse, and, in particular, a frantic 911 call in which an enraged O.J. was heard verbally threatening Nicole.

Could it be, then, that the killing was cold-blooded revenge for Nicole's refusal to reconcile with him? Was it, rather, a crime of passion when Goldman, whom O.J. apparently disliked, suddenly appeared at Nicole's house? Indeed, did O.J. have anything at all to do with their deaths? For, despite an embarrassingly-obvious motive, and despite whatever physical evidence the police may have found, from the very beginning O.J. steadfastly denied any knowledge of the double-homicide.

After all, does someone murder his ex-wife only four hours after both attending their eight-year-old daughter's dance recital? Is it likely that the time frame of events on that evening would even allow for his having been at the scene of the crime when the deaths occurred? Why was there not more blood all over O.J.? Whoever did this supremely nasty killing must surely have been awash in his victims' blood. And, mystery of mysteries, where is the murder weapon?

No easy case, this. No smoking gun; no tearful confession. Just questions. And drama unparalleled in the annals of crime. For years to come, it will be one of those days like Pearl Harbor, J.F.K.'s assassination, and the space shuttle Challenger disaster. Odds are, you'll never forget where you were when the television networks suddenly dropped normal programming to show the now-famous low-speed freeway chase, as life-long friend Al Cowlings drove his white Bronco fifty miles along L.A. freeways with O.J. reportedly holding a gun to his own head. And everyone wondered, "Could this be the act of an innocent man?" With collective sadness, an entire nation cried, "Say it isn't so, O.J."

❧

What If You Were a Juror?

When the last of the evidence is in, and the final impassioned arguments have been made, it will all come down to one dramatic moment of truth: either the O.J. Simpson we all know and love is a maniacal killer capable of slashing two people to death, or he is wholly innocent of the charge and stands wrongfully accused in the worst miscarriage of justice of our time. But who is to decide?

In the real trial, of course, the decision will be left to a jury of twelve quite ordinary citizens, whose own lives will have been forever altered by one of the most grueling trials ever to take place. But in this book, YOU WILL DECIDE. For better or for worse, O.J.'s fate is in *your* hands. As a juror, you no longer have the luxury of idle speculation like everybody else. The eyes of the world are watching, and millions are holding their breaths with anticipation as you return to the jury box to read out your verdict. And, of course, no one is more anxious than O.J. himself

Are you ready for such a responsibility? Can you give O.J. Simpson the fair trial to which he is entitled? Have you already made up your mind, based on the unprecedented barrage of media coverage?

The purpose of this book is to serve as your own personal trial guide. Unlike the many sensational books which undoubtedly will continue to spew forth from the popular press, *The Trial of the Century* has been specifically designed to give you a front row seat in the jury box, and to help you understand the trial process as it unfolds before you. Apart from sitting in the courtroom itself, this book unquestionably is the best seat in the house.

Whether you watch every minute of gavel-to-gavel television coverage or are able to catch only regular updates and evening wrap-ups, this book promises to provide one of the most interesting experiences of your life: *being a juror in the O.J. case.* And if at any point in the trial the judge should bar cameras from the courtroom (as he has a duty to do if their presence threatens Simpson's right to a fair trial), then this book could be your *only* "live-action" window to the proceedings.

☙❧

Not Just Another O.J. Book

Unlike any other "O.J. book," *The Trial of the Century* is interactive. At each step of the proceedings, you will not only get a crash course in trial law to help you navigate through all the confusing legalese, but you will also be invited to personally participate in the decision-making process. For example, you will have the opportunity to complete sample questions from the 79-page questionnaire filled out by the 304 prospective jurors initially screened in the case. You will get to summarize the testimony of each witness and evaluate for yourself each item of physical evidence. And at the end of the trial you will be asked to sit in on jury deliberations and cast your own crucial vote.

With the help of this book, you will quickly and easily be introduced to criminal trial procedure, legal terminology, prosecution and defense strategy, and a wide range of motions and objections. You will also become a fledgling expert in the field of scientific proof, including hair comparisons, blood samples, and the highly controversial DNA analysis test. Because of its sheer educational value, this is one book where the melody of understanding will linger on long after the music of the trial has ended. And along the way, you will surely gain a new appreciation for America's love affair with the jury system and the adversarial trial process.

Indeed, the book's lasting value could well be its contribution to learning, especially on the part of students who are unfamiliar with trial procedure. Long after the final verdict is in, the notoriety surrounding this case will likely prove to be the best incentive yet to encourage young people to explore what criminal justice in America is all about.

Until the real trial is over, however, you have a unique opportunity to interact with it in an unprecedented way—through the eyes of a juror. Perhaps you will wish to heighten the experience by getting together with a group of your friends and having your own jury deliberations. As each of you looks back over the notes you have made in *The Trial of the Century*, you can discuss and debate each point. Were the witnesses credible? Do you believe that the hair and blood samples were compelling evidence? How do you feel about DNA testing? Whose version of the time sequence do you accept? If these questions don't provide a lively and informative evening, nothing will!

Now that you are set for one of the most fascinating experiences you will ever have, we need first of all to make sure that you are *qualified* to be a juror in this case, and that you are actually *selected* to serve. After all, no one just walks in off the street and volunteers for the job!

Your role as a juror must begin where it began for the actual jurors in the case—with a Summons to Appear. You will find it in your "mailbox" as the next chapter begins.

Welcome to the trial of the century.

2

You are Summoned to Appear

꒰꒱

Jury Panel Selection

The jury system puts a ban upon intelligence and honesty, and a premium upon ignorance, stupidity and perjury.

—Mark Twain

"By order of the Superior Court for the County of Los Angeles, you are hereby summoned to appear for jury duty."

Had you been one of a thousand citizens in Los Angeles County who received that notice in the early fall of 1994, you very likely would have been asked to participate in one of the largest jury screening processes ever to take place. Upon arrival at the downtown Criminal Courts Building, you would have had to make your way through an army of media personnel into crowded, uncomfortable rooms designated for prospective jurors.

Once there, you would have been informed that you were being considered as a potential juror in the case of *People v. O.J. Simpson,* a case that could literally last for months. If you considered your unique opportunity to be a juror in "the trial of the century" to be good news, the bad news is that, if selected from the panel to serve in the case, you could quite possibly be cut off from all contact with your family, friends, and employment for the duration of the trial. And that could stretch into several months.

This enforced isolation of the jury is called *sequestration*. The purpose of sequestering the jury is to shield them from the media and anyone else who might intentionally or inadvertently influence their decision. It is for the judge to decide whether sequestration is needed in order to insure a fair trial for the accused. In the event this extraordinary custodial device is ordered by the judge, then you and the other jurors—all strangers—would be locked up twenty-four hours a day. From your hotel rooms, you would be herded to and from the courtroom, almost as if you yourselves were under arrest.

For some prospective jurors, any lengthy trial—even if there were no sequestration—would mean extreme hardship. Suppose, for example, that there are relatives who need care; or a professional licensing exam to be taken; or, if you're lucky, non-refundable tickets already purchased for an around-the-world luxury cruise. For those who find themselves in a lower tax bracket, there may be the economic burden of loss of employment to consider. Many companies will not compensate their employees for more than ten days of jury duty. Who can afford to live for months on the paltry five dollars a day that is paid for jury service?

⚘

Phase One: Would It Be a Hardship?

Here now is your first opportunity to personally interact with the O.J. case. Knowing what you now know about the potential rewards and risks of being further considered for the jury panel, are there any hardships which you would bring to the Court's attention? Be careful. Any hardships which you list here might well preclude your going any further as a juror in the trial of the century. On the other hand, you should be honest and disclose any legitimate hardships. (For purposes of this book, of course, you will not be disqualified whatever you write down.)

I wish to be excused from jury duty because of the

following hardship it would impose:_____

_____

_____

Despite the unusual commitment which serving in the Simpson case would involve, the surprise is that relatively few (only 90) actual prospective jurors in the case claimed hardship. Compared with previous cases, the Court discovered that there were 25 to 30 percent more jurors who said they would be able to serve. But what does that eagerness to serve say about these "volunteer jurors?"

Does it mean that their lives are so dull they would do anything to "get a life?" Is there a risk that they might want to serve, simply because they could cash in on their notoriety after the trial has ended? A positive answer to either of those questions hardly gives one a great reason to have faith in the system.

~×~

Phase Two: Screening for Bias

Now that those who have pleaded hardship have been excused (following personal interviews with the judge and lawyers), there is the enormous task of screening the remaining pool of prospective jurors for potential bias. In a case such as this, there are many hidden biases which everyone concerned with the case would like to expose. Naturally, the race factor is of concern. O.J., a black man, is accused of killing two white victims. Since one of those victims was his ex-wife, the issue of interracial marriage becomes important. Then there is the spousal abuse factor. What kind of emotional response will O.J.'s violent history with Nicole evoke in this juror or that?

For some issues—particularly those dealing with the physical evidence to be introduced—everyone wants to know individual attitudes toward the police (who gathered the evidence), expert witnesses (who tested the evidence), and the lawyers themselves (who will be questioning the evidence). How will each juror respond to complex issues like DNA testing? Do they have any background in science? Are they well educated?

These and many other concerns prompted the judge and lawyers to formulate a 79-page Juror Questionnaire to be used as a basis for evaluating the 304 people who, as it turned out, would comprise the jury panel in this case. (From that panel, twelve jurors and up to fifteen alternates would eventually be chosen to hear the case.)

You now have the opportunity to complete a Sample Juror Questionnaire, drawn from the exact questions used in the Simpson case. Approximately 75 of the 294 questions have been selected as representative of the questionnaire. (Sheer length prohibited the inclusion of every question.) As you will see, in addition to the expected personal background questions there are also a number of attitudinal questions, aimed less at biographical information and more at the prospective juror's subjective feelings.

Remember that, if you were a real juror, you would be completing the following questions under penalty of perjury. So your own answers should be true and correct to the best of your knowledge.

~×~

SAMPLE JUROR QUESTIONNAIRE

(Question Numbers Correspond to Actual Questionnaire)

JUROR NUMBER ....

1.   Age: ....

2.   Are you male .... or female .... ?

3.   What is your race?   (please circle)

   a) White/Caucasian   b) Black/African American

   c) Hispanic/Latino   d) Asian/Pacific Islander

   e) Other (please state) ....

4.   Marital status:

   .... Single and never married

   .... Single, but living with non-marital mate

   For how long? ....

   .... Currently married

   Length of marriage ....

   .... Divorced

   When divorced: ....

   Length of previous marriage ....

   Did you initiate the divorce?

   No .... Yes ....

   .... Widowed

   Length of marriage: ....

12.   Which of the following best describes your current type of residence?

   .... Rental apartment   .... Own apartment or condo

   .... Own home   .... Own mobile home

   .... Rental house

.... Rental (other)

.... Other (specify) ....

19. Are you currently employed outside the home?

No .... Yes ....

26. Have you ever worked in the entertainment industry in any capacity?

No .... Yes ....

If yes, please describe: ....

....

28. Have you ever worked in journalism or the news industry in any capacity?

No .... Yes ....

30. Have you ever worked in a laboratory or in any medical research or testing facility?

No .... Yes ....

31. What is the last level of education you completed?

.... Grade school or less

Please circle one: 1 - 2 - 3 - 4 - 5 - 6

.... Junior High School

Please circle one: 7 - 8 - 9

.... High School

Please circle one: 10 - 11 - 12

.... Technical, Vocational or Business school

For the above answers, please indicate number of years attended, field of study and any degrees achieved:

....

....

.... College

Please circle one: 13 - 14 - 15 - 16

Please indicate degree(s) achieved, if any:

....

.... Post graduate work

Please indicate degree achieved:

....

39. While in school, what was your favorite subject?

....

40. What was your least favorite subject?

....

41. Have you ever served in the military?

Yes .... No ....

45. While serving in the military, did you ever see someone being killed or who had been killed?

Yes .... No ....

If yes, please describe:

....

....

69. Do you believe that a defendant in a criminal case should testify or produce some evidence to prove that he or she is not guilty?

Yes .... No ....

If yes, please explain why: ....

....

72. Why do you feel that you would be a good juror for this case?

....

....

....

74. As part of your service on this case, the Court will order you not to read, listen to or watch any accounts of this case reported by television, radio or other news media. Will you have any difficulty following this order?

    Yes .... No .... Do not know ....

75. If you are selected as a trial juror in this case the Court will order you not to discuss this case with *anyone* unless and until permitted to do so by the Court. Will you have any difficulty in following this order?

    Yes .... No .... Do not know ....

78. Because this case has received extensive publicity many, if not all, of you will have heard and/or read something about this case at some time. It is vitally important that you truthfully answer the following questions concerning what you have learned about this case from the media. There are no right or wrong answers. There should only be truthful and forthright answers.

    Please indicate from what sources you have learned about this case (check as many as apply):

    .... Television   .... Books

    .... Newspapers   .... Tabloids

    .... Radio   .... Have had conversations w/ others

    .... Magazines   .... Have overheard others discuss it

    .... Other (please specify): ....

    ....

The preliminary hearing on this case was broadcast live on both radio and television from June 30, 1994 through July 8, 1994.

81. Did you watch any portion of the preliminary hearing on television?

    Yes .... No ....

92. Which of the following best describes how you would describe the media coverage overall?

    .... Biased in favor of the prosecution

.... Biased in favor of the defense

.... Basically fair to both sides

93. If you have discussed this case with friends and/or relatives, do your friends/relatives overall seem to lean toward thinking that O.J. Simpson is:

.... Not guilty

.... Probably not guilty

.... Not sure

.... Probably guilty

.... Guilty

101. Did you call the police, the judge, or either the defense or prosecution "800" hotline number regarding this case?

Yes .... No ....

If yes, please explain: ....

....

103. What do you think about jurors appearing on talk shows after serving on a criminal trial jury?

....

....

....

110. Based on what you know of this case thus far, what are your views concerning the LAPD?

....

....

....

111. Have you followed any criminal cases in the media in the last 5 years? (e.g. Menendez, Damian Williams [Reginald Denny Beating Case], Rodney King, etc.)

Yes .... No ....

114.   Have you visited the location of 875 So. Bundy since the date of the killings of Nicole Brown Simpson and Ronald Goldman?

Yes .... No ....

If yes, how many times have you gone there? ....

Please describe your reason(s) for going there: ....

....

127.   What is you opinion, if any, about prosecuting attorneys in general?

....

....

....

128.   What are your opinions, if any, about criminal defense attorneys in general?

....

....

....

131.   What was your first reaction to hearing that O.J. Simpson was a suspect in this case?

....

....

....

135.   Did you see O.J. Simpson play football in college or as a professional football player?

Yes .... No ....

If yes, describe the circumstances and your feelings toward O.J. Simpson as a football player:

....

....

....

137. Have you seen O.J. Simpson as he appeared in movies such as *Roots* or *Naked Gun 2 1/2* ?

Yes .... No ....

If yes, describe your feeling toward O.J. Simpson based upon your observations of him as an actor:

....

....

....

138. Based upon your feelings toward O.J. Simpson, are you inclined to believe him guilty of the crimes with which he has been charged?

Yes .... No ....

Please explain: ....

....

....

....

139. Based upon your feelings toward O.J. Simpson, are you inclined to believe him not guilty of the crimes with which he has been charged?

Yes .... No ....

Please explain: ....

....

....

....

143. Have you ever asked a celebrity for an autograph?

Yes .... No ....

If yes, whom did you ask: ....

....

....

....

145. Please name the person for whom you are a great fan and describe why you are a fan of that person.

    ....

146. Will you hold the prosecution to a higher standard than is legally required because the defendant is:

    African/American?   Yes .... No ....

    Wealthy   Yes .... No ....

    Famous   Yes .... No ....

148. Do you feel you know O.J. Simpson because of his background and fame?

    Yes .... No ....

    Please explain: ....

    ....

    ....

    ....

    ....

151. Have you seen, heard or read any portion of the freeway pursuit of O.J. Simpson and Al Cowlings?

    Yes .... No ....

    A. If yes, approximately how many hours/minutes of the freeway pursuit did you watch on television or listen to on the radio?

    ....

    ....

    B. What did you think about the chase?

    ....

    ....

153. Have you seen, read, or heard any portion of the 911 calls made by Nicole Brown Simpson?

    Yes .... No ....

If yes, what did you think about the calls:

....

....

156. Have you purchased, or otherwise obtained any commercial item relating to this case? (For example a T-shirt, book, video or trading card)

Yes .... No ....

If yes, please describe the item(s) and what was depicted on the item(s).

....

....

160. Do you have any affiliation of any kind with the University of Southern California?

Yes .... No ....

If yes, please explain: ....

....

162. Have you ever experienced domestic violence in your home either growing up or as an adult?

Yes .... No ....

Please describe the circumstances and what impact it has had on you:

....

....

....

....

....

....

....

....

170. When is violence an appropriate response to domestic trouble?

_____

_____

_____

173. Do you think that violence that occurs in the home or between adult intimates should be looked at differently than violence that occurs between strangers?

_____

_____

_____

_____

175. Do you believe people with professional lives that involve physical confrontation or the use of violence are more susceptible to imposing violent solutions in their personal lives?

Yes .... No ....

Please explain your answer: _____

_____

_____

_____

181. "Male professional athletes who participate in contact sports are more aggressive towards women."

.... Strongly agree

.... Agree

.... No opinion

.... Disagree

.... Strongly disagree

183. Have you ever experienced fear of a person of another race?

.... Yes .... No

If yes, please explain the circumstances: ....

....

....

184.   How do you feel about interracial marriage?

....

....

....

185.   How would you feel if a close family member or relative married someone of a different race?

.... Would favor it.

.... Would not oppose it.

.... Would oppose it.

Please explain: ....

....

....

186.   Have you ever dated a person of a different race?

Yes .... No ....

If yes, how did you feel about it:

....

....

188.   "Some races and/or ethnic groups tend to be more violent than others."

.... Strongly agree

.... Agree

.... Disagree

.... Strongly disagree

.... No opinion

If you wish to do so, please explain your answer:

....

....

The ability of DNA analysis to prove the identity of the person(s) whose blood or hair is found at a crime scene has been the subject of some television and radio shows, and magazine and newspaper articles.

The following questions pertain to this subject.

193. Before the Simpson case, did you read any book, articles or magazines concerning DNA analysis?

Yes .... No ....

If yes, please name the book, magazine, newspaper or other periodical where you read about it and briefly describe what you recall having read.

....

....

196. What is your view concerning the reliability of DNA analysis to accurately identify a person as the possible source of blood or hair found at a crime scene?

.... Very reliable .... Not very reliable .... Don't know

.... Somewhat reliable .... Unreliable

Please explain your answer: ....

....

....

....

....

201. A. Do you have a religious affiliation or preference?

Yes .... No ....

B. If yes, please describe: _____

C. How important would you say religion is in your life?

_____

D. Would anything about your religious beliefs make it difficult for you to sit in judgment of another person?

_____ Yes _____ No _____ Possibly

E. How often do you attend religious services?

_____

202. What is your political affiliation? (please circle)

1) Democrat 2) Republican 3) Independent

4) Other (please specify) _____

204. Did you vote in the June, 1994 primary elections?

Yes _____ No _____

206. Have you ever consulted with an expert other than a medical doctor?

Yes _____ No _____

If yes, please specify the type of expert and the purpose for which s/he was consulted.

_____

_____

_____

211. Have you ever provided a urine sample to be analyzed for any purpose?

Yes _____ No _____

If yes, did you feel comfortable with the accuracy of the results?

Yes _____ No _____

212. Do you believe it is immoral or wrong to do an amniocentesis to determine whether a fetus has a genetic defect?

Yes _____ No _____ Don't have an opinion _____

Please explain: ....

....

216. Please check the answer which best describes how comfortable you usually feel dealing with mathematical concepts:

.... Usually very comfortable

.... Usually fairly comfortable

.... Usually fairly uncomfortable

.... Usually very uncomfortable

217. Do you have any knowledge of the field of population genetics?

Yes .... No ....

If yes, please describe your understanding of this subject and how it relates to DNA analysis:

....

....

....

221. Are you or have you been a member of Neighborhood Watch?

Yes .... No ....

If yes, what was the nature of your involvement? ....

....

222. Do you have: (please check)

Security bars .... Alarms ....

Guard dog .... Weapons for self-protection ....

224. Have you ever been a victim of a crime? Yes .... No ....

If yes, how many times? ....

What kind of crime(s)? ....

....

....

228. Do you feel the job the police did on it was:

Satisfactory .... Why? ....

....

Unsatisfactory .... Why? ....

....

244. What types of books do you prefer? (Example: Non-fiction, historical, romance, espionage, mystery)

....

....

246. Which "news" magazines, if any, do you read on either a regular or occasional basis?

.... Time

.... Newsweek

.... People

.... The New Yorker

.... Los Angeles Magazine

.... Other. Please specify:

....

....

249. Which tabloids do you read on an occasional or regular basis?

		Occasionally	Regularly
....	The National Enquirer	....	....
....	The Star	....	....
....	The Globe	....	....
....	The National Examiner	....	....
....	Other: Please specify:		

....

252. Do you ever watch TV programs that show real life police activities such as "Cops", "America's Most Wanted", or "Unsolved Mysteries"?

Yes .... No ....

If yes, Very often .... Occasionally .... Almost never ....

[Note: Questions 248, 249, and 252, following, were out of sequence and repetitive on the original questionnaire.]

248. Do you watch any of the afternoon "talk" shows? Such as "Maury Povich", "Donahue", "Oprah", "Sally Jessy Raphael", etc.

Yes .... No ....

If yes, how often? (please check)

Daily .... Occasionally ....

249. Do you watch any of the early evening "tabloid news" programs? Such as "Hard Copy", "Current Affair", "American Journal", etc.

Yes .... No ....

If yes, how often? (please check)

Daily .... Occasionally ....

252. What are your leisure time interests, hobbies and activities?

....

....

255. What groups or organizations do you belong to now or have you belonged to for a significant period of time in the past? (For example, bowling leagues, church groups, AA, Sierra Club, MECLA, National Rifle Association, ACLU, YWCA, YMCA, PTA, NAACP, etc.)

A. Now: ....

B. Previously: ....

Have you served as an officer in any one of these groups?

Yes .... No ....

If yes, which group(s): ....

....

265.   Are you a fan of the USC Trojans football team?

Yes .... No ....

If yes, for how many years? ....

269.   During football season, do you watch Monday night football: (Check the one answer which most applies:)

.... Every Monday night, without fail

.... Almost every Monday night

.... Frequently

.... Occasionally

.... Seldom

.... Almost never

.... Never

275.   Does playing sports build an individual's character?

Yes .... No ....

Please explain your answer whether you answer yes or no:

....

....

....

....

276.   Do you seek out positions of leadership (please check answer)

Always .... Often .... Seldom .... Never ....

279.   Do you think celebrities are held less responsible for their actions than the average person?

Yes .... No ....

281.   Do you own any special knives (other than for cooking), such as for hunting or pen knives?

Yes .... No ....

If yes, please describe the knife or knives and your reasons for owning it or them:

....

....

....

285.   Would you like to be a juror in this case?

Yes .... No ....

Please explain:

....

....

....

....

....

....

291.   If you are selected to serve as a juror on this case, would you be concerned about reactions to the verdict by:

Friends?	Yes	No ....
Relatives?	Yes	No ....
The media?	Yes	No ....
People in the community?	Yes	No ....

If yes, what kind of concern(s) do you have? Please explain:

....

....

....

....

....

293. Is there any matter not covered by this questionnaire that you think the attorneys or Court might want to know about you when considering you as a juror in this case?

....

....

....

....

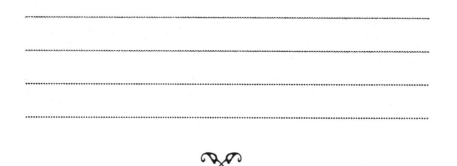

Based upon the answers you have now given to the questionnaire, the Court and the lawyers will determine whether you should be included in the panel of jurors from which the actual trial jurors will be chosen. Have you fudged your answers so as to sway them one way or the other? Do you think you have passed the test? What, if anything, do you think might cause you to be eliminated from the panel?

....

....

....

....

Other Background Investigation

Suppose at this point that you have in fact been selected to be one of the jury panel members. There is yet another process of evaluation that will take place before you step foot into the courtroom for the final elimination round. Unbeknownst to you, investigators for both prosecution and defense may be sent to scout out your neighborhood and your home, looking for anything which might tip them off as to what kind of a juror you might be. (Due to the great expense involved, this kind of investigation takes place only in high-profile, well-financed cases.)

How would you complete the investigator's field report on yourself?

Field Report On Prospective Juror

1. Character of neighborhood ....
   ....

2. Description of home ....
   ....

3. Condition of lawn, driveway (neat or cluttered?) ....
   ....

4. Type and condition of vehicle/s ....
   ....

5. Messages on any bumper stickers ....
   ....

6. Personalized license plate ....

7. "Neighborhood Watch" or other signs on house or in yard
   ....

8. Other indications which might reveal bias ....
   ....
   ....

   One's economic status and ethnic comfort zone can usually be determined right away, depending upon the neighborhood in which he or she lives. Upper-middle-class white neighborhoods may suggest a bias against lower economic and non-white ethnic groups. A well-kept house with a neatly-mowed lawn tends to indicate responsibility, and, typically, a more conservative perspective. "Neighborhood Watch" signs may hint of "law and order" types, whereas rainbows and crystals hanging in the window might point to more independent-minded free spirits.

   Pay special attention to those personalized license plates and bumper stickers. You can tell a lot by the ones which read: "Abortion Stops a Beating Heart" or "Pro-Child, Pro-Family, Pro-Choice." On the political side, who do you think you are dealing with when the sticker reads, "Don't Blame Me, I Voted for Bush" or simply "Clinton/Gore"? One of the more interesting stickers from the point of view of juror selection is the one which reads, "Question Authority." But who knows what goes through the mind of someone whose sticker proudly proclaims, "My karma just ran over your dogma"!

Time For Self-Evaluation

For the moment, step out of your shoes as a potential juror and assume the roles of judge and lawyer. Knowing your own answers in the Juror Questionnaire, and knowing how you would complete the investigator's field report, what kind of a juror do you think you would be?

A. Do you appear to have any particular biases? ....

....

....

B. Does it look like you could sit as a fair and impartial juror despite any apparent biases?

Yes .... No ....

C. If you were the judge, would you feel comfortable having a person like yourself on the jury panel?

Yes .... No ....

D. Which side would most want you to be on the jury panel?

The Prosecution .... or the Defense ....?

If you have been fortunate enough in your answers not to be excused from the jury panel, you are just one small step away from serving on the jury that will hear the trial of the century. Whether you will actually serve will depend upon the judgment that is made by the attorneys in the final selection process. They want to examine you up close and personal at the opening of the trial. So get a good night's sleep when you're called to appear. It may be the most crucial interview of your life.

3

Making the Final Twelve

Voir Dire and Seating of the Jury

When you see a lawyer trying to pick a smart jury, you know he's got a strong case. Percy Foreman and I once had an argument as to which one of us had picked the most stupid jury.

—F. Lee Bailey

You've already seen the courtroom on television weeks before you were instructed not to watch any further broadcasts of the proceedings. The setting seems more austere than you might have guessed, a bit cold and impersonal for such a momentous occasion. And, of course, the courtroom is overcrowded. This is no ordinary case.

The first person you notice is the judge, 44-year-old Lance A. Ito, whose bespectacled, bearded face is now almost as recognizable around the world as is O.J.'s. His calm demeanor instantly puts everyone at ease. This may be your first time in the big leagues, but it is not Lance Ito's. In 1992, Judge Ito presided in the highly publicized Charles Keating, Jr. securities fraud case, in the wake of which Ito was named Trial Judge of the Year by the Los Angeles Bar Association. And in case anyone wants to speculate about what might happen in the event O.J. is found guilty, it should be remembered that Ito slapped Keating with the maximum sentence possible.

Knowing that Judge Ito is a former prosecutor married to the highest-ranking woman in the LAPD, Capt. Margaret York, one might be tempted to think that Ito would be squarely within the prosecution's camp. However, his reputation for fairness and patience with both sides is widely heralded. The son of Japanese-American schoolteachers who met in a California internment camp during World War II, Ito quietly personifies a sense of justice perhaps made all the sharper by the tragic injustice of his own roots.

What catches you off guard about an otherwise serious-looking Judge Ito is his personal warmth and ready sense of humor. As he began the arduous process of questioning prospective jurors, the first number he drew was for juror number 0032. (For most of his football career, O.J. wore the number 32.) At that, Ito immediately quipped, "I don't know if this is an omen." O.J. nodded his head, as if in agreement.

On another occasion, when cautioning prospective jurors against reading or watching publicity about the case, the judge obviously had the Simpson case heavy on his mind. "When you see it on TV, switch to "The Simpsons," he said, pausing briefly to recognize his inadvertent "Simpson" reference. "The TV show, I mean," he quickly added with a smile.

There Sits the Prosecution

At the right-hand counsel table, you easily spot the two district attorneys, Marcia Clark and William Hodgman. They will be presenting the prosecution's case on behalf of the People of California. The two deputy DA's were handpicked by Los Angeles County District Attorney Gil Garcetti, whose slick political savvy fired the first volley in what turned out to be a trial by media. He knew he had seasoned veterans in Clark and Hodgman.

Marcia Clark gained her "tough-as-nails" reputation through a series of twenty murder cases, successfully winning the 1991 conviction of Robert Bardo, who had stalked and killed actress Rebecca Schaeffer of *My Sister Sam*. At 41 and twice divorced, Clark has a no-nonsense personality, often to the point of being prickly. Her early brusqueness and sarcasm have now been toned down in an attempt to make her look less combative. But combative she must be if she is to go toe to toe with some of the nation's toughest defense lawyers.

Sitting next to Clark is the low-key William Hodgman. It was the 41-year-old Hodgman who had feathered his reputation with a conviction against Charles Keating, Jr. in the case tried by Judge Ito. His somewhat less aggressive style nicely complements Marcia Clark's much caricatured persona. They undoubtedly will prove to be a tough prosecutorial team to beat.

Alongside them from time to time you may also see deputy DA Chris Darden, recently drafted onto the prosecution team at the close of the Al Cowlings grand jury probe. Lisa Kahn's departure from the team for maternity leave has meant that DNA issues will be handled by Rockne Harmon of the Alameda County prosecutor's office.

O.J.'s Dream Team

If you had tried to script a movie about a sensational trial, you could never have done better than in real life. O.J.'s defense team is perfectly typecast to play the role of spoiler. None is more suited to his role than lead attorney, 52-year-old Robert Shapiro, counsel to the stars. He literally reeks of celebrity connections. It was Shapiro who made it possible for Johnny Carson to plead "no contest" to drunk driving in 1982. It was Shapiro again who skillfully negotiated a short prison term for Christian Brando who had killed his half-sister's boyfriend. And it was Shapiro who made sure that baseball star Darryl Strawberry was safe at home plate when he was charged with hitting his girlfriend. Not one to mince words, Shapiro, like Marcia Clark, is a seasoned gladiator ready to pounce on any weakness that may be exposed in the prosecution's case.

With Shapiro at the table to the left is the rest of O.J.'s dream team. Seated next to O.J. himself is 57-year-old Johnnie Cochran, a longtime friend of O.J.'s, who, like Shapiro, has a file full of celebrity clients. His claim to fame ironically includes a winning defense of another football legend and actor, Jim Brown, who was acquitted of rape charges in 1985. More recently, Cochran brokered a $15- to $20-million settlement in the case of the 13-year-old boy who accused Michael Jackson of indecent molestation. As a highly successful black attorney, Cochran adds an important dimension to any racial factor which might be at work in the case.

If any criminal defense attorney's name is a household word, it would be that of F. Lee Bailey. Senior partner on the team at age 61, the mere mention of Bailey's name still conjures images of Dr. Sam Sheppard (the case which inspired *The Fugitive*) whose conviction for killing his wife was reversed; Boston Strangler Albert DeSalvo; and Patty Hearst, hostage turned convicted bank robber. In each of those cases, it was F. Lee Bailey who made his way into the limelight. In a twist of fate back in 1982, it was Bailey himself who turned to Robert Shapiro for help in obtaining an acquittal on a charge of drunk driving. Now in the Simpson case, Bailey will once again work his magic in an attempt to charm the jury into a favorable verdict.

By contrast with the more flamboyant members of the defense team, there are two legal academic experts standing by to deal with the more complex legal issues and to set the stage for the inevitable appeal process which would follow any conviction. You may have read editorials on the Op-Ed page by Harvard's Alan

Dershowitz. Although he was unsuccessful in his defense of Leona Helmsley on her tax charges, Dershowitz gained notoriety when he managed to win an appeal for Claus von Bulow, as chronicled in his book and film, *Reversal of Fortune.* Dershowitz has also been associated with such celebrities as defrocked televangelist, Jim Bakker, and convicted rapist, Mike Tyson. Dershowitz's job is to make sure that, if all else fails, O.J. will get a second bite at the apple on appeal.

Finally, the distinguished former Santa Clara Law School dean, Gerald Uelmen, brings a measure of professional dignity to the team, along with his own impressive portfolio of past cases. In the late '60's, Uelmen was a mob-busting prosecutor. In 1972, he took on the defense of Pentagon Papers protestor, Daniel Ellsberg. From his all-white hair to his hearing aid, Uelmen is the perfect "kindly legal scholar" whom the jurors can trust.

All in all, it's a formidable team which O.J. has huddled around him. Their game plan is simple: get O.J. off the defensive and open up the offense. Like any other front five, their job is to create the holes up the middle so that O.J. can run through untouched.

What In the World Is Voir Dire?

Just about the time you've had a chance to sit down and take all this in, the judge will introduce the case, the lawyers, and the defendant. Members of the jury panel will then be called one by one into the jury box so that they can be questioned in a process known as voir dire. *Voir dire* is an odd term of Anglo-French origins meaning something like *to speak the truth.* Sometimes it is used to refer to the qualifications of a person to testify, but more often it refers to the process of jury selection.

In this case, the lawyers already know a great deal about you. In fact, you would think that the questionnaires told them more than they would ever need to know. But it's one thing to read the cold responses to a written questionnaire, another to look you in the eye and watch your body language. Some (few) lawyers swear that they can pick the right jurors without ever asking a single question.

But sizing someone up is a two-way street. Just as you are evaluated by the lawyers, you in turn will have the opportunity to evaluate them. Do you like one better than another? More importantly, do you *trust* one more than another? Knowing that it is a two-way street, good trial lawyers intentionally curry favor with the jury during the voir dire process, hoping the jurors will like them so well that they would believe anything they say.

If voir dire means to speak the truth, it must be said that prospective jurors can often be terribly economical with the truth. Sometimes it is because they are uncomfortable under the scrutiny of interrogation-level questioning which threatens to invade their privacy. Sometimes it is because they are willing to say whatever it takes to insure that they are chosen. Or perhaps *not* chosen.

If voir dire means to speak the truth, it must also be said in candor that selection of the jury is not the only purpose of the exercise. As important as it is to get the right people on one's jury, the lawyers will be trying their best to win you over to their side. Johnnie Cochran, for example, may read jury instructions to you that call on you to not convict unless there has been proof beyond a reasonable doubt. He will then ask you if you will *promise* to bring in a not guilty verdict if the proof falls short of that standard. With that, he knows he has you in his grasp. It's hard to turn your back on a *promise.*

Following a favorite ploy of prosecutors, William Hodgman might well ask a potential juror, "And if the People prove beyond a reasonable doubt that O.J. Simpson is guilty of murder, what will your verdict be?" The likely response will be "Guilty." To the next juror he might say, "And you?" Again, "Guilty" is the expected response. He might then go down the row asking each of you in turn the same question. One right after another will come the words, "Guilty," "Guilty," "Guilty," "Guilty," "Guilty"—even before the first witness is called to testify!

Yet another purpose of voir dire is to allow the lawyers an opportunity to see how you react to certain key issues. Which issues look like they might be easy winners; which ones will take more effort? They are probing their own cases as well as your particular biases. They are also looking to see which of you might end up being the jury foreman or the most persuasive advocate during deliberations. You can bet those jurors will get special attention during the arguments at the close of trial.

More than anything else, this is the first opportunity both sides have to personalize their cases. There is a lot of dry—frankly *boring*—trial time ahead. It's not always the exciting stuff of television drama. Therefore, it behooves the defense in particular to use voir dire to make the jury *like* the defendant—to personalize him and make him their friend. In O.J.'s case, that may not be a difficult job. In fact, in this case the shoe may be on the other foot. The prosecution will have to work very hard during voir dire to get across the point that, regardless of how you feel about O.J., you must not let your emotions override the evidence.

From Shapiro and the defense, you can be sure that you will be told three things during voir dire. First, that O.J. is presumed to be innocent. Second, that the prosecution has the burden of proving him guilty, beyond a reasonable doubt. And third, that O.J. doesn't have to prove anything, or even to testify.

Marcia Clark and the prosecution team will also want you to know three things. First, that the People of California are looking to you to do justice.

Second, that you must follow the law in this case, even if you might disagree with it. And third, that if the evidence shows O.J. to be guilty beyond a reasonable doubt, then you have a sworn duty to convict him, regardless of your personal feelings toward him.

Commitment. That is the key word during voir dire. If you happen to be included in the final twelve, what both sides want from you even now is your commitment that you will be fair. The prosecution wants you to commit that you will base your decision strictly on the evidence. The defense wants you to commit that you will keep an open mind until you have heard "the other side." Are you willing to make those commitments? The time is coming closer and closer to when the trial is no longer just fun and games, but terribly serious business.

Cause To Be Excused

When all the questioning has ceased, the lawyers must then decide whom they will accept as jurors and whom they will excuse. Jurors may be excused on one of two very different bases. The first, known as *challenges for cause*, will not likely be involved at this stage in the Simpson case. Any legally-recognized reason for dismissing a juror should already have been discovered by use of the lengthy Juror Questionnaire. This explains section XI of the questionnaire, and in particular questions like the following:

116. Do you know personally, or are you personally acquainted with, the judge or any members of the court staff?

 .... Hon. Lance A. Ito, Judge

 .... Court clerk Deirdre Robertson

 .... Court reporters Janet Moxham or Christine Olson

 .... Bailiff - Deputy Sheriff Guy Magnera

Other questions in section XI probed to see if any of the prospective jurors had any familiarity with the attorneys, victims, witnesses, or even O.J. himself. Naturally, any familiarity could automatically prevent someone from being an unbiased juror. Suppose, for example, that one of Nicole's sisters had randomly received a notice for jury duty and been called to sit on the Simpson case. Certainly, no one would expect her to serve.

Other examples of "cause" include felony conviction, mental infirmity, difficulty with the English language, and hearing impairment, etc. With regard to challenges for cause, then, there should be no surprises at this point. If something unusual does happen to be unearthed during voir dire, the attorneys are given the right to excuse as many jurors as might be necessary to protect the integrity of the jury process.

❧

A Matter of Choice

The second basis for excusing a juror is known as a *peremptory challenge*. Within certain Constitutional limitations (guarding against racial or gender discrimination, for example), the peremptory challenges may be exercised arbitrarily with whim and caprice. In theory, a potential juror could be dismissed for no other reason than that the lawyer didn't like his looks. In practice, jurors are rejected by counsel whenever they feel an individual would not be favorably inclined to their particular side. Perhaps something in their answers indicates that they are definitely biased toward the opposite side; or that they are not likely to follow the judge's instructions in a case where the law is terribly important; or that they don't seem sufficiently well educated to grasp complex issues which might be central to the case.

Perhaps someone is too docile, or perhaps too strong-headed. Perhaps their world view is too liberal or too conservative. It may be that they are too materially comfortable to identify with a client who is unemployed and homeless. There are a thousand and one reasons why a lawyer might have apprehension about a particular individual serving on his jury. Whatever those reasons might be, the individual will never be told why he or she is excused. Since no reason is needed, no reason is given.

The number of peremptories which each side can use to challenge jurors from the case will vary from state to state and from case to case. In the Simpson case, each side will be permitted to exercise twenty challenges (or strikes, as they are sometimes called). After the judge and the lawyers have completed voir dire, the jury panel will be excused and then called in at random, one at a time, until there are twelve people seated in the jury box.

At that point, the prosecution and the defense, alternating back and forth with each juror, will either accept or challenge that juror. Whenever any juror is challenged, he will be excused and another juror called to fill his seat. This process will continue until each side has used up all twenty of its peremptories. The twenty-seven jurors who remain will be sworn in as the jurors and alternates for the trial. The trial of the century!

A quick word about the alternates. The alternate jurors will sit with the first twelve jurors throughout the entire case, but they will only be used in the event that one or more of the original twelve jurors becomes incapacitated in some way, such as suddenly being beset by a serious medical problem.

As you can see, just becoming a member of this once-in-a-lifetime jury is rather much of a trial in itself. Through *The Trial of the Century*, you have been spared all of the grief associated with the grueling elimination process, without any fear of being rejected by the lawyers. Congratulations on being one of the final twelve!

Your Job Description as a Juror

Now that you have been chosen to serve as a juror, you may wish to know what you are expected to do. First and foremost, you are to be a judge of the facts in this case. In the eyes of the law, no one else in the entire world—only you—will know whether the evidence points to O.J.'s guilt. No one but you—not even Judge Ito—knows whether O.J. was actually at the scene of the crime at the time alleged and actually killed Nicole Simpson and Ronald Goldman. It will be strictly up to you to decide whether the police officers lied about what they found and how they found it. You alone must decide whether you believe the scientific experts, who presumably will claim that there is a DNA match between Nicole's blood and the blood found on various items of evidence, like the two gloves which were found.

At the end of the trial, Judge Ito will read to you the relevant law of the case and instruct you regarding its meaning. It will then be your job to apply that law to the facts as you have determined them to be and to render your verdict accordingly. Sound simple? If it were, we might never need twelve good people tried and true. As it is, the task before you is a daunting one, demanding concentration, patience, courage, clear thinking, good judgment, accurate recall, and good interactive social skills when you join with the other eleven jurors for your deliberations.

As if to further impress upon you the seriousness of your duties as a juror, you will be asked to take a solemn oath that you will "well and truly try the matters in issue and a true verdict render according to the evidence and the law." Do you so swear?

And So It Begins...

Judge: Are counsel ready to proceed?

Prosecutor: Ready, Your Honor.

Counsel for the Defense: Ready, Your Honor.

With that, the overture has ended, and the curtain is about to rise on the prosecution's case. All around the courtroom, palms are getting sweaty. And the earth is slightly tilted toward L.A.

4

Curtain Rises on the Prosecution's Case

✎

Prosecution's Opening Statement

A jury consists of 12 persons chosen to decide who has the better lawyer.

—Robert Frost, poet

"Good morning, ladies and gentlemen. Let me once again introduce myself. I'm Marcia Clark, representing the People of California for the prosecution of this important case. As you well know by now, Mr. O.J. Simpson has been charged with two counts of murder in the first degree in the deaths of Nicole Brown Simpson and Ronald Lyle Goldman.

"My purpose this morning is to help you anticipate what you will be hearing over the next weeks and months as you listen to the evidence. Neither what I am about to say, nor what defense counsel will tell you in their opening statement, is to be considered by you as evidence. The evidence will come to you by way of the witnesses who take the stand and testify, and by way of physical items which are admitted by the Court for your consideration.

"It is important also to realize that this is not the time for either myself or defense counsel to present arguments in this case. We will both have opportuni-

47

ty to comment on the evidence at the close of the trial. For now, I simply want to give you an overview of the People's case against Mr. Simpson and to thank you in advance for your patience and attention. As all of us who are involved in this case already know, the next several weeks will be very demanding. Your willingness to serve as jurors in this unique case speaks well of your sense of civic duty and commitment to justice.

"Let me say right up front that the People are well aware of the burden of proof which we bear in this case. It is our responsibility to prove Mr. Simpson's guilt beyond a reasonable doubt, and we welcome that responsibility. We are confident that by the end of the trial you will be able to see that we have more than met that burden. In fact, that is our promise to you. As alleged in counts one and two of the Information filed in this case, we will show beyond a reasonable doubt that, on or about June 12, 1994, Mr. Simpson did willfully, unlawfully, and with malice aforethought murder Nicole Brown Simpson and Ronald Lyle Goldman."

∽✕∽

A Horrendous Homicide

With words to similar effect, we can anticipate that Marcia Clark will begin her opening statement, exuding the kind of confidence that only a prosecutor, backed by every investigative resource available to the State, can have. She knows exactly what evidence she has, some of which will be dramatically revealed for the first time during the presentation of her case. What she must do now is to lay out the prosecution's case with enough of her hand showing so as to give the jury confidence that the People have an air-tight case, but without revealing any wild cards that she may be holding. They will come in time.

"It was a grisly scene," Clark might quietly muse as she begins to chronicle the events surrounding the brutal double-homicide. If she has done her homework correctly—and she will have—her account of the murders will be factual, emotional, and powerful. Without a hint of being argumentative, she will stir the jury's imagination by weaving a web of who, what, when, where, and why—drawn from events already widely reported by the media, but only now being fleshed out. With the exception of the killer himself, Clark may know more than anyone about what happened on the fateful night of June 12.

As the gruesome details begin to emerge, watch the body language of your fellow jurors. And O.J. How should one react to horrific stab wounds, hands slashed as they were instinctively raised into a defensive position, and throats being cut to the spinal column? Play it back in slow motion and just imagine the horror.

If O.J. really did do it, imagine what must be going through his mind.

And if he *didn't* do it, imagine even more what must be going through his mind.

Given the barbaric nature of the killings, you can pretty much bet that, throughout the trial from the prosecution side, O.J. will be referred to only as "Mr. Simpson" or "the defendant." Nothing will be done to contribute to a personalized "O.J" and the sympathy vote that it might garner. By contrast, the victims will likely be referred to simply as "Nicole" and "Ronald." *That* is the sympathy vote the prosecution wishes to cultivate.

Whatever it takes, Clark must make the jury feel as sorry for two relatively-unknown victims as they do for America's super-hero. To that end, Clark may describe in detail their robust health and active lives. There will be references to their families and friends, their future prospects and dreams—all of that now taken away by a frenzied knife attack.

Not only will O.J. be de-personalized by stiff references to "Mr. Simpson, the defendant," but he will hear the prosecution characterize him as anything but an all-American hero. The Los Angeles Coliseum where O.J. was cheered on as USC's beloved "Number 32" in crimson and gold may be only a short distance from this downtown courtroom, but the distance between the picture of a smiling, affable O.J. and a calculating, vengeful, and cold-blooded *defendant* could not be greater.

❧

But Why?

At some point, Marcia Clark will highlight that picture with scenes and sounds of domestic turmoil in which Mr. Nice Guy turns ugly, cruel, and violent. It's the dark side of O.J. Simpson that few people knew. It's what went on with this popular actor behind the scenes. It's what he did after the game and between commercials. The damage, when it comes, will be devastating. It will be anything but the O.J. America knows and loves. And, worse yet for O.J., it provides Clark the all-important motive for the killing. What O.J. had threatened to do to Nicole all along has now—sadly, tragically, brutally—been done.

❧

Could O.J. Have Done It?

Motive, then, is the first of the four crucial cornerstones of Clark's case. The second cornerstone is *opportunity*. To establish that the defendant had opportunity to be at the scene of the crime at the very time the killings took place, Clark will promise to present witnesses who will place the defendant well within easy driving distance of Nicole's condominium during what the prosecution will promote as a roughly one-hour time frame (10:00-11:00 p.m.) in which she and Ronald most likely were killed.

As Clark previews the expected testimony, a guesthouse resident at O.J.'s estate, "Kato" Kaelin, will testify that he and O.J. returned from McDonald's around 9:30-9:45. He knows nothing more about O.J.'s whereabouts until about an hour later when he hears three loud thumps outside his guesthouse. Limo driver, Allan Park, who was to pick up O.J. for an airport run that evening, will testify that O.J. was not ready on time—and apparently was not even home until shortly before 10:55 p.m., at which time Park will testify he saw a six-foot-tall, 200-pound black person crossing the lawn and entering O.J.'s house.

Opportunity? According to the prosecution, there won't be any doubt about it at the end of the trial.

The third cornerstone of the prosecution's case is the *means.* Did the defendant have the means to kill his ex-wife and her friend? Here, Clark is probably haunted by two problems. First, she is going to have to disappoint the jury and tell them that she doesn't have the actual murder weapon. Nothing has been found. Second, she is already anticipating that she may run into trouble with her medical investigator, Irwin Golden, who was butchered by Robert Shapiro at the preliminary hearing when Golden failed to match the fatal wounds with a potential murder weapon. Therefore, Clark's opening statement will undoubtedly attempt to underplay the significance of Golden's findings, pointing instead to a more speculative theory about the murder weapon.

Could it have been the 15-inch stiletto which O.J. purchased from Ross Cutlery salesman, Jose Camacho, for $81.17 five weeks before the murders? Clark could tell the jury that she is going to subpoena Camacho, or even Allen Wattenberg, co-owner of Ross Cutlery, who sharpened the stiletto for O.J. But she has a problem here. Camacho and Wattenberg sold their story to the *National Enquirer* for $12,500. Will the defense be able to impeach their credibility, suggesting that they likewise might be willing to sensationalize what they know even while under oath?

It is here that we may observe a calculated gamble on the part of the prosecution. Sometimes it is advisable to "air your dirty laundry" as soon as possible. What Marcia Clark may decide to do is bring up the *National Enquirer* article herself, rather than wait for the defense to use it as a weapon against her. It's a preemptive strike. Call it "damage control," if you will. Every good lawyer knows when and how to do it, and we will probably see an example of it in the defense's opening statement as well.

But Marcia Clark is still not home free on this particular issue. One of the most intriguing mysteries of the whole trial will be what was turned over by the defense to Municipal Judge Kathleen Kennedy-Powell who presided at the preliminary hearing. You may recall that, on July 1, Robert Shapiro handed the judge a sealed manila envelope, the contents of which have yet to be revealed. Suppose what's inside is the stiletto O.J. bought from Ross Cutlery—*sans* blood and in mint condition!

If the opening statement is directed at the jury, for the defense lawyers it is also a window to the prosecution's case. What you may see in Clark's opening statement is a cat and mouse game going on. But Clark still has a trump card which she can play with regard to *means*. That card is O.J. himself—a man whose very strength earned him his fame. It will be surprising if Clark doesn't minimize the *knife* and maximize the *person* she believes was wielding the instrument, whatever the instrument may have been and whatever may have happened to it after the killing. Using that approach, Clark can once again comfortably promise to provide the third cornerstone beyond a reasonable doubt.

Who Dunnit?

The last cornerstone, *the identity of the killer*, may prove to be the most difficult of all for the prosecution. Even if O.J. had the opportunity, the means, and the motive to kill Nicole, the crucial question remains: did he do it? That's as in, did *he* do it? Could it even remotely be that someone else *might possibly* have done it? In the absence of eyewitnesses, all the prosecution has to go on is circumstantial evidence.

And that brings us to one of the biggest hurdles Marcia Clark will have to cross during her opening statement. Somehow, some way, she will have to overcome the naivete of laymen about the nature of circumstantial evidence. The one thing about which there is no doubt is that laymen have great doubts about circumstantial evidence. ("*Merely* circumstantial evidence," as it is usually put.) "What kind of a case do you have," someone asks, "if all you have is circumstantial evidence?" The answer, of course, is the normal, usual, typical court case. Where there is direct, eyewitness evidence of a crime, there is rarely any likelihood of a trial. That kind of evidence gives the prosecutor such a slam-dunk case that the defendant is probably going to plead guilty and get on with serving his time.

Without an eyewitness or a confession, all anyone ever has to go on are the circumstances surrounding a case. What Marcia Clark will have to explain to the jury in her opening statement is that circumstantial evidence in a murder case is little different from the kind of circumstantial evidence each one of us relies on every day of our lives. More often than not, we make our most important decisions based upon nothing more than circumstantial evidence. That is, we carefully consider *all of the circumstances* and confidently act thereon. And in this case, *all of the circumstances* weigh heavily against the defendant.

The *circumstances*? They will be catalogued one after another in a long list of prosecution exhibits, mostly centering around blood. If Marcia Clark is familiar with the old hymn, "There is Power in the Blood," she must be singing it over and over again in the shower. For the prosecution in the Simpson case, there is indeed power in the blood. It has the capability of pointing to O.J. as surely as if it were an eyewitness to the killing.

But Clark must first lay the evidentiary foundation. For that she will anticipate the testimony of LAPD Officer Robert Riske, who was the first to respond to the emergency call alerting police to discovery of the bodies. He will tell of the pools of blood surrounding the two bodies, and blood on the paws of Nicole's pet Akita, and more bloody footsteps leading toward the alleyway. Clark will then call to the stand Det. Mark Fuhrman who arrived two hours later, and detectives Philip Vannatter and Thomas Lange who were called out to complete the investigative team.

Four officers, including detectives Vannatter and Fuhrman, will testify that as they made the connection between Nicole and O.J., they proceeded to his Brentwood estate where they then noticed what appeared to be blood on the driver's side door of a white Bronco parked askew to the curb. In the course of events, as they will testify, they discovered a trail of blood drops leading up the driveway from the Bronco to the front door. Perhaps most significant of all, Det. Fuhrman discovered a bloodied glove between a fence and the outer wall of the guest wing.

✂

Power in the Blood

Blood, blood, everywhere; and all the doubts did shrink. But still the prosecution must proceed with caution. The question remains, whose blood is it? Given normal blood groupings, it is easy to *eliminate* individuals from certain blood types, but in the past it has been difficult to *exclusively identify* them. For example, if the accused's blood is type A and the blood on an item of evidence—say a baseball cap—is type B, then it could not possibly be the accused's blood on the cap. But if the blood on the cap happens instead to be type A, then the accused might *or might not* be the person from whom the blood came. There are millions of other people who are also type A.

But, as Clark will at some point explain to the jury, that is somewhat ancient history. Modern science has given the prosecution—and in many cases the defense—a gift from out of the blue. ("Out of the blue" having been medical research into the genetic structure of sickle cell anemia.) As used in criminology, it is a relatively new method of scientific "fingerprinting" known as DNA analysis, by which it is possible to narrow down one's identity to the likes of a unique, never to be duplicated fingerprint. At least in theory.

Naturally, the prosecution would like to present this kind of "conclusive" evidence to the jury at the earliest possible moment, and that would be during the opening statement. However, there are at least two concerns for the prosecution to consider. One is whether in pre-trial hearings the Court has indicated it will admit evidence from DNA testing. Because other courts have often been skeptical, its admission is not a foregone conclusion.

Even if the test is admitted (and, therefore, can be referred to in Ms. Clark's opening), the other concern is how to articulate the degree of accuracy and exclusiveness of the analysis. There may not be much rancor in the scientific community about the validity of the procedure itself, but there is great debate over how the odds ought to be calculated. When we consider the chances of a second person having an identical DNA pattern, are we talking one in tens of millions, or perhaps one in a quarter of a million or something far less?

Naturally, the prosecution would hope to be able to talk in terms of one in several million. However, one of the most interesting things to listen for is how Marcia Clark introduces the jury to DNA testing. Will she be restricted in what she can say by some prior Court ruling? Will she boldly go for the highest odds she can reasonably expect to get out of her DNA experts? Or, indeed, will she simply refer to the analysis in general terms and wait until the end of the trial before trying to press home her position on the controversial test?

Veteran court watchers might find all the buzz about DNA testing to be somewhat distracting. In the midst of all the expert testimony you will soon hear from the witness box, even you as a juror might wonder if we haven't gotten too sophisticated for our own good. Suppose the blood on the glove found at O.J.'s estate matches his basic blood-type. (A safe assumption since, if it didn't at least pass that test, no one would be talking about further narrowing the odds.) Therefore, given even the most rudimentary blood-type match, if the brown leather right-hand glove found at O.J.'s house is one of a pair with the brown leather left-hand glove found at the murder scene, then what doubt can there be?

Will Marcia Clark out-technology herself from the very start? Will she be so enamored with the latest scientific proof that she fails to realize a conviction is being handed to her in a brown leather glove? Or does even the glove make her nervous?

Just when it looks like the prosecution's case is in the bag, a black cloud creeps into the courtroom, casting what could be a pall of doubt over the bloody glove. Clark knows exactly what that cloud is, but the question is, does she dare mention it? Does she dare *not* mention it?

On the strength of the fact that she has done such a good job of tying together the trail of blood with the accused in the case, Clark may leave well enough alone and bring her opening statement to a close. Her package is complete. For the moment, her job is done. In anticipation of the evidence which she knows she can produce, Marcia Clark has laid a solid foundation using the four cornerstones of motive, opportunity, means, and identity.

All that remains is to remind the jurors of their duty to convict the defendant on the basis of the evidence which they are about to hear. "After you have heard all of the evidence, ladies and gentlemen, we are confident that you will find Orenthal James Simpson guilty of murder in the first degree on both counts as alleged."

A Brief Interlude

Well, what do you think? Were you surprised at some of the evidence she promises to deliver? Did she talk about any evidence that had never been reported by the media? From what you can tell, what is likely to be the key evidence for the prosecution?

What did you think of Marcia Clark personally? Do you have the feeling that she is sincere? Does she seem pushy and aggressive—as if she were going to shove a murder verdict down your throat—or were you impressed with her demeanor and presentation?

If you had to decide right now, what would your verdict be, and why?

....

....

....

....

....

....

....

What Can They Possibly Say?

In answering that last question, did you just violate the commitment you made to defense counsel during voir dire—that you would keep an open mind throughout the trial, and that you would wait to hear the other side of the story before making up your mind? Perhaps, but the mind does have a funny way of being fickle. At one moment there can be complete certainty; the next moment, nagging doubt. After all, there really is another side to every story, *isn't there?* Would we even be in court today if there weren't *another side?*

That sounds good, but what can that "other side" possibly be? Given what Marcia Clark promised to deliver, what possible defense could O.J. have? How will O.J.'s Dream Team try to explain away the blood? What can they possibly say about the gloves? Who else could possibly have had a motive for killing Nicole and Ronald? Could their deaths and O.J.'s strange movements that night really have been nothing more than a tragic coincidence?

You haven't long to wait. Defense counsel has pushed back his chair and is confidently approaching the jury box. Hold onto your seat. Here we go again.

5

There's Always Another Side to the Story

∽✕∾

Defense's Opening Statement

*Our national nostrum, "Not Proven" . . . a
verdict which has been construed by the profane to
mean "Not Guilty, but don't do it again."*

—William Roughead
The Art of Murder

"Ladies and gentlemen, we are assembled here today because a great tragedy has occurred. On the night of June 12, two quite innocent, unsuspecting individuals were viciously attacked and brutally murdered on a quiet street in west Los Angeles. One of the victims, Nicole Brown Simpson, was an unusually beautiful lady—vivacious, intelligent, the mother of eight-year-old Sydney and six-year-old Justin, who were sleeping upstairs in the house at the time. The other victim was her friend, Ronald Lyle Goldman, who apparently turned out to be the classic case of someone being at the wrong place at the wrong time. He had done nothing more wrong than attempt to return a pair of mislaid glasses. But his timing was bad. And now they are both dead. Senselessly dead.

"The frightening thought is that, given the slightest change in circumstances, you and I might well have been in their shoes that evening.

"But that is not the end of this tragic story. Sadly, the original tragedy was compounded many times over, and continues even to this moment. The father of those two young children—a man who loves them more than his own life—has been wrongfully accused of their mother's murder.

"And, of course, it's not just any father we are talking about, but O.J. Simpson—a man all of America knows and loves. A man whom we have laughed with, and cried with—who has exhilarated us and entertained us and been our friend. There were not just two killings on that fateful night. The incredible events of that night and the bizarre events that followed in the ensuing days have also killed O.J.'s very soul. Try to imagine what it must be like to be falsely accused of murdering your children's mother. How could you or I even begin to imagine what that might be like? Or how we might react?

"What the prosecution has failed to tell you is that there was not just a homicide that night, but a *robbery*-homicide. Within hours of the killings, O.J. himself was robbed. Robbed of his most valuable and precious possession—his reputation. Apart from being reunited with his children, what O.J. most desperately wants to get back is the goodwill of a nation of admirers who had come to love him as much as he loved them.

"Sadly, we cannot bring Nicole Brown Simpson and Ronald Lyle Goldman back to life. Would that we could! It's a tragedy that simply can't be undone. But there is another tragedy which it is within your power to prevent: the wrongful conviction of an innocent man. And that, ladies and gentlemen, is what this trial is all about—restoring the impeccable reputation of one good, decent and honorable man."

If He's Innocent, Why Is He Here Today?

"But surely you must have asked yourself, 'If O.J. is truly innocent, then why has he been arrested and charged with this heinous crime?' To that question there is only one answer: O.J. was an easy target. The police weren't just jumping fences to get into his estate when they had no right to; worse by far, as we're going to show, they were jumping to conclusions in order to probe into his private life when they had no right to. Contrary to rumor, even superstars have a right of privacy.

"But that is where O.J. himself fumbled, and fumbled badly. It's not something he is proud of. In fact, it's the greatest embarrassment of his life. But by now you and the whole world know that his relationship with Nicole was stormy, to say the least. It's no secret that O.J.'s love for Nicole often bubbled over into jealousy. It was as if Nicole had a mystical hold over O.J. from which he could never quite escape. As best as either of them could make of it, the tension between them was that of star-crossed lovers—destined, it seemed, for as much mutual hurt, anger, and pain as there was love.

"However, to say that O.J. had a violent dark side which was hidden from public view would be grossly overstating the case. Is there a history of spousal abuse with his first wife, Marguerite? Is there any suggestion that O.J. has ever acted violently with any other woman? The picture which the prosecution will attempt to paint of O.J.—as a man who stalked and abused Nicole and threatened to kill her—does not tell the whole story.

"Have you ever gotten so mad at someone that you wanted to kill them? You'd be in a small minority indeed if your answer is 'no'. Most of us at some point in our lives have known that feeling. Some of us have even verbally expressed our anger in those very terms. But who among us has ever actually killed someone under those circumstances? As you sit here in the days ahead and keep hearing about all the threats which O.J. allegedly made, keep asking yourself, 'Should you or I or anyone be put on trial simply for what we have thought, or perhaps said?'

"When the prosecution brings to your attention O.J.'s single incident of being charged with hitting Nicole, keep in mind that this time it is *murder* with which O.J. is being charged, not battery. One sin is not every sin. And somewhere it was written, 'Let him who is without any sin cast the first stone.'

"O.J. himself will be the first to admit that he is not the perfect human specimen his fans want him to be. In particular, he has messed up big-time with Nicole. But when he did, he pleaded 'no contest' and underwent the counseling he knew he needed. When he's guilty, he's man enough to admit it and take his punishment. But when he's not guilty, he's also man enough not to let himself be run over by a mob of headline seekers."

Keep Asking Yourself the Hard Questions

"As you listen to the prosecution's case, what you must keep supremely in mind is that they will not tell you the whole story. It's not their job to do that, so they won't. Also keep in mind that, at this point, they have too much time, money, and misdirected effort invested in O.J.'s guilt to admit that they could be wrong. For that reason, the prosecutors will not even explore with you the difficulties of their own scenario. If there are obvious questions to be asked, they'll certainly be in no rush to ask them. It will be left for you, and for us, to shine the light of truth on their darkened alleyway which leads in whatever wishful direction they want it to go.

"What you must keep asking yourself throughout the prosecution's case is, 'Why aren't they at least interested in answering the obvious questions?'"

Could It Be a Well-Intentioned Setup?

"As we will show, both in our cross-examination of the prosecution's witnesses, and by O.J.'s own witnesses, the prosecution and the police don't really care to know who the real killers were. Once the police focused in on O.J.—undoubtedly because Det. Fuhrman just happened to be aware of O.J.'s and Nicole's stormy relationship—they went into their own frenzy in an all-out attack on a defenseless O.J. Simpson.

"I don't know. Maybe you think it's O.K. for the police to do whatever it takes to convict some guy they sincerely believe has committed a terrible crime—that the end somehow justifies the means. But if we are able to show, as we believe we *will* be able to show, that the police went completely over the top in their zeal to nail O.J., then we're talking nothing less than lies, deception, and perhaps even—dare we say it—intentionally planted evidence.

"We will show, for example, that the lead detective in this case, Mark Fuhrman, is not only a racist, but certainly not the salesman you want to buy from when you're shopping for the truth. What you're going to want to ask yourself is why Det. Fuhrman kept the coroner's office away from the scene of the crime for an incredible ten hours. Was it because he knew it would make it more difficult to pin down the time of death and thus interfere with any legitimate alibi O.J. might have?

"The prosecution will be talking about a 75-minute 'window of opportunity,' conveniently designed to correspond to the only hour during which O.J. isn't with anyone who can verify his whereabouts. But had the coroner's office been allowed merely to take the temperatures of the victim's livers, they may well have determined a time of death that was after O.J. had already left for the airport. When you hear the coroner testify, ask yourself, 'Why would the police violate their own department rules of investigation so blatantly in this particular case?'

"You're also going to want to ask Det. Fuhrman about the leather glove which he supposedly found at O.J.'s Brentwood estate. Were any of the other officers near him when he allegedly discovered the glove? Can they verify that Det. Fuhrman was not alone when he came upon the glove? One of the things we are going to want to know is whether perhaps Fuhrman thought it might be a plum for his career if he could lay claim to having made the flying tackle on O.J. But if it were merely the game that Det. Fuhrman may well think it is, the evidence is going to show that he'd be thrown out of the game for unsportsmanlike conduct. No Buffalo Bills crowd would stand for it if somebody hit O.J. out of bounds. In the course of this trial, neither should you.

"As the prosecution's case unfolds, you are going to see a litany of police mistakes. We're going to point out broken chains of custody, confused samples, and contaminated evidence. Throughout the trial, keep asking yourself, 'Is that the kind of evidence upon which you will want to convict a man for murder?'

"But it's worse than that. What you are going to see on the part of the LAPD is not only sloppy police work, but a carnival atmosphere unparalleled since Roman soldiers cast lots for Jesus' cloak at the foot of the cross. You will hear testimony that, during one three-hour search of O.J.'s residence, ten police officers took time out to watch a video in which O.J. starred, and further desecrated his dignity by setting up photos of Nicole Simpson to resemble a 'shrine.'

"By the time we get through with this case, we can fairly promise you that it is the LAPD you will want to convict—not O.J."

Why Are We Hiding the Ball?

"Of course, I can almost hear one of you saying to yourself, 'But if O.J. has nothing to hide, then why are his lawyers trying to cover up all the evidence?' But just think about it. If the police are filling in the missing pieces with pieces which only they themselves have provided, why shouldn't we do everything we possibly can to keep out such bogus evidence?

"Ladies and gentlemen, if in the course of the prosecution's case you get even the slightest whiff of manufactured evidence, then shut this case down in your minds immediately! This is no hanging you will want to have any part of.

"During the trial, you undoubtedly will hear us make repeated objections to either certain witness testimony or to specific items of physical evidence. Bear in mind that it will not be because O.J. fears the truth. It will only be because the other side is trying desperately to *distort* the truth.

"You have already heard the prosecutor refer to certain DNA tests that will be used in an effort to point the finger at O.J. And you can bet those tests will be impressively presented. Simply keep this in mind as the prosecution's experts testify: scientific tests are only as good as the people who use them. That bears repeating: *Scientific tests are only as good as the people who use them.* With all the contamination, mislabeling, and confusion at both the crime scene and the crime lab, no scientific test in this case can bear the stamp of reliability. Again, O.J. doesn't fear the truth from any legitimate evidence. But neither should he have to run the risk of false identification simply because the police, the medical examiner, and the criminologists all royally blew it.

"And therein, ladies and gentlemen, lies the tale of this trial. One after another, you will see that reasonable doubts abound in this case. But at the end of all the testimony and evidence it will be abundantly clear that there is at least one thing about which there can be no doubt: that justice has been turned on its head. In this extraordinarily convoluted case, we are confident that over the course of the trial you will come to see that the *system* is the culprit, and O.J. its innocent victim.

"At the end of the case, ladies and gentlemen, we will be asking that you recognize this trial for what it really is, and appropriately bring in a verdict of not guilty. For our part, we promise that it will be a verdict which not only will be *just,* but also *right.* Absolutely, 100% right!"

Time Again to Reflect

What do you think at this point? Has the defense damaged the prosecution's case as presented in its opening statement?

_____

_____

_____

_____

What is your understanding of the defense's theory of the case?

_____

_____

_____

_____

From what you can tell, which items of evidence are likely to be the key evidence in favor of O.J.?

_____

_____

_____

_____

What did you think of the defense counsel personally? Do you have the feeling that he is sincere? Does he seem too slick and smooth—as if he were going to charm you into believing in O.J.'s innocence—or were you impressed with his professional demeanor and presentation?

Trial rules do not permit counsel on opening statements to *argue* their case. That must wait until after the evidence is presented. Did the defense's opening statement (either in this chapter or in the actual trial) cross the line from being an *introduction* to being an *argument?*

If you had to decide right now, what would your verdict be, and why?

Analyzing the Defense's Opening

Naturally, it's only a matter of speculation as to what opening statement O.J.'s defense team will actually make. But their opening will likely include many of the strategies reflected in the mock presentation which you have just read. Did you catch what the defense was trying to accomplish?

First, they will make every effort to take the sting out of the gruesomeness of the murders. It won't be long before you are shown some absolutely horrendous crime scene photos. It won't be a pretty sight. So if the defense can join in with the grief and horror, then the outrage is shared by the defense, and the case remains balanced from the very beginning.

The defense will also want to go out of its way to identify with the victims: they were innocent. They didn't deserve to die. It could have been any one of us that night. This approach takes the sympathy vote away from the prosecution and cements a common bond with the jury. Is *anyone* glad this tragedy has happened? Of course not. Least of all, the defendant.

Having identified with the sympathy naturally flowing toward the victims of the homicide, the defense draws on that sympathy and turns it into O.J.'s advantage: While we're talking about victims and sympathy, how about O.J. himself? He, too, is a victim deserving our sympathy. He is not just a jealous ex-husband of one of the victims, but the father of that victim's two children. With Nicole's death, O.J. has lost a crucial family link. What's more, he has also been "robbed" of his reputation. It is no longer O.J. the *accused*, but O.J. the *victim*. Look how the tables have turned.

Did you notice throughout the defense's opening that every opportunity possible was taken to make use of football analogies? It's one thing for O.J. to say, "Don't acquit me only because of who I am;" but his superstar persona will always be the trump card. In whatever way they choose to do it, the defense will make a concerted effort to keep before the jury an image of the same likeable, believable O.J. who sold orange juice and promoted Hertz rental cars.

Call it courageous, or simply the only option the defense team has, but you can be sure that they won't be relying solely upon a hoped-for sympathy vote. Leading with O.J.'s own confident jaw, the opening statement will be a *tour-de-force* of aggressive challenge to the prosecution. With every skill at their command, the defense team will promote the idea that O.J.'s plea was not merely a technical pleading device ("Not Guilty, *so now prove it*"), but a genuine claim of innocence ("Not Guilty, *because I honestly, really, truly did not do it!*").

For that very reason, it will be no surprise to anyone when the defense team airs O.J.'s "dirty laundry" right up front. What else can they do? O.J.'s history of jealousy, stalking, threats, and even physical abuse against Nicole is tailor-made for the prosecution's assertion of a motive. All that the defense can do is try to make the jury personally identify with his anger, and perhaps even his physical abuse. Of course, in today's climate of heightened sensitivity regarding spousal abuse, the defense must carefully walk a thin line. If they're smart, they'll acknowledge the evil of spousal abuse, show appropriate contrition on O.J.'s part, then cut and run as fast as possible in a different direction.

That direction? Head straight for the police. After all, their bungling of the evidence—even if there is nothing at all nefarious about it—has handed the defense a golden opportunity. Being able to capitalize on police mistakes helps to shift the spotlight away from O.J. and onto a system that many people love to hate. When you pit the system versus O.J., he immediately becomes the under-dog. And everybody pulls for the underdog.

In the trial of the century, there aren't many people who *want* O.J. to lose. Hoping against hope, their hearts continue to ask what the defense team wants you, yourself, to ask: "Can you really say there isn't *some* reason to doubt?"

A Minor Tactical Decision

When it comes to the defense's opening statement, there are many "unknowns" that will be revealed only as the actual trial proceeds. The defense's case is not as easily predictable as that of the prosecution. For openers, the defense has the option of waiving an opening statement altogether (almost never a good idea) or waiting to present it until after the prosecution's case-in-chief and immediately before their own. The advantage of waiting would be that the defense could have a better idea of the prosecution's evidence before telling the jury their own theory of the case. However, the advantages of waiting are usually heavily outweighed by the disadvantages.

The defense clearly does not want to leave an impression with you that they have no case—but instead are just hoping for some lucky break. To the contrary, the defense usually wants to take the initiative as soon as they have the opportunity. The last thing they want is to let the prosecution's version of the facts go unchallenged. Therefore, it can be expected that the defense's opening statement will come on the heels of Marcia Clark's.

A Major Tactical Decision

Far more crucial is the question of which theory of the case will be presented by the defense. Are they going to take the all-or-nothing gamble: Murder One or Not Guilty? Or will they hedge their bets and hope to get a jury verdict for Voluntary Manslaughter? That may depend on how strong they believe the People's case is at the end of the prosecution's case-in-chief.

If the DNA and other physical evidence seems insurmountable, then the defense might consider having O.J. admit that he did the killings, but only in the heat of passion, not with premeditation. The problem with that approach is two-fold: 1) O.J. probably told the police that he was at home the entire time and therefore could not have done the killing; and 2) if he admits the killing, there is no way that he is going to be found not guilty.

Given the downsides to introducing the Voluntary Manslaughter theory, the defense most likely will continue to maintain O.J.'s complete denial, and hope either that they get a not guilty verdict or that the jury on its own will bring back Voluntary Manslaughter as a compromise verdict.

Voluntary Manslaughter is a kind of mitigated murder. Mitigation is most often found where there is evidence of a killing done in the heat of passion. That passion must be caused by provocation of a type that would cause the rational mind of an average reasonable person to be temporarily derailed. (It is not to be confused with insanity, which is always based upon some mental disease or defect and is a complete defense.)

Who Among the Who's Who?

The third great unknown has to do more with personalities and egos than purely trial tactics. Unfortunately for purposes of this chapter, we don't know in advance which of O.J.'s Dream Team will take the spotlight on the first day. Will it be Robert Shapiro, the original lead lawyer in the case? Or will it be Johnnie Cochran, who, over the weeks and months leading up to the trial, has taken an ever-increasing role? It's Cochran, of course, with whom O.J. has a bond of a personal friendship. Will that be the deciding factor?

Not just here, but throughout the trial it will be interesting to see how the dynamics of the Dream Team plays itself out. If it is felt that the most important presentation is the defense's closing argument at the conclusion of the trial, then perhaps Cochran will covet that role for himself. And O.J. may concur. If so, the opening statement will probably fall by default to Shapiro. For O.J., of course, it's a win-win situation. On the Dream Team, there is no such thing as a second string.

O.J. Simpson—Defense Exhibit Number One

While everyone is talking about O.J.'s Dream Team, his lawyers, in turn, have the distinct advantage of representing a Dream Client. O.J. Simpson is no ordinary criminal defendant. What other criminal defendant has ever been so comfortable before the cameras and the eyes of the world? Who ever has had so many people pulling for him? Who possibly could look more respectable and less likely to have done the dastardly deed?

As every defense lawyer knows, most of their clients have to be "dressed up" for the occasion. Cut the hair, trim the beard, get some decent clothes. With

O.J., you are already dealing with a clean-cut male model, right down to the silk tie, expensive dress shirt, and softly tailored, conservative suit.

And then there is that patented O.J. smile. As one dismissed prospective juror reported to *Los Angeles Times'* Bill Boyarsky, the magic was still there. "I turned forward. He was still looking at me. We made eye contact a couple of times. He was gorgeous."

Adding that she felt somehow connected to O.J., her bottom line assessment is exactly what O.J.'s lawyers hope will come through to the jury in their opening statement: "Here he was, a real, tangible person." To be precise, a real, tangible, *innocent* person.

6

We'll Take a Brief Recess

Trial Procedure and Objections

*We find the defendant guilty and recommend
that he be sentenced to one year of jury service.*

—Cartoon

In a good book or movie, the action never stops. Non-stop action is manda-tory to keep the reader's or viewer's attention. But one of the first things you are going to learn about the real world of legal trials is that it's always a case of hurry up and wait. For much of the time, the conversation of justice is on hold. Just when the excitement mounts, the judge—as if on cue—turns to the jury and says, "Ladies and gentlemen, we'll take a brief recess."

In the course of this trial, you can expect to have hundreds of recesses—some brief, some long; some when you expect them, some when you don't. At times you will welcome a break from the tension of fierce cross-examination or a sobbing witness. At other times, you will *beg* for a "brief recess" just to escape the monotony of endless—seemingly pointless—questioning. Low-speed trials are not as riveting as low-speed freeway chases.

So as we come to the end of the opening statements, you can fully expect that the Court will break for a recess. This will give counsel time to catch their breaths, line up their witnesses, and set the stage for what promises to be a no-holds-barred donnybrook.

✎

Rules of Engagement

Before the prosecution's first witness takes the stand and is sworn "to tell the truth, the whole truth, and nothing but the truth," there are certain "rules of the game" which you need to quickly understand. On direct examination, the party calling the witness (here, the prosecution) must not ask "leading questions." Except for initial background questions which help to introduce you to each witness, it is forbidden for counsel to ask a question which suggests an answer. The aim of direct examination is to let the witness tell what he or she knows, not what the lawyer knows. You and the Court want to hear it in the witness' own spontaneous words, not in the carefully-crafted words of some lawyer.

On cross-examination, by contrast, the opposing counsel may "lead" a witness with sharply pointed questions if he so chooses. The reason is that it is assumed the witness might not be favorably inclined to respond with complete candor to a lawyer on "the other side." Therefore, greater latitude is given to make the process a fair one. When the defense later calls its own witnesses, then the tables will be turned and it will be the prosecution who can ask leading questions.

✎

A Word About Cross-Examination

Before we embark on the direct examinations and cross-examinations of the People's witnesses, we need to discuss the true purpose and nature of cross-examination. Unlike the cross-examinations we are used to seeing on "L.A. Law" and "Perry Mason," in the real world of criminal trials, witnesses don't break down and confess under the pressure of the rapier cross-exam of some lawyer. Most witnesses have been coached and prepared to withstand the rigors of cross-examination.

Furthermore, good trial lawyers recognize that their cases are won on the strength of the evidence they produce during their direct examination. Since only perhaps ten percent of evidence needed to win will come from cross-examination, the good lawyer will not press his cross examination nearly as far as the "movie lawyer."

For the layman, it is useful to imagine cross-examination as a guerilla raid behind enemy lines. There are fixed targets which are hit, then a hasty retreat is made. If the lawyer goes further into enemy territory than he should, he may well hit an unexpected land mine and lose his case.

So here's what you can expect to hear on cross-examination in the O.J. case: first, a ton of leading questions. A leading question not only suggests the answer the lawyer wants to get, but it also permits the lawyer to control the agenda. Keep in mind here that the *question* is more important than the *answer*! It's almost as if the *lawyer* is testifying rather than the *witness*.

Second, both you and the witness will become extremely frustrated when the lawyer won't allow the witness to explain his answer. (If an answer needs further explanation, the other side can elicit that explanation with rebuttal questions.)

Third, you can be sure that a good lawyer will never ask a question to which he does not already know the answer. Don't think for one minute that lawyers of this caliber are just making up some interesting questions to fill time! See if you can figure out what their game plan is with each witness.

Fourth, don't be surprised if a lawyer leaves you hanging by not asking the final question which you expect him to ask. You can bet that he will argue that very point to you in his closing argument! (But for now, why alert the opposing counsel to the bomb intended to be dropped later?)

As we proceed to the prosecution's case-in-chief, we will demonstrate the unique style of cross-examination by focusing in on the prosecution's first witness.

Trial Objections

To avoid convicting someone solely on the basis of rumor and innuendo, there are also strict rules forbidding the introduction of hearsay. What everyone wants to know from a witness is what he or she *personally* saw or heard—not what someone else may have seen or heard. As with most rules, the rule against the admission of hearsay also has certain well-recognized exceptions. But law school students, and even many practicing trial lawyers, will tell you that the "well-recognized" exceptions are not always easy to discern. For that reason, we have included in the Appendix a whole section on hearsay and other rules of evidence which you may find helpful as you observe the O.J. trial.

When you hear counsel for the prosecution or defense say, "Objection, Your Honor," then listen carefully for the reason given. Is it "leading the witness"? Or "hearsay"? Or "irrelevant"? Or "narrative"? Does it call for a "conclusion, opinion, or speculation"? Perhaps it is "failure to lay a proper foundation," or "assumes facts not in evidence." Or perhaps the question is a "compound question," or is "argumentative," or "beyond the scope." If you don't already understand why the objection is being made, quickly refer to the Rules of Evidence section and you will soon be right up to speed along with the lawyers themselves.

With the raising of each objection, Judge Ito will either *sustain* the objection (agreeing that the witness should not answer the question asked) or *overrule* the objection (allowing the question to be answered). Sometimes objections are made solely to set the stage for a later appeal, claiming that the information elicited by the question should not have been admitted.

If at any time Judge Ito asks counsel to "approach the bench," it means that there is something he needs to talk to them about without your hearing it. He may be allowing counsel an opportunity to argue how he ought to rule on an objection; or anticipating an evidentiary problem that he needs to rule on before you have already heard something which is not admissible; or, perhaps, even issuing a warning to one or both counsel for unprofessional conduct. It may prove frustrating to you not to know what everyone else seems to know. But don't forget that the rules of evidence are carefully designed for the purpose of maintaining fairness to all parties. You will get to hear everything you need to hear in order to render a proper verdict.

What to Look For in the Witnesses

With the appearance of each witness, you will have both the opportunity and the responsibility to assess the witness' credibility. You must continually ask yourself, "Is this witness to be believed?" But how are you supposed to know the answer to such a subjective question? The law itself suggests how you will do that by specifically telling you what you may consider. Among those factors are the following:

a. The witness' demeanor while testifying

   Does he appear unusually nervous, defensive, aggressive, uninterested?

b. The character of his testimony

   Is he testifying about something he has reason to know about?

c. Extent of his capacity to perceive or recollect

   Are there any physical problems such as hearing or eyesight?

d. Opportunity to perceive

   How long did he have to register the event?

Where was he when he claims to have seen the event?

e. Character for honesty

Is there any evidence of prior dishonesty?

f. Existence of bias, interest, or other motive

Is the witness related to any of the parties or have something else to gain by testifying?

g. Previous consistent statement

Has he said the same thing before under trustworthy circumstances?

h. Inconsistency with any other testimony

Has he previously given conflicting testimony?

i. Accuracy of any fact testified to by him

Is his testimony directly contradicted by another proven fact?

j. Attitude toward the case

Does he give the appearance that he takes his duty to testify seriously?

k. Any admission of untruthfulness

Has he previously been caught in a lie and acknowledged it?

If all these guidelines seem a bit artificial, they are. As of yet, there is no "credibility detector" that we can use to scan across the witness and know whether he or she is being honest, or even completely candid. And that is exactly why you have been asked to serve as a juror—to use your own common sense and human experience to make just such a judgment. So be listening, not only with your ears, but also with your eyes and your heart.

❧

Benefit of the Burden

It is almost time for the recess to end. The court bailiff is motioning for you and your fellow jurors to follow him back into the courtroom. As you proceed down an inner hallway, you pass an open door and happen to hear a passer-by exclaim, "Well, I for one believe that O.J. is innocent." What should you do? Close your ears and run so as not to be unduly influenced?

Under normal circumstances, yes. But the fact of the matter is that the passerby was right. O.J. is indeed innocent! Innocent until *proven* guilty. When you go back into the courtroom and see O.J. seated at counsel table, remind yourself that, as of this moment in time—as a matter of law—O.J. Simpson is an innocent man. What's more, he will remain innocent throughout the trial until—as declared by your own verdict—the prosecution has met its burden of proof to show *beyond a reasonable doubt* that O.J. is guilty.

And that is the burden which the prosecution bears regarding each and every element of the crimes charged. O.J. himself has no burden of proof. He need not present any evidence whatsoever. Nor must he testify on his own behalf. It is up to the prosecution alone to prove O.J.'s guilt. For that reason, the prosecution is given the first opportunity to present its case-in-chief.

Now, as a hush comes over the courtroom, it's "all rise" as Judge Ito takes the bench, and the spotlight moves from the jury box to the witness stand.

Judge: Are the People ready to proceed?

Prosecutor: We are, Your Honor.

Judge: Very well. You may call your first witness.

7

It's Time to Hear the Evidence

୶ଵୠ

Prosecution's Case-in-Chief

*Human blood is heavy; the man who has shed it
cannot run away.*

—African proverb

The great drama is about to unfold. As if it were an epic movie with a cast of thousands, the O.J. Simpson trial will be told through the eyes of scores of witnesses. It's a plot with many twists and turns; a human jigsaw puzzle with many pieces. Where does one begin to tell the story?

Marcia Clark and the prosecution team will have spent many hours casting just the right actors, deciding their sequence of appearance, and scripting exactly what they want each of those actors to say. There will have been many late-night rehearsals. And then there are the many, perhaps hundreds, of props. Some of the props were found at the murder scene or at O.J.'s Brentwood estate. Others will have been designed and created by the art department to be used as backdrop. All in all, it will be an impressive, no-cost-spared production.

This particular production, however, will resemble a high-tech *interactive* video, where the viewer is able to stop the action and make certain decisions which can change the direction of the plot. The *viewer* in this instance is the defense team. With the appearance of each actor—or, in reality, witness—the defense lawyers will have the right, following the prosecution's direct examination, to cross-examine that witness. The routine will be direct and cross; direct and cross; and sometimes even re-direct and re-cross. Therefore, that is how we, too, will proceed in our presentation of the prosecution's case-in-chief.

But for the moment, there is more strategy to consider.

Who's On First?

As the prosecution looks at its list of no fewer than thirty witnesses, it will see eight natural groupings:

1. Witnesses who can testify to events leading up to the homicides.

2. Witnesses who can tell how and when the bodies were discovered.

3. Witnesses who can testify as to Simpson's whereabouts before his flight to Chicago.

4. Police officers and other investigators who collected items of physical evidence and any statements which Simpson may have made.

5. Criminologists, medical examiners, and other experts who have made crucial tests or observations in the case.

6. Background witnesses who can testify to Simpson's whereabouts and activities from the time he left L.A. until he was arrested and questioned.

7. Witnesses who can speak to the issues of motive and possible means.

8. Witnesses who can testify regarding Simpson's low-speed-chase "flight" as seen by millions on television.

How the prosecution might choose to present these groupings is yet to be seen. But the order suggested above is as logical as any, and it has many distinct advantages, as you will soon see.

Lead-up to Nicole's Death

One of the great media curiosities is who will be the first witness for the prosecution. Of course, we won't know until the actual trial, but counsel normally would like to begin and end with witnesses whose testimony is strong and mind-sticking. That might suggest someone who could lay a foundation for the murder scene photos. The photos would certainly make a tremendous visual impact.

On the other hand, the prosecution in particular would like to tell you a story, in as close to actual chronological order as possible. A time sequence helps give you an overview of events and assists you in keeping all the facts in place. If that turns out to be the strategy, then we might expect to hear how Nicole and Ronald spent their last hours, and what eventually led to the discovery of their bodies. Such a chronological sequencing can also serve the dual purpose of establishing the time frame in which the homicides took place, a fact which will become crucial in linking Simpson to the murders.

One final factor to consider could give us a clue to the prosecution's first witness. When possible, the prosecution in a murder case wants to make living, breathing persons out of the victims. It's like an instant-replay resurrection of the deceased. By going back in time before their deaths, the impersonal "victims" become your own personal "friends" who have been brutally murdered.

So who could achieve this goal for the prosecution? Perhaps a family member, especially one who also knows some of the specific events leading up to the killing. The only drawback in this case is that the defendant himself was formerly tied by marriage to whomever might testify. That could make for a particularly tense opening. So, for the moment, let's skip over Nicole's mother, Juditha Brown (whom the prosecution may need later in any event), and nominate one of Nicole's three sisters, Denise Brown.

↬☓↫

Denise Brown (Nicole's sister) — On Direct Examination

As a former model, Denise, 37, should have the poise it will take to be the first to walk on stage and endure the glare of media lights. Not only would she be able to help bring Nicole's memory back from the dead, but she was with Nicole in her final hours. In one stroke, the prosecution has a witness who can make Nicole look good and Simpson look bad. Denise would know all about the stormy relationship between the two since their divorce in 1992, and certainly about Simpson's smothering possessiveness.

Denise could also set the scene for something that might possibly have led to the killings. At 4:30 that Sunday afternoon, the family had attended 8-year-old Sydney's western dance recital at Paul Revere Middle School in Brentwood. Simpson arrived late in his 1988 Bentley, and sat away from the family, apparently because Nicole failed to save him a seat. Denise can confirm that Simpson tried unsuccessfully to get the family together for a photograph. For later reference, the prosecution will want to establish that Nicole was wearing a black cocktail dress. Around 6:00 p.m. in the school parking lot, Nicole and Simpson had a brief talk.

At 6:30 p.m., the party proceeded to the Mezzaluna restaurant, three long blocks from Nicole's home. Around the table were Nicole, daughter Sydney, son Justin, mother Juditha, father Louis, sister Denise, and four other friends. Apparently, Simpson had been specifically uninvited. Over an order of rigatoni, Nicole and Denise talked about "all the trips we were going to take." Nicole chatted about her new life as a single woman and her idea for opening a cafe. At 8:30 p.m., the party was over and Nicole and the kids crossed the street to get an ice cream at Ben and Jerry's. Presumably, that is the last time Denise saw Nicole.

Denise Brown — On Cross-examination

As promised, we will focus on Denise Brown's testimony in order to demonstrate the unique kinds of questions typically asked on cross-examination.

The first point the defense will wish to develop is that the relationship between O.J. and Nicole must not have been all that bad, and therefore that O.J.'s involvement in the killings would have been out of character for him. Listen to the leading questions Denise will be asked:

— You were real close to Nicole, weren't you?

— In fact, you and Nicole discussed everything with each other, isn't that true?

— In fact, you and Nicole discussed her relationship with O.J. on numerous occasions?

— Isn't it true that Nicole continued to make attempts at reconciliation with O.J. long after their divorce?

— The relationship between Nicole and O.J. was such that you were shocked when you heard Nicole's 911 call, weren't you?

The second point to develop is that everything was "right" in Nicole's world during dinner, just before the homicides.

— You and the family, including Nicole, all had dinner together that night, didn't you?

— Would you describe Nicole as upbeat and buoyant that night?

— And isn't it true that the two of you talked about all the trips you were going to make?

— Isn't it also true that Nicole talked about her new life as a single woman?

— She was pleased about that wasn't she?

— Isn't it also true that Nicole talked about maybe opening a restaurant and planning for the future?

— As the party broke up around 8:30 p.m., Nicole was in good spirits, wasn't she?

[Space prohibits complete cross-examination with each witness, but perhaps from this brief demonstration you will appreciate how different cross-examination is from direct examination.]

It is a dangerous gamble, but the defense might wish to portray Nicole as a promiscuous woman who might have gotten in over her head with some jilted lover. If they choose this strategy, then they will want to begin even now to probe regarding Nicole's dating habits. Of course, a loving sister may not be their best source of damning information.

Bill Chang (Ice Cream Manager) — On Direct Examination

As manager of the Brentwood Ben and Jerry's, 21-year-old Bill Chang will testify that Nicole and her children came into the store between 8:30-9:00 p.m. The prosecution will have Chang identify a picture of Nicole and the children, and then likely will move to head off impeachment of Chang by the defense. At one point, Chang had told police that Nicole and the children were accompanied by a man whom he could not identify. He later changed his story, now believing that the man was just another customer. The prosecution will ask Chang about his change of mind and why he was mistaken the first time.

Bill Chang — On Cross-Examination

The defense will want to rule out O.J. as being the man Chang saw, and plant the idea of some stranger possibly stalking Nicole: Could the man you thought you saw with Nicole have been O.J.? Did that man leave before or after Nicole? Did you see in what direction he walked away?

Juditha Brown (Nicole's mother) — On Direct Examination

Juditha, 63, undoubtedly will not find it easy to take the stand and testify against her former son-in-law. But the prosecution almost certainly needs her testimony to establish the time of the killing. In the process, we may learn more about the relationship between Simpson and Nicole. But of special interest is a phone call which Nicole made to her mother at approximately 9:40 p.m. (Phone company records will likely be introduced as verification.)

Juditha will set up that phone call by telling of having dropped her prescription glasses near the valet parking stand outside Mezzaluna. When she called Mezzaluna, the glasses were found and put into an envelope by bar manager Karen Crawford, since Juditha couldn't go to pick them up. Apparently Juditha will testify that Nicole called Mezzaluna and that her friend, Ronald Goldman, a waiter there, said he would drop off the glasses at Nicole's after he got off work. The phone conversation between Juditha and Nicole ended at approximately 10:00 p.m. That is the last known contact anyone had with Nicole before her death.

Juditha Brown — On Cross-Examination

Isn't it true that you cannot recall the precise time your phone conversation with Nicole ended?

Nicole didn't express any anxiety or fear during that call, did she?

[Given what may be a great deal of hostility toward O.J., as well as possible insider information about the tempestuous relationship between her daughter and O.J.—which could turn out to be a can of worms—the defense may choose not to cross-examine Juditha.]

Lead-up to Ronald's Death

For the moment, the prosecution might pause in the sequence of events to catch us up with the events leading to Ron Goldman's involvement. His and Nicole's destinies are about to intersect, and both deaths need to be considered simultaneously. Once again, the prosecution will want to call someone who can humanize Ron and help the jury to identify more closely with his death. It is unknown who that might be, but it could well be Ron's father, Frederic Goldman, 53, a businessman.

Frederic Goldman (Ron's father) — On Direct Examination

Mr. Goldman could tell us that, after he and his first wife, Sharon Rufo, divorced in 1974, he retained custody of Ron and daughter Kim, now 22. In 1987, Frederic married Patti Glass, mother of three. The merged families now live together in Agoura Hills, just outside L.A.

Frederic may or may not be able to testify to rumors that Simpson disliked Ron. He may be asked to repeat what he had said in an interview with Barbara Walters on *20/20*, including his denial of rumors indicating that Ron was gay, into fast living, and was one of Nicole's lovers. In the positive way that only a father could remember his son, Frederic will present a good image of his son and perhaps lay a foundation for photos to be shown.

Frederic Goldman — On Cross-Examination

If Mr. Goldman has testified to any animosity between O.J. and Ron, the defense may follow up to clarify whether there were any overt threats involved. Otherwise, it might be prudent not to cross-examine the father of one of the victims.

Jeff Keller (Friend of Ron) — On Direct Examination

Jeff, or someone else like him, may be called to further personalize Ron for the jury. He and Ron played softball weekly at the Barrington Recreation Center and had a game together at 1:00 p.m. that Sunday. Jeff could testify that Ron seemed happy and was loose and relaxed. Ron had played well that afternoon.

Jeff Keller — On Cross-Examination

There is little for the defense to pursue, except to capitalize on what they will guess to be a lack of knowledge on Jeff's part about any animosity between Ron and Simpson. If they wish to pursue that line of questioning, any ignorance on Jeff's part about such animosity will be taken as evidence of a lack of any such animosity. The defense may ask either Jeff, or any other of Ron's friends who may be called to testify, if they can shed any light on the relationship (particularly sexual, if any) between Ron and Nicole. The less intimate they can make that relationship, the less motive O.J. would have for killing Ron.

Karen Crawford (Bar manager) — On Direct Examination

Karen, bar manager at Mezzaluna, talked to Juditha Brown about the lost glasses. She will testify that within a few minutes after she put the glasses into an envelope, Nicole called and asked to speak with Ron. It is not known whether Karen overheard their conversation, but she will be able to testify as to when Ron got off work and left Mezzaluna. He clocked out at 9:33. Apparently he changed clothes before heading for Nicole's around 9:45.

Karen Crawford — On Cross-Examination

Ron indicated it was not an imposition to drop off the glasses, didn't he? Did he say anything that would indicate he was happy to have the opportunity to go to Nicole's house?

Did Ron leave the restaurant alone? Was he driving or walking?

A Special Problem

There may not have been an eyewitness to the killing, but there may have been an "earwitness" to the killer. That witness may have been eight-year-old Sydney, who, at the time of her mother's death, was asleep inside the house. It has been reported that, while temporarily in police custody following discovery of the bodies, Sydney said: "I heard Mommy's best friend and heard Mommy crying." So far, the identity of that "best friend" has not been revealed, if it is even known.

Naturally, the prosecution has a real dilemma here. How can you put a nine-year-old child on the stand to testify against her own father? For a time, she apparently didn't even know he was in jail. (She had been told only that her Mommy was in heaven.) On the other hand, if the voice she heard was in fact Simpson's, then his denial that he was at Nicole's house that night—his alibi—is completely blown out of the water. It could be the most damning evidence of all!

But if Sydney did in fact make the reported statement, is it reasonable to believe that she would have referred to her own father as "Mommy's best friend"? Which only raises the interesting question as to who that might be, if not Simpson. Could the mystery "best friend" be Ron Goldman? Was he or she someone else altogether? If anything, the "best friend" reference may also help the prosecution to rule out some freakish coincidence of an ordinary street crime committed by a complete stranger.

Any way you look at it, this potential wild card could be one of the most fascinating surprises in the whole trial. If either side wishes this reported information to come in, the likelihood is that it would have to be introduced in some manner other than putting Sydney on the witness stand. She could be questioned prior to trial under highly protective circumstances (perhaps by the judge, with lawyers for both sides in attendance), and the transcript of her testimony read to you at the appropriate time.

The problem is that thorny legal issues are presented when a child is testifying against her own parent (which typically occurs in sexual abuse cases). The Constitution guarantees a defendant the right to confront witnesses against him. But what is the court to do when the witness is a frightened child having to face the very one who has abused her? Under those unique circumstances, as well as a few others, some courts have permitted the questioning to proceed outside the presence of the parent.

In a leading case, the U.S. Supreme Court endorsed this practice upon a showing of necessity. Almost all states now have a procedure by which child victims can testify, either by deposition or otherwise out of the defendant's presence.

The Simpson case, however, presents a still tougher issue. Suppose Sydney does in fact have information that would literally decide the case one way or the other. Can the prosecution or the defense be precluded from using that information? Should Lady Justice be required to wear her blindfold in the face of unimpeachable evidence which would positively identify the killer of Sydney's mother? Would it be in Sydney's best interest to tell what she knows and thereby send her own father to jail? At this point, Judge Ito may send out an urgent appeal for some assistance from his fellow jurist, Solomon!

Given the difficulties inherent in presenting such evidence (and the tentative assurance that such evidence even exists), you may or may not hear from Sydney as a witness.

∾✗∾

Discovery of the Bodies

Having traced the steps leading up to the hours and minutes before the homicides occurred, the prosecution will play the tape forward to the circumstances surrounding the finding of the bodies. The effort will be to close the "window of opportunity" at the earliest possible time. If the homicides occurred after 11:00 p.m., Simpson has a perfect alibi. On the other hand, if they occurred between Nicole's phone call to her mother (sometime between 9:40 and 10:00) and sometime around 10:45 or 11:00, then the prosecution's "window of opportunity" is wide open for Simpson.

∾✗∾

Pablo Fenjves (Nicole's neighbor) — On Direct Examination

Screenwriter Pablo Fenjves, who lives near Nicole's condo, will testify that, around 10:15 p.m., he heard a dog's "plaintive wail."

Pablo Fenjves — On Cross-Examination

Isn't it true that you cannot be certain of the time?

Isn't it true that you did not go out to investigate?

And isn't it true that you cannot testify with any degree of certainty that the bark came from the direction of Nicole's condo?

Steven Schwab (Walking dog) — On Direct Examination

A neighbor of Nicole's, screenwriter Steven Schwab, 37, will testify that he left his house shortly after 10:35 p.m. to walk his dog. He soon encountered a white Akita, with bloody paws, barking non-stop. Noticing that the dog was not wearing any tags, he took the dog in tow.

If there is any question about the identity of the dog, the prosecution undoubtedly will have Schwab point out the dog, perhaps even in the courtroom. (Ironically, the children named the dog Kato after "Kato" Kaelin, Simpson's resident house guest who will soon figure prominently in the case.)

Schwab's testimony is extremely important to the prosecution's case. Not only does he fix the time that he spotted the Akita as somewhere around 10:35 p.m. to 10:45 p.m., but he has a specific time-frame reference. He left his house at the end of an episode of *The Dick Van Dyke Show*—at 10:30 p.m.—returning before the beginning of *The Mary Tyler Moore Show*—at 11:00 p.m.

Steven Schwab — On Cross-Examination

Isn't it true that the distance between your house and Nicole's condo is _____?

Isn't it true that you did not see, or hear, or sense anything was amiss at her condo?

You have no way of knowing whether the blood you saw on the dog's paws was human blood, do you?

Isn't it true that you had never seen the Akita before? You don't know whether or not it often barks incessantly, do you?

Sukru Boztepe (Discovered bodies) — On Direct Examination

Boztepe, 28, and his wife, Bettina Rasmussen, 25, are neighbors of Steven Schwab. Boztepe arrived home at 11:40 and saw Schwab with the Akita. Boztepe told Schwab he would be happy to keep the dog for the night and take it to the animal shelter the next morning. When the Akita became agitated inside the house, the Boztepes decided to see if the dog would lead them to its owner. The Akita led them to 875 South Bundy, Nicole's condo. The time was just at 12:00 midnight.

It was then that in the dim light of the gated entrance, Boztepe noticed a body sprawled on the Spanish-tile walk. Boztepe will testify that he saw a lot of blood, and turned around. He and his wife roused a nearby resident, who called the police.

[Note: It is not known whether the prosecution will call the neighbor who alerted the police. That neighbor might or might not know any more about the relevant facts. Also, the prosecution may wish to call Boztepe's wife, whose testimony at the preliminary hearing was far more dramatic.]

Sukru Boztepe — On Cross-Examination

— Isn't it true that you never went inside the gate?

— To your knowledge, no one else did, isn't that right?

— Who was the first person to enter the premises?

— How long did it take for the police to arrive?

— How many officers responded?

— Isn't it true that the officers arrived with flashing lights and sirens?

— How long did you stay at the scene?

— What did you see regarding the investigation by the police?

— Bystanders began to gather, didn't they?

— Isn't it true that the police first went to the bodies?

— Were you there when the paramedics arrived?

— How much time passed from the police's arrival to the paramedics' arrival?

— Isn't it true that the police's first priority was the bodies?

— Did the police eventually cordon off the area?

— Did that include the area outside the gate?

— Within a half hour after the police were called, how many people would you estimate were in the area?

[Note: Counsel will not ask the final question: "Could someone have picked up any crucial evidence?" That point will be saved for argument.]

— Oh, one last question. You didn't see anyone from the coroner's office on the scene while you were there, did you?

ॐ

Reconstructing Simpson's Whereabouts

With the foregoing testimony, the prosecution will have attempted to establish what it believes to be the only "window of opportunity" in which the homicides could have occurred: sometime between 9:40-10:00 p.m. and approximately 10:45-11:00 p.m. What remains to be shown is that Simpson's whereabouts that evening perfectly fit that precise "window." To prove that scenario, the prosecution will call at least four witnesses, the first two of whom are crucial.

ॐ

Brian "Kato" Kaelin (Resident Guest) — On Direct Examination

Kaelin, 35, is an aspiring actor with a reputation as a popular ladies' man on the hip Hollywood party scene. For some time, he has lived in guest quarters at Simpson's Brentwood estate, located at 360 North Rockingham Avenue. Kaelin and Simpson are good friends, and even Nicole's now-famous Akita is named for him.

Kaelin will testify that he was with Simpson in the kitchen of the main house around 7:00 p.m. when Simpson jokingly criticized Nicole's friends for wearing tight-fitting clothes. Simpson wondered aloud if Nicole would still be wearing dresses like the black cocktail dress she wore to Sydney's dance recital even when she was a "grandma."

Two hours later, around 9:10 p.m., Kaelin and Simpson made a McDonald's run in O.J.'s Bentley. Simpson wanted to grab something to eat before catching an 11:45 p.m. flight to Chicago. He was to play in a Hertz golf outing the next day. Kaelin will testify that Simpson was wearing a black long-sleeved sweatsuit.

After returning to the estate around 9:45 p.m., Kaelin and Simpson parted company. Kaelin retired to his apartment in the guest wing.

The next thing Kaelin recalls as being out of the ordinary happened around 10:40 while he was talking on the phone with friend, Rachel Ferrara, an aspiring actress. Suddenly, Kaelin heard three loud thumps on the outside wall. Grabbing a flashlight, he went outside to investigate.

After searching around for several minutes, Kaelin went to the front of the house where he saw Allan Park, a limo driver who had come to take Simpson to the airport. Kaelin waved briefly. After an interval of a few minutes, Kaelin opened the gate for Park and the two men talked together until Simpson emerged. At that point, Simpson got into the limo with Park and they drove away.

Somewhere along the way, the prosecution will want to establish the distance between Simpson's Brentwood estate and Nicole's condominium. Kaelin would be as good a witness as any to get this information into the record. He could testify that the driving time between the two residences is a short 5-10 minute ride.

"Kato" Kaelin — On Cross-Examination

The defense will want to establish through Kaelin that O.J.'s demeanor throughout the evening was typical of the affable O.J.—that O.J. was neither (1) a man who was nervous or distracted because he knew he was about to pull off a premeditated murder of his ex-wife, nor (2) an angry or brooding man who was on the verge of exploding at the least provocation.

It will be important for the defense to clarify that O.J. was "joking" about how Nicole and her friends dressed—that he was not outraged about her wearing the black cocktail dress. They want to leave no possible motive arising out of what they will characterize as playful banter about Nicole.

An attempt will probably be made to capitalize on the fact that Kaelin made an extensive investigative sweep of the estate with his flashlight. Did he see anyone? Did he hear any further noise? Did he discover anything unusual? Most important of all, did he see a leather glove on the ground by the wall where he had heard the three loud thumps? If not, the foundation is laid for future cross-examination of the detective who claims to have found the glove.

The defense will likely also want to ask whether Kaelin saw or heard O.J. either leave the estate or return between the time they got back from McDonald's and when O.J. came out of the house to get into the limo.

Allan William Park (Chauffeur) — On Direct Examination

Park, 24, is a chauffeur for Town & Country Limo. At 10:25 p.m., Park pulled up in his white stretch limousine and parked it across the street from the Ashford Street gate to Simpson's estate. He was twenty minutes early, so he waited in the limo. At approximately 10:40 p.m., Park swung the limo around to the North Rockingham Avenue gate of Simpson's estate and looked for a car in the driveway. Seeing none, he returned to the Ashford gate, where he got out and repeatedly rang the buzzer. There was no response.

At 10:50 p.m., Park beeped his boss, Dale St. John, who returned Park's page two minutes later, at 10:52 p.m. While Park was explaining to St. John that the house was dark and nobody seemed to be at home, he turned and saw Kaelin coming from the backyard with a flashlight. Kaelin waved but did not immediately open the gate.

Within moments, Park observed a six-foot-tall black person wearing dark clothes entering the house through the front door, and then first-floor lights coming on.

At 10:56, Park again buzzed the intercom and Simpson said, "Sorry, I overslept, and I just got out of the shower. I'll be down in a minute." Park and Kaelin talked together while waiting for Simpson to emerge. He came out of the house at approximately 11:10 to 11:15 p.m., wearing a white short-sleeved shirt and stonewashed jeans. Simpson was carrying a garment bag.

Park will further testify that on the way to the airport Simpson kept his window rolled down, despite the fact that the limo was air-conditioned. Park recalls Simpson repeatedly saying, "Whew, I'm hot. Whew, man, I'm hot."

Allan Park — On Cross-Examination

Defense counsel will definitely want to zero in on the fleeting figure whom Park describes as a "six-foot tall black person." Has Park chauffeured O.J. on previous occasions? Would he not have recognized O.J. if, in fact, it had *been* O.J.?

And did Park see any vehicle approaching the estate? Where would the "mystery man" have come from? [It is critical to position Park at the gate (perhaps with a diagram) to show that while he was waiting no one drove into the estate.]

If O.J. had in fact overslept, wouldn't the events which Park described be consistent with that scenario? For example, lights coming on in the house as Park's repeated buzzing finally awakens O.J.?

Did Park learn anything about O.J.'s whereabouts from Kaelin?

Does Kaelin confirm to Park the sighting of the "mystery man?" If not, where was Kaelin when Park saw the "mystery man"? As for O.J.'s complaints about being hot inside the limo, did Park get the impression that it was anything more than a man oversleeping, taking a hot shower, and then rushing out late to catch his plane?

❧

Rachel Ferrara (Kaelin's friend)

[The prosecution could call Kaelin's actress friend, Rachel Ferrara, to confirm that Kaelin reacted to the loud thumping by hanging up so that he could investigate the noise. Ms. Ferrara might also be able to help identify the time of the call itself and when the call abruptly ended.]

❧

Dale St. John (Allan Park's boss)

[Simply to corroborate the time sequence of Allan Park's observations, the prosecution might decide to call his boss, Dale St. John.]

❧

The Police Investigation

The prosecution knows in advance that the weak link in its case is the process of police investigation. The defense has already served notice that they are going to hammer away at what they believe to have been—at a minimum—sloppy investigative techniques, and perhaps even willful deception. For that reason the prosecution may decide to sandwich this phase of the case between the highly damaging testimony already received from their occurrence witnesses and what they believe will be additional strong testimony from "motive" and "means" witnesses yet to come.

That said, however, there is another sense in which this part of the prosecution's case-in-chief could be the clincher. For it is the physical and scientific evidence which trains the big guns in on O.J. Simpson. If the prosecution can persuade you that the evidence was properly collected, identified, handled, and tested, then their scientific experts can later drop some incredible evidentiary bombshells.

It can't be known prior to the trial how many officers and detectives the prosecution intends to call as witnesses. It could be an impressive (if, perhaps, boringly repetitive) lineup of the LAPD's finest. It is during this phase, too, that you are likely to long for all the "short recesses" you can get. The method of establishing the *chain of custody* is nothing if not dulling to the senses. In fact, why don't we take that "brief recess" you've been wanting and explain what chain of custody is all about.

❧

Establishing the Chain of Custody

Before a scientific expert can give you his opinion regarding, say, matching blood or hairs with similar characteristics, or bloody gloves, it must first be established that these items are relevant to this particular case and are tied to identifiable individuals. How is that done? Typically, officer A testifies as to the circumstances of his finding an item of evidence (for example, a hat) which he turned over to Detective B, who, in turn, delivered the hat to crime lab expert C. Each witness will have to testify that he carefully marked the hat for identification, affixing to it either his signature or some other identifying symbol. He will further have to satisfy the Court that, while the hat was in his possession, there was no opportunity for anyone else to have access to it. The hat must be free from any possible taint or tampering. Once this chain of custody has been established, then the expert who performed the test can testify, for instance, that he found a hair on the hat which has similar characteristics as hair taken from the accused. (And that hair sample, itself, would need a similar chain of custody established.)

Given the large number of physical items seized and tested in this case, the sheer process of painstakingly establishing the chain of custody for each one could turn into an evidentiary marathon. Call it a nightmare. But there is no getting around it, so steel yourself for the tedium. If it is any comfort, along the way there ought to be some real fireworks as the defense team attempts to discredit as much of the physical evidence as they possibly can.

Incidentally, even though crime scene photos or diagrams do not need a chain of custody to be introduced, witnesses will have to show that they are familiar with the scenes shown, and that the photos or diagrams are an accurate depiction of that which they purport to show. That's fairly obvious with photos; less so with diagrams, which are more easily manipulable.

With this brief explanation of what you are about to see over and over during this phase, we turn now to the witnesses themselves. Again, the officers and detectives listed here are representative of a number of others who likely will be called to testify in the case.

❧

Ofc. Robert Riske (First to respond) — On Direct Examination

At 12:09 a.m., Monday, June 13, Officer Robert Riske arrived at the scene and was led to the gated entrance of Nicole's condo by Boztepe and his wife.

The body of Nicole Brown Simpson, 5'5", 129 lbs., was lying in a fetal position inside the gate at the foot of a flight of stairs. The much-talked-about black cocktail dress was torn, and her bloodied hands were raised in a position suggesting that she had been trying to defend herself. Multiple stab wounds were visible, and a pool of blood told all that needed to be told.

Ofc. Riske discovered the body of Ronald Lyle Goldman, 5'9", 171 lbs., in the bushes ten feet from Nicole's body. His body also exhibited multiple stab wounds, with cuts to his hands, just as with Nicole.

This may be the point in the trial when Marcia Clark decides to offer into evidence the crime scene photos. After a proper foundation is laid as indicated above, the photos will be admitted as People's exhibits, say, 1 through 10. Once admitted, it is likely that Clark will want to have the jury see the photos. Get ready for a grisly sight. (You will also have these photos, as well as other items of physical evidence, available to you in the jury room during deliberations.)

Ofc. Riske will testify that, at Goldman's feet he also discovered a brown leather left-hand glove and a knit cap. Near his knees was an envelope containing prescription glasses. At his back was a beeper.

When Ofc. Riske proceeded toward the house, he found the door to Nicole's condo ajar, and Sydney and Justin upstairs asleep. Lights were on throughout the house. Candles were flickering in the bathroom.

Back outside, Ofc. Riske found bloody footsteps leading to the alley. He called for backup, and other officers arrived at the scene, cordoning it off with police crime-scene tape.

Sydney and Justin were taken to the West Los Angeles police station.

Ofc. Riske — On Cross-Examination

The defense will begin right away to establish their main theory—that the police bungled their investigation. Therefore you can expect to hear Ofc. Riske being closely examined regarding the physical evidence.

— Who was at the scene when you arrived?

— Did you arrive with lights and siren?

— Did backup arrive with lights and siren?

— Did the paramedics arrive with lights and siren?

— How much time passed before the area was cordoned off?

—   Did you touch the bodies?

—   Please describe.

—   When did you check the condo?

—   How long did that take?

—   How much time elapsed before you called for backup?

—   Isn't it true that when you examined the bodies you had to step into the blood on the walkway?

—   Isn't it possible that you could have tracked the blood in the direction of the alleyway?

—   Isn't it possible that a dog could have tracked blood?

—   Did you notify the coroner's office regarding the homicides?

—   In fact, isn't it true that it wasn't until 6:55 a.m.—almost seven hours after you discovered the bodies—that the coroner was officially notified?

—   Did you take any medical or scientific steps to ascertain when the killings might have taken place?

—   Are you qualified to determine the time of death?

—   Would it not be important to know the time of death?

—   Were you still present at the scene when Det. Mark Fuhrman arrived?

—   Had any items been taken from the scene prior to his arrival?

—   You testified that you found only one bloody glove?

—   It's possible that another glove might have been discovered by Det. Fuhrman in some location you may have overlooked, isn't it?

—   From what you saw of the bodies and their relative positions, it's possible that more than one person did the killing, isn't it?

—   Did you ever discover a knife?

Det. Mark Fuhrman (Found second glove) — On Direct Examination

Det. Fuhrman, 42, is a twice-divorced former Marine who finished second in his class at the Police Academy in 1975. At 1:05 a.m., Fuhrman was contacted at his home and summoned to the crime scene. He arrived at Nicole's condominium at 2:10 a.m., whereupon he conducted his investigation for two hours until later joined by other detectives.

Det. Fuhrman will testify that at 5:00 a.m., he and Det. Vannatter and two other officers drove to Simpson's estate. They buzzed the intercom at the Ashford gate with no response. They then tried to phone Simpson, but again got no response. Det. Fuhrman saw a white Bronco parked askew to the curb near the Rockingham Avenue gate and proceeded to check it out. On the driver's side door of the Bronco, he saw what appeared to be blood. He then briefly discussed with his fellow officers what they should do. They returned to the Ashford Street gate, and Det. Fuhrman scaled the wall and let the others in.

Once inside the estate, the officers woke Kaelin and also, in a separate part of the guest wing, Simpson's daughter (by his first wife), Arnelle. When Kaelin told Det. Fuhrman about the "three thumps," Fuhrman went between the guest wing wall and a fence, where he discovered a bloody right-hand leather glove. He discovered more blood in a driveway leading from the Bronco to the front door, and also on the garage wall and on a wire near the south wall.

Det. Fuhrman is expected to testify that, while Det. Vannatter left to get a search warrant, the rest went inside the main house where Arnelle helped police get in touch with Simpson's assistant, Cathy Randa. Learning that Simpson was in Chicago, the officers called him and informed him of Nicole's death.

Inside the house, officers found red stains in the foyer and master bathroom. They seized a pair of navy blue socks from the master bedroom; a baggage tag found on a bench outside the front door; an airline ticket from a trash can; a wooden stick and a blue plastic bag found lying on the grass; a Marlboro cigarette butt found in the street; and a note from Nicole breaking off contact with Simpson.

Det. Fuhrman — On Cross-Examination

If you want to see a classic cross-examination confrontation, this one promises to live up to its pre-trial billing. The defense team has already done everything it can do—including requesting various personnel records—in an effort to discredit Det. Fuhrman. His claimed discovery of the right-hand glove is particularly threatening to the defense, especially if it turns out that it matches the left-hand glove found at Nicole's. In whatever way they can, the defense hopes to create an implication that Det. Fuhrman actually planted the glove at the Brentwood estate in an effort to frame O.J.

Why should Fuhrman do that? It will be the defense's contention that Fuhrman is a racist. Maybe he even realized that a conviction of O.J. would be a feather in his cap and, therefore, did whatever was necessary to pin the murders on O.J.

The defense team may attempt to make some connection between this case and a 1985 incident in which Fuhrman went to the Simpson home to investigate a domestic disturbance call. Could Fuhrman have it in for Simpson because of something that happened on that occasion?

[There has been much pre-trial legal wrangling over the admissibility of the various items of evidence seized at O.J.'s estate. The defense will want to reiterate their objections based upon what they believe to be illegal searches and seizures. It will be interesting to see whether there are any last-minute surprises as to what items may or may not be admitted by Judge Ito.]

Det. Philip Vannatter (Robbery-Homicide) — On Direct Examination

Detective Vannatter, 53, is a big, strong, raspy-talking detective, known to his friends as "Dutch." A 25-year veteran of the LAPD, Vannatter was first alerted of the homicides at 3:00 a.m. (When it had become apparent who was involved in this case, it was decided that the elite detective corps of Robbery-Homicide should be brought in.) Vannatter rolled to the scene at about 4:00 a.m. where he joined Det. Fuhrman. Vannatter's partner, Det. Thomas Lange, arrived thirty minutes later.

Det. Vannatter was one of the four officers who went to the Brentwood estate at 5:00 a.m. It was Vannatter who left the estate to obtain a search warrant from the L.A. municipal court.

In the absence of a legal hurdle to its admission, it is possible that the prosecution will use Vannatter to introduce a video of a television pilot titled "Frogmen," which at some point was seized from the Simpson residence. In the show, Simpson the actor holds a knife to a woman's throat, a coincidence which the prosecution will hope to turn into a demonstration of how Simpson might have committed the killings. [The prosecution may decide to bring in a witness from the Navy SEALS, who reportedly gave Simpson special knife training in preparation for the film.]

Det. Vannatter — On Cross-Examination

The defense can be expected to keep up its blistering attack on every aspect of the police investigation. They will probe Det. Vannatter's whereabouts at the time Det. Fuhrman found the bloody glove, and possibly attempt to link him to any "planting" theory they may have established in their cross-examination of Fuhrman.

If the prosecution uses Det. Vannatter to introduce the "Frogmen" video, the defense will jump all over the circumstances of its being found and played during a "leisurely," sometimes party-like, three-hour search of the house. The defense will attempt to show that the police acted unprofessionally in making their search, and to that end will nitpick almost everything that was done, as well as probe its relevance in the apprehension of the killer.

Det. Thomas Lange (Vannatter's partner)

Det. Ronald Phillips (Part of investigative team)

[The prosecution may call both of these detectives (and as many as ten other officers who participated in the search of the Simpson estate), not only to verify the physical evidence which was discovered and seized, but, more importantly, to corroborate and bolster Det. Fuhrman's testimony. Yet there is a risk involved. While there may be a high degree of fraternal loyalty among the officers, the more who testify, the greater the chance for the defense to find discrepancies in their testimony.]

Andrea Mazzola (Criminalist) — On Direct Examination

Mazzola will testify to the many blood samples and other items of evidence which she collected from the Brentwood estate. In many instances, she will provide the first link in the chain of custody leading to the testing of the physical evidence for purposes of identity.

Andrea Mazzola — On Cross-Examination

Apparently, the defense team will attempt to capitalize on Mazzola's comparative inexperience, hoping to throw her off guard and reveal mistakes in the way her samples were collected. With each mistake which they might be able to show, there is greater chance that you will begin to accept their argument that scientific tests are only as good as the people who use them.

Mazzola's time of arrival and any relative contamination of the scene is crucial.

Battle of the Experts Begins

Once the prosecution has laid a proper chain of custody through the testimony of all the investigators and criminalists who seized or collected tangible physical evidence in the case, it remains for the experts to take the stand and testify about the results. Expert witnesses are permitted to testify, at the judge's discretion, when it can be proved that they are qualified in their fields of expertise and that their testimony would aid the jury in better understanding the evidence. Because many scientific tests and procedures are controversial, the experts called by either side may sharply disagree as to the accuracy of a given test or the interpretation which should be given to any results.

For that reason, counsel on direct examination are only permitted to elicit the expert's *opinions*, which you the jury may either accept or reject. On cross-examination, counsel are permitted to impeach the expert in a number of ways, including challenges to his qualification, scrutiny of his methodology, and the consistency of his opinion with the rest of the scientific community.

In this case, you can expect to witness not just a "battle of the experts"—typical of many cases—but an all-out war.

Irwin Golden (Medical Examiner) — On Direct Examination

Irwin Golden is the deputy L.A. medical examiner who performed the autopsy on the victims' bodies. Golden is a board-certified forensic pathologist who joined the coroner's office in 1982. He has testified in court some 700 times. Among the 6,500 autopsies he has conducted are such high-profile cases as Jose and Kitty Menendez and some of the Night Stalker victims.

Golden will testify that Nicole Brown Simpson's throat had been slashed all the way to the spinal column. A gash 5 1/2 by 2 1/2-inches ran from left to right up to her ear. There were four more wounds in the left side of the neck and three punctures at the back of her head. Her hands had been repeatedly slashed.

An autopsy of Ronald Lyle Goldman's body revealed much the same story as with Nicole. Goldman's hands had been slashed, and also his neck. In addition, there were three stab wounds in the chest, one in the abdomen, and one in the thigh.

As for the crucial time of death, Golden can only guess that it might have been sometime between 9:00 p.m. and 12:00 midnight.

Without a known murder weapon, Golden can only speculate as to what kind of an instrument was used.

Irwin Golden — On Cross-Examination

When Golden's cross-examination begins, it will be round two in what has already proved to be an embarrassment to the prosecution. At the preliminary hearing, Robert Shapiro performed his own autopsy on Golden, leaving him looking tentative and confused. Shapiro will hope for a rerun, although you can count on the prosecution's having done everything it can to make Golden look better this time around.

Golden, 54, has a reputation for what some consider to be inappropriate gallows humor. For example, it is reported that a few years back Golden was examining a suicide victim when somebody walked into the morgue and asked what he was doing. Wrapping the still-attached noose around his own neck, Golden reportedly said, "Just hangin' around with my friend here."

Some weeks after his disappointing performance in the Simpson preliminary hearing, he allegedly waved a gun in the lobby of the coroner's office and said, in effect, "This is all you need to take out six or seven lawyers!"

Shapiro will want to use both of these instances, if allowed, in order to establish that Golden has a bad attitude toward his work, an attitude that might have hindered his performance in the Simpson case autopsies.

More serious, Shapiro may wish to impeach Golden's qualifications by pointing to a 1990 shooting case in which he had the fatal bullet exiting the body the wrong way. (The case against the suspect was dropped as a result.) Additionally, the fact that Golden has written almost no professional articles and has had no academic appointments will no doubt be highlighted to help create an atmosphere of distrust.

The heart of Shapiro's attack on Golden will center around Golden's failure to preserve the contents of Ms. Simpson's stomach, which, had he done so, might have more closely nailed down the time of death. In this connection, Shapiro will once again establish that there was a highly unusual 10-hour delay before the coroner's investigator was permitted to test the bodies.

Shapiro will also press the point that Golden did not perform a rape test, thought to be standard procedure in murders involving women. The tie is tenuous at best, but the failure to ascertain if a rape occurred plays into the hands of any defense theory that Nicole may have been the victim of rogue street criminals.

As a final blow, Shapiro undoubtedly will want to revive his line of questioning at the preliminary hearing about Golden's refusal to match the death wounds with a knife which the police had thought to be similar to the murder weapon. Golden says he didn't think such a comparison was necessary, since the wound indicated a single sharp cutting edge—which could fit innumerable knives or other instruments.

In particular, Shapiro will want to raise the possibility that the two victims might have had their throats slashed with two different knives, a possibility that would give credence to the defense's suggestion that more than one killer was involved. If Golden was unwilling to do that kind of testing on the bodies, then Shapiro will claim that O.J. was denied the opportunity of a fair defense.

❧

Possible Medical Examiner Backup?

[Because of Golden's embarrassing showing at the preliminary hearing, it is quite possible that at the trial the prosecution may bring in a more dependable expert who will have reviewed Golden's work and can justify his actions and bolster his conclusions. District Attorney Gil Garcetti has tried to get San Francisco's highly respected Medical Examiner Boyd Stephens, but it remains to be seen whether Stephens will agree to appear on behalf of the prosecution.]

❧

Gregory Matheson (Blood analyst) — On Direct Examination

Matheson, 39, is a blood analyst for the LAPD crime lab. He will testify, as he did at the preliminary hearing, that Simpson's blood characteristics link him to the crime scene. Matheson's testimony will be helpful to the prosecution, but not anywhere near as conclusive as any DNA analysis which may be introduced.

Gregory Matheson — On Cross-Examination

The defense will probably have little success in attacking Matheson's blood comparisons, as such; but they will be consoled knowing that their best success will have been their attack on the methods by which the samples were taken. Problems with the chain of custody, including apparent mislabeling, could be highlighted by asking Matheson how important it is for his expert opinions to be based upon accurate samples.

❧

Unknown Criminologists — On Direct Examination

Various criminologists from the crime lab will be testifying to a wide variety of forensic evidence. Perhaps most crucial out of all that evidence will be hair samples allegedly found at the crime scene. As reported, hair was found in the knit cap. Also, there was a single hair on Goldman's body.

Unlike DNA hair testing, traditional hair comparisons are limited to *similar* characteristics. If reports are to be trusted, one of the criminologists will testify that the hair samples taken from the crime scene are from an African American. The odds of making a closer identification (apart from DNA analysis itself) will depend upon whether the particular hair happens to share unusual characteristics, such as cracks, splits, or diseases.

Unknown Criminologists — On Cross-examination

What the defense will want to emphasize is the limitation inherent within standard hair comparisons. Unlike fingerprints, hairs do not single out any one individual. Hair comparisons can *rule out* individuals, but not specifically identify them.

One possible line of questioning will proceed on the basis that O.J. was a frequent visitor to Nicole's condo. The criminologist may be asked whether it might have been possible that a hair from O.J., perhaps dropped on the ground, might attach itself onto Goldman's body when he fell.

This may not be the right witness, but the defense may want to raise the question of whether, in the kind of violent struggle which apparently took place, only *one* hair would have fallen from O.J.'s head.

The worst case scenario for the defense is if the prosecution presents DNA testing of the hair and not simply standard hair comparisons.

Cellmark DNA Experts — On Direct Examination

The centerfold of the entire trial could be the testimony from DNA experts representing Cellmark, the lab which is responsible for the DNA analysis of the many blood samples collected at both Nicole's condominium and Simpson's residence. A number of matching possibilities could arise. By precisely identifying the blood of both Simpson and the two victims, it could be shown that Simpson's blood was at the crime scene itself, or at his residence, or perhaps in both places.

More damning yet would be any proof that either of the victim's blood was among the samples collected at Simpson's residence. Certainly that would be true of the bloody right-hand glove which Det. Fuhrman says he found there, but (because the defense is attempting to cast doubt on the glove) it would be even more significant if there was a match of either of the victim's blood on Simpson's driveway.

Standard blood comparisons would be strong proof in and of themselves.

However, they tend simply to *exclude* rather than *include* a given individual. By contrast, DNA analysis points the finger of identity, not simply to groups of individuals, but to single, uniquely identifiable individuals. Each of us has a DNA composition that is different from every other person who has ever lived. And, while current DNA analysis is not capable of drawing quite that fine a line, the odds of there being any other person out there closely matching the same DNA tend to get rather slim.

The issue of DNA analysis has already received massive attention before this moment in the trial. Many, if not most, of the thorny legal issues have already been resolved, and Judge Ito has made it known that he will probably allow the experts to testify about DNA results.

Given that green light, experts for the prosecution will attempt to reduce to layman-like understanding the mysterious science of DNA analysis. What they will explain is that human chromosomes are made up of deoxyribonucleic acid (DNA), a highly complex, two-stranded molecule wound into a double helix. The DNA has a certain sequencing—as if you were to randomly scramble the alphabet—which is unique to each individual. That sequencing, in turn, becomes a blueprint for all of an individual's inherited traits, and—like snowflakes—no two blueprints are exactly alike.

Since DNA is resident in blood, semen, skin, saliva, and hair follicles, any of those items discovered at a crime scene can be tested to determine what its unique DNA blueprint is. That sample, in turn, can be compared with the unique DNA blueprint of either the victims or the suspect. Any match is, well, extraordinary. However, the $64,000 question is, *just how extraordinary?* And you can be sure that you will witness an epic battle over that single question. Are the odds one in 800? Or 4,000? Or 250,000? Or, indeed, one in tens of millions?

What kind of gambler are you willing to be with justice? Indeed, what kind of gambler will Judge Ito allow you to be? He might decide to limit the range of odds that counsel can talk about. On the other hand, he may let counsel each have their own experts testify in an attempt to win you over to their particular view of what the odds ought to be. Suffice it to say that a confirmed match at any odds will be damaging to the defense.

[For cases dealing with the legal admissibility of DNA analysis, see Appendix C.]

The prosecution's specialist DNA deputies will want to have their expert witnesses point out that DNA has proved to be as successful in *exonerating* persons accused of crimes as in *convicting* them. In more than 25,000 criminal cases in North America alone, more than a quarter of the accused have been ruled out by DNA *mismatches.* That fact not only tends to show the fairness of the process, but bolsters the psychological punch when what is proved is a *match.*

Cellmark DNA Experts — On Cross-Examination

Because of the potential implications of the DNA results, the defense will have its work cut out for it. That explains why the defense team has called in two lawyers who are DNA specialists, Barry Scheck and Peter Neufeld. What Scheck and Neufeld will want to challenge right off is the particular test that might have been used on each sample. There are two basic tests, each yielding different odds.

The first test, RFLP (for restriction fragment length polymorphism), is the more accurate of the two, but the trick is that it requires a greater quantity of genetic material—probably no less than the size of a dime. That amount of material is required in order to radioactively "photograph" the DNA, which appears as two dark bands on X-ray film. If the pattern of bands from the genetic sample (blood, hair, saliva, etc.) matches the pattern of bands from the exemplar drawn from the victim or the accused, then we could be talking odds of one in tens of millions. Obviously, that is not the test the defense will hope for.

The second test, known as PCR (for polymerase chain reaction), needs no more genetic material than that which would fit on the head of a pin. DNA experts liken the process to a kind of molecular Xeroxing in which individual genes are copied millions of times to form a composite picture—in a series of blue dots—that can then be tested for common chemical sequences. This low-tech approach to high-tech DNA analysis reduces the odds to somewhere around one in 800 to 4,000 people sharing the same characteristics. Naturally, this test would be far more favorable to the defense.

Most people who have followed the pre-trial DNA debate expect there to be some DNA matching of some sort with either Simpson's or the victims' blood. What could be the sensation of the century, however, is something no one is expecting: an actual *mismatch*. Short of that, all the defense can expect to do is demonstrate the lowest possible odds coming out of the analysis, and once again hammer on the problems they uncover with the collection of the samples themselves. No matter how accurate the analysis, if the wrong samples are being analyzed, then the spectacular results mean nothing.

Steps Leading to O.J.'s Arrest

Having established the events surrounding the crime itself, the prosecution will want to go back and pick up the chronology of events which occurred from the time Simpson flew out of LAX until he returned the following day and was eventually arrested. What they will be looking for is any indication that Simpson was distressed, nervous, or unusually tense—anything that might be consistent with a man who had just murdered two people.

The specific witnesses in this category are not as well identified as in the other categories, nor is it known how many different people will be called. Therefore, we will simply list here some of the generic witnesses you can expect to hear testify.

❧

Airline personnel on flight to Chicago

It will be established that O.J. arrived at LAX at 11:35 p.m. for his 11:45 p.m. flight to Chicago on American Airlines Flight #688. His demeanor on this flight will be the subject of inquiry, perhaps from a flight attendant or fellow passengers who may have observed Simpson that night. Did he eat? Did he sleep? Was he restless, nervous, agitated?

❧

Hertz Driver in Chicago

Simpson was due to play in a Hertz-sponsored golf outing on Monday in Chicago. Around 4:15 a.m. (6:15 Central), he was picked up at the Chicago O'Hare Airport by a Hertz driver who delivered Simpson to the O'Hare Plaza Hotel where he checked in. Same questions: "Did you observe anything unusual about Simpson's demeanor?"

Personnel at O'Hare Plaza

Reception desk personnel, bell hops, or others at the O'Hare Plaza Hotel will be called to testify for the same purpose. Whatever they may say regarding his checking in, they will testify that Simpson checked out sometime after 6:00 a.m. (8:00 Central), and that he was visibly upset. By then he had received the 5:45 a.m. (7:45 Central) call from Arnelle and the LAPD notifying him of Nicole's death.

❧

Driver back to O'Hare

If the driver back to O'Hare International knows anything significant regarding Simpson's demeanor, he will be called to give the jury that information.

❧

Airline personnel on flight to L.A.

As before, airline personnel, or perhaps fellow passengers, will probably testify as to what they observed of Simpson on his 7:41 a.m. (9:41 Central) flight to Los Angeles.

❧

Chicago police

At 9:30 a.m. (10:30 Central), the Chicago police searched Simpson's hotel room. They discovered a broken glass, a washcloth with blood on it, and drops of blood on the bathroom sink.

❧

Det. Vannatter — Recalled for Further Direct Examination

Back in Los Angeles at approximately 12:00 noon, Simpson arrived at the Brentwood estate carrying a leather travel bag. Det. Vannatter noticed a bandage on the knuckle of the middle finger of Simpson's left hand.

Simpson's attorney, Howard Weitzman, had arrived earlier. Weitzman and Simpson conferred privately for a brief time, and then Simpson was temporarily handcuffed. Afterwards, Simpson voluntarily accompanied LAPD officers to police headquarters and participated in 3 1/2 hours of questioning.

What Simpson said to the police during this period of interrogation could prove to be of great interest. Det. Vannatter, or other detectives, likely will disclose anything that may have contributed to their formally arresting Simpson four days later. On the other hand, at this time the prosecution may choose not to reveal everything that came out of the interrogation. Perhaps anticipating that Simpson will testify in his own defense, the prosecution might decide to hold in reserve any statements by Simpson that could be used to impeach him should he tell a different story on the witness stand.

Det. Vannatter — Again on Cross-Examination

The defense will want to capitalize on the bandaged finger by asking if such a wound would be consistent with the broken glass found in O.J.'s Chicago hotel room. They may also try to relate it back to the blood found earlier at O.J.'s residence.

The temporary handcuffing of O.J. will also likely be the subject of defense questioning. Did the police have sufficient probable cause to arrest O.J.

at that time? If so, why did they need four days to come up with the formal charge? If his guilt was so obvious from the evidence they already had, why wait?

And that only serves to further sharpen the focus on what O.J. may have said to the police. (There was consternation from criminal defense attorneys nationwide when it was learned that Weitzman had let O.J. talk to the police before the case had been more carefully studied.) For that reason, the defense may downplay this whole line of questioning, fearing more harm than good.

O.J. apparently told police that he had been home the entire time between the McDonald's run and leaving for the airport.

The defense will want to make much out of the fact that O.J. *voluntarily* went to police headquarters and *voluntarily* agreed to answer police questions.

What Motive? What Means?

It is time now to go back and tie up loose ends—two in particular: motive and means. With this category of witnesses, the prosecution will want to go back and answer questions that it thinks may still be nagging at the jury. Questions like, "Why in the world would O.J. do such a thing?" And, "If there is no murder weapon that can be traced to O.J., then how could we possibly convict him?"

One of the curious questions from the very beginning has been, "What happened to the murder weapon?" Of course, a knife could easily have been disposed of in any number of dumpsters or sewer drains along the streets of Brentwood. However, jurors have seen enough crime films to want to see the macabre weapon for themselves. No murder weapon, no crime!

In this case, the best the prosecution can do is to point to a knife that *might* have been the weapon. (For the moment we'll hold off on explaining why, but to take that approach in this particular instance could turn out to be a high-stakes gamble which fails.) Let's assume that the prosecution proceeds as expected.

Jose Camacho (Sold knife) — On Direct Examination

Five weeks before the homicides occurred, Jose Camacho was a salesman at Ross Cutlery in downtown Los Angeles. He will testify that he sold Simpson a 15-inch stiletto for $81.17. Undoubtedly, he will be asked to show you a similar stiletto to demonstrate the one he actually sold to Simpson. You want a murder weapon? You have a murder weapon! But there may yet be problems....

Jose Camacho — On Cross-Examination

This witness is ripe for being impeached as having acquired a financial interest in the case. Camacho and his former boss, Allen Wattenberg, sold their story to the *National Enquirer* for $12,500. The defense might want to raise this issue as a means of discrediting anything negative Camacho might say regarding O.J.

At this point, a heavy anticipation will almost literally hover over the courtroom. Is this to be the moment that the defense will finally unwrap the mystery envelope which Robert Shapiro handed to Judge Kathleen Kennedy-Powell at the preliminary hearing back in July? If so, will he reach in and pull out the very knife that Camacho sold to O.J.? It could be a dramatic moment, implying as it undoubtedly would that the weapon which the prosecution wanted to put into O.J.'s hand was bogus. Confident that tests would show the knife had never been used (or certainly never in so violent a manner as would have been required by the victims' wounds), the defense could leave the prosecution hanging in the breeze of embarrassment. Will the defense play this trump?

[Note: If in fact the mystery envelope does not contain the knife in question, the prosecution is likely to call Ross Cutlery co-owner, Allen Wattenberg, to confirm Simpson's purchase of the stiletto.]

Would the prosecution be better off to leave the knife well enough alone? After all, if everything else in their case ties Simpson to the crime scene, what real need do they have to provide the actual weapon? Satisfying the jury's curiosity is not sufficient reason to take such a gamble with an unknown outcome. Rather, the prosecution may decide to avoid this pitfall and turn to the even more intriguing question of motive. *Why* O.J.? *Why?*

Facts, times, dates, physical evidence, expert opinions, crime scene photos, and DNA results are all impressive, but they have a strange way of missing the point. At least for a watching world, the real question is, "Why would O.J. Simpson want to kill the mother of his two children? Just because he was insanely jealous? Is there any evidence that Simpson had ever actually threatened Nicole? Had he ever been a man of violence off the football field?" Here, we return to the dark side of O.J. Simpson. No one wants to believe it, much less dwell on it. But the prosecution cannot afford to let you forget it.

❧

Keith Zlomsowitch (Nicole's lover) — On Direct Examination

Thirty-three-year-old Keith Zlomsowitch, an erstwhile restaurant manager, may or may not be called as a witness. He dated Nicole in 1992, after she had filed for a divorce from Simpson. Zlomsowitch says that Simpson was so hysterically jealous of his association with Nicole that he hounded them—even to the point, on one occasion, of peering through a window when they were "having an intimate encounter" at Nicole's condo.

Keith Zlomsowitch — On Cross-Examination

Oddly enough, the defense would probably welcome Zlomsowitch's testimony. If it is to be believed, then the questions from the defense seem all too obvious: "Mr. Zlomsowitch, you've testified that O.J. was hysterically jealous of you, and that he hounded you and Nicole. Is that right? And you say he even peered through a window, and *actually watched* as you were being intimate with his ex-wife. Is that right? On that occasion, did he bang on the window, or try to force open a door, or pull out a gun, or brandish a knife? You say *none of the above?* Let me see if I have this straight. You were being intimate with Nicole right in front of his very eyes, and O.J. *did not react violently?*"

Paula Barbieri (Simpson's girlfriend) — On Direct Examination

Barbieri, 27, a model for *Vogue* and Victoria's Secret, enjoyed an ongoing relationship with Simpson for some time. He had given her what seems to have been the vehicle of choice, a white Ford Bronco, which afterwards was stolen. Prior to this point in the trial, some earlier police witness will have testified that the stolen Bronco was recovered, and that in it was a notebook which reportedly contained a log of Nicole's daily routine. If all of this proves to be the case, the prosecution will want to use that information to bolster the theory that Simpson was stalking Nicole, and even planning her death.

As a friend of Simpson's, Barbieri will not likely appreciate contributing in any way to his conviction. In fact, rumors have it that Barbieri is living in O.J.'s Brentwood residence even as the trial progresses. The prosecution may wish to establish whether this rumor is true in order to treat Barbieri as a "hostile witness." This would entitle the prosecution to use leading questions, as if on cross-examination, and relieve them of any responsibility of having "sponsored" the witness.

Paula Barbieri — On Cross-Examination

If the notebook says what it reportedly says, and if the defense lawyers are not successful in keeping it out of evidence, then their next step will be to turn her testimony into an advantage. First of all, they may wish to know whether the tabloids are right—that she spent time with pop star Michael Bolton on the night of June 12. Next, they may want to confirm what may be more than a rumor that O.J. called her at 10:05 p.m. that night. Supposedly, O.J. called from his cellular phone and left a message for her to call him back on that same phone.

Is it true that O.J. called and left a message? Was it at 10:05 p.m.? So he called you during the one-hour time frame in which he was supposed to be busy killing Nicole and Ron? And he asked you to call him back, presumably as soon as possible?

Paula Barbieri — On Re-Direct

The prosecution will want to pursue what was brought out by the defense on cross-examination: "You've said that you received a call from Simpson, but it was on his cellular phone, was it not? Would that not indicate that he was calling from some place other than his home?"

Paula Barbieri — On Re-Cross

The defense will want to follow up that exchange on re-direct: "Were you aware that O.J. was taking a red-eye to Chicago that night? Is it possible that he wanted you to call him at the airport, if necessary, or even on the way to the airport?"

❦

Susan Forward (Psychotherapist) — Probably NOT a witness

Early on, you may have read an article or watched a program featuring Susan Forward, Nicole's psychotherapist and author of the bestselling *Men Who Hate Women and the Women Who Love Them*. Forward claims that Nicole told her in various therapy sessions that O.J. had battered her and stalked her. Fellow psychotherapists have been outraged, believing that she has breached professional ethics in making such revelations.

A somewhat different problem arises from the prosecution's standpoint. Even if the prosecution would like to use a witness like Forward to establish stalking on Simpson's part, it is probably precluded from doing so because of a legal privilege that Nicole, were she still alive, would have had to keep Forward from testifying as to confidential conversations. As a matter of public policy, there are any number of legally-recognized privileges, including the priest-penitent, doctor-patient, and lawyer-client privileges. Legal privileges are designed to encourage the free flow of information on behalf of one who needs services and advice without fear that one's most intimate details will somehow seep into the public arena.

Since the privilege is "owned" by the party giving the information (e.g., the patient in a therapy relationship), it would be reasonable to ask whether the privilege survives after one's death. While there is not complete agreement about this, it may be possible for one's executor to waive the privilege on behalf of the deceased in a murder case. Even if this were a closer question legally, the mere fact that Susan Forward is selling her story to the tabloid media is enough to disqualify her as a potential witness.

So if you don't see Susan Forward making a cameo appearance as a witness in the trial, you can tell all of your daytime television friends why.

✧

Police Officer "A" — On Direct examination

Some police officer (Det. Fuhrman?) could be called to relate an incident in which O.J. shattered the windshield of Nicole's car with a baseball bat. The year was 1985, the same year of their marriage. (They had been living together since 1978, a year before Simpson and his first wife, Marguerite, were officially divorced.) Such testimony, however, may not be permitted.

While the law does sometimes allow evidence of prior misconduct to be introduced for the purpose of showing *motive*, such evidence should not be permitted if its only purpose is to show *tendency*. The problem, of course, is how to show *motive* without, at the same time, suggesting *tendency*.

If not admissible in the prosecution's case-in-chief, this evidence of prior spousal abuse could be used to impeach any later testimony by Simpson himself that his relationship with Nicole was absent threats and violence.

Police Officer "A" — On Cross-Examination

The defense might pursue this series of questions: Have you witnessed a lot of domestic violence in your years on the force? If a man knocks out a window of a car with a baseball bat, does that mean the next thing he is going to do is kill his wife? How often does that sequence of events happen?

✧

Police Officer "B" — On Direct Examination

This officer will testify that, in 1989, at 3:30 a.m. after a New Year's Eve party, Nicole called 911 (police emergency) to report a fight. When the police arrived, Simpson had vanished, but Nicole was fearful that O.J. was going to kill her. Her injuries that night were serious enough to require hospitalization. Simpson was eventually arrested.

In court on a charge of battery, Simpson pleaded "no contest," an alternative to a "guilty" plea which falls short of an actual conviction. He was fined and ordered to undergo psychiatric counseling.

Again, for the reasons cited above, such testimony may not be admissible except for impeachment purposes at a later time.

Police Officer "B" — On Cross-Examination

The defense may want to emphasize that O.J. knew he had a problem and voluntarily went through psychiatric counselling.

They may also pursue the fact that O.J. may have been drinking too heavily at the New Year's Eve party, and that it was his drunkenness that made him violent.

ॐ

911 Operator — On Direct Examination

Released to the public when it should not have been, a now-famous 911 tape (recording an emergency police call in 1993) reveals what purportedly is a frantic call from Nicole to the police. In the background can be heard a man's voice (assumed to be that of Simpson), yelling and screaming after breaking down her door. Foundationally, the tape could be introduced into evidence by the 911 officer who took the call (and who, therefore, can testify to its authenticity as a true representation of what the operator personally heard over the phone).

As before, a huge question mark hovers over the introduction into evidence of this recording. Even if Judge Ito were inclined to admit the 911 tape for the purpose of showing motive, there is yet another hurdle which must be crossed. The law does not permit such evidence when it is unduly inflammatory. One could hardly imagine a more inflammatory piece of evidence than the 911 tape! The prosecution might conceivably argue, however, that—given the uniqueness of this case and the fact that the jurors have all likely heard the 911 tape—the shocking nature of the tape has lost its sting.

An alternative strategy available to the prosecution is to hold the 911 tape over Simpson's head, should he wish to testify on his own behalf. Any testimony which Simpson would offer promises to characterize his relationship with Nicole as non-violent and non-threatening. Such testimony would literally beg to be rebutted by the prosecution, and what would serve better for that purpose than the 911 tape? At that point, the prosecution would likely be permitted to introduce the tape for the limited purpose of impeaching the witness' testimony.

The long and the short of it is this: unless that rebuttal scenario takes place, don't be surprised if you do *not* hear the infamous 911 tape being played for your listening enjoyment!

911 Operator — On Cross-Examination

Assume at this point that the 911 tape is admitted (either on direct examination in the prosecution's case-in-chief, or on cross-examination in the defense's case-in-chief). As with the 1989 New Year's incident, the defense may try to build a link between O.J.'s violence and heavy drinking. The 911 operator may be asked if there was any indication that O.J. had *not* been drinking heavily immediately prior to the incident. If, by this negative implication, the defense can keep alive the connection between drinking and domestic violence, then a comparison with the night of June 12 might take some of the sting out of the emotional 911 tape and also set up an interesting point for the defense in closing argument.

O.J. On the Run

As you will be instructed at the end of the trial, the prosecution is permitted to enter evidence of conduct by which an admission of guilt may be implied by the jury. Such conduct includes two elements which may have been involved in the famous "low-speed freeway chase," witnessed by millions either in person or on television. Those two elements? Flight and attempted suicide. Because of its mind-sticking impact, and because it suddenly made a whole nation wonder if the unthinkable were not true after all, the prosecution will undoubtedly "save the best for last."

Apprehending Officers — On Direct Examination

The prosecution has available to it as witnesses a whole platoon of police officers who participated in the fifty-mile-long low-speed chase from Orange County back to Simpson's Brentwood estate, where he was placed into custody and jailed. They will testify that, on June 17, Simpson and his lifelong friend, Al Cowlings, eluded apprehension for hours until they finally surrendered at Simpson's Brentwood estate. Police will testify that, inside Cowlings' white Ford Bronco, they found a large amount of cash (perhaps as much as $7,000 or $8,000), a gun, a passport, and a fake beard and mustache. Given the location of the Bronco when first sighted, police believe Simpson was attempting to flee to Mexico.

The second element of attempted suicide may or may not have been a factor in the low-speed chase. As widely reported, Cowlings indicated that Simpson was lying down in the back of the vehicle, holding a gun to his own head.

Apprehending Officers — On Cross-Examination

The defense will likely try to establish its viewpoint on the low-speed chase through its own witnesses when they finally have that opportunity. For now, they will simply attempt to inject doubt regarding the prosecution's interpretation of events.

The defense faces somewhat of a dilemma at this point: Do they play up a suicidal O.J. to suggest that he wasn't fleeing but simply doing something very irrational? Or do they intentionally downplay any real threat of suicide, suggesting instead that O.J. merely wanted to hold off police long enough for him to see his mother? If O.J. was not in fact suicidal, then he must face the "flight" argument head on. If, on the other hand, his suicidal state was all too real, then O.J. is saddled with "suicide" being a second way for the jury to find an admission of guilt.

Jennifer Peace (Cowling's friend) — Probably NOT a Witness

You may have seen media coverage of Jennifer Peace, 23, a porn-film actress whose stage name is Devon Shire. Her relationship with Al Cowlings won her a day in court with the Grand Jury. Peace allegedly testified that Cowlings told her that he and O.J. were, in fact, headed to Mexico prior to the low-speed chase. Additionally, Peace claims Cowlings told her that the bloody gloves were his, and that Simpson had asked him to dispose of a bloody knife.

Given the tenuousness of Ms. Peace's relationship with Cowlings and the absurdity of Cowlings making any such admissions to anyone (implicating his best friend), it would be surprising indeed if the prosecution were to call her as a witness. The prosecution has already established the globally witnessed "flight" in the now-famous white Bronco. There is no reason for the prosecution to leave a bad taste in the jury's mouth as it comes to the end of its case.

Time to Rest

The prosecution's case has lived up to its every expectation. It was excruciatingly lengthy, extraordinarily complex, and absolutely riveting. After surely weeks, if not months, of testimony on behalf of the People of the State of California, the prosecution's case-in-chief has finally come to a close. Marcia Clark and her team (along with everyone else, including yourself) will probably be totally exhausted by the time she rises to confidently proclaim, "Your Honor, the People rest."

As a matter of standard trial practice, defense counsel can be expected to immediately move for a dismissal of the case for lack of sufficient evidence. It is a perfunctory motion which counsel in this case knows full well will be denied. The defense will have to proceed with their own case-in-chief. But only after, hopefully, more than just a brief recess at this point!

A Few Moments to Reflect

Now that you have heard the prosecution's case-in-chief, what surprises or disappointments were there for you?

_____

_____

_____

_____

_____

_____

_____

_____

_____

Do you think the prosecution succeeded in proving

Motive? _____

Means? _____

Opportunity? _____

Identity? _____

What did you think of the People's DNA evidence?

Do you believe that DNA analysis is valid? _____

What odds would you put on its accuracy? _____

Do you think the DNA chain of custody was safe? _____

Was there sufficient DNA evidence to link either O.J.
to the crime scene, or either of the victims to O.J.'s house?

....

....

How much damage did the defense do on cross-examination, particularly
regarding the collection and handling of the physical evidence?

....

....

....

....

....

....

....

....

....

Is there any evidence which you distrust at this point?

....

....

....

....

....

....

....

....

What do you believe was the prosecution's strongest evidence?

....

....

....

....

....

....

What evidence or prosecution theory did you definitely not believe?

....

....

....

....

....

....

....

....

If you had to decide the outcome of the case at this point in the trial, what would be your verdict?

....

On to the Defense

However you may feel about the evidence at this point, you must recall that you promised defense counsel you would keep an open mind until you heard O.J.'s side of the story. You never know. The defense's case-in-chief could make you change your mind either way. It could create doubts where you may now have certainty about O.J.'s guilt. It could even make O.J look guilty, where at present you may think him to be innocent. Stranger things have happened.

So, we return now to the courtroom to see what the defense has to say about the case. And we will soon find out the answer to one of the most intriguing questions in the whole trial: Will O.J. himself take the stand and testify? Here we go!

8

What Does the Accused Have to Say for Himself?

❧

Defense's Case-in-Chief

The defendant wants to hide the truth because he's generally guilty. The defense attorney's job is to make sure the jury does not arrive at that truth.

—Alan M. Dershowitz, 1982

Just how prophetic is the above quote from Harvard law professor, Alan Dershowitz? Now that he is assisting in O.J.'s defense, does he believe O.J. is guilty, and does he believe it is his job to help O.J. hide the truth? It's one thing for a law professor to be an observer of the process and tell it like it is. It is another thing altogether to represent a client—guilty or not—and present his side of the story with as much clarity as is possible, given whatever favorable evidence is available.

That evidence will go a long way towards shaping the defense strategy. Unlike the prosecution, which can know pretty well in advance what its case is and what witnesses will be needed to substantiate that case, the defense pretty much has to play it by ear. For the most part, defense counsel are placed in a position of reacting to the prosecution's case. Naturally, the defense will know in advance where their own strengths and weaknesses lie, so they will want to exploit the one while downplaying the other. That accounts for their overall strategy of bitterly contesting the sloppy police work (as they see it) that was done in this case. Anything at all to create doubt.

However, there are other strategies which must also be decided. Are they going to stick with the alibi defense—that O.J. could not have been at the scene at the time of the killings? Or might they decide that the prosecution's DNA evidence is simply too overwhelming to deny O.J. was there? If so, you could see them shift to a "heat-of-passion" killing theory in hopes of getting voluntary manslaughter rather than murder.

The low-speed freeway chase also presents a considerable headache for the defense. Should they make an attempt to explain it away, or might it be best to gamble on simply ignoring it. They can always argue that it was an emotional aftermath to the trauma of being falsely accused, without having to risk highlighting it once again through their own witnesses.

Decisions. Decisions.

Whatever their theory, the defense may consider calling various witnesses in at least four natural groupings:

1.   Witnesses who can attack the police's handling of
      the evidence.

2.   Expert witnesses who can counter the prosecution's
      own expert witnesses.

3.   Witnesses who can make O.J. look good on the day of
      the homicides.

4.   Witnesses who can shed light on the low-speed
      chase.

How to Make the Cops Look Bad

Since the bedrock of the defense's case is to shift the spotlight from O.J. to the police, you can expect to hear from the defense's own investigators. These private eyes will attempt to convince you that the cops did it all wrong—and that in the process the evidence was mangled more than the corpses of Ms. Simpson and Mr. Goldman.

John McNally (Retired NYPD) — On Direct Examination

McNally's white hair and white beard give this soft-spoken investigator the look of real respectability. Nor will it hurt that McNally has the reputation of capturing Jack "Murph the Surf" Murphy, the jewel thief, while a detective with the New York Police Department. Just having a former police officer giving a critical review of shoddy police work is sure to take its toll. Apparently, McNally's job is to help the defense establish a sequence-of-events time-line that will shatter the prosecution's "window of opportunity."

Perhaps that time-line will include such things as the driving time between O.J.'s estate and Nicole's condo. Or the time it would take for O.J. (had he done the killings) to get back to the Brentwood estate, dispose of the alleged glove behind Kaelin's room, change out of bloody clothes, and take a shower before emerging from the house for his ride to the airport. Or perhaps the time in which the deaths themselves would had to have occurred. Such a time-line could go a long way in establishing an alibi for O.J.

John McNally — On Cross-Examination

The prosecution will already have established their own time-line of events. It will only remain for them to point out any "convenient" discrepancies between McNally's time-line and facts brought out by other witnesses. Or, perhaps, to note for the jury any smokescreen analysis that appears in McNally's testimony on direct examination. McNally, however, is a seasoned veteran at both investigation and in-court testimony. He will not be easily dislodged from his position, whatever it turns out to be.

❧

Patrick McKenna (McNally's colleague) — On Direct Examination

It will not be surprising if you see Patrick McKenna taking direct aim at police investigative procedures in the O.J. investigation. McKenna, a West Palm Beach associate of McNally's, and a former Chicago probation officer and Florida public defender, worked with McNally in the notorious William Kennedy Smith case. He would be well qualified to walk the jury through any number of claimed police miscues in this case. He might, for example, point out how inexperienced personnel were used to collect crucial samples; and how there was sophomoric mislabelling of evidence; and how police can "slant" evidence if they choose to do so.

You can almost bet that McKenna or some other similar witness will be used to cast as much doubt as possible on the investigative process. No detail will be overlooked. Every move of the police will be excruciatingly scrutinized.

Patrick McKenna — On Cross-Examination

Naturally, the prosecution will be on the defensive, desperately attempting to minimize the damage which even they know they will have suffered at the hands of the defense. It is in this one area more than any other that they are vulnerable. So it will be a tedious game of mutual nitpicking. In whatever way possible, the prosecution will attempt to rehabilitate its own witnesses by trying to demonstrate that, with perhaps a few possible exceptions, the LAPD investigators followed standard police practice in their investigation.

❧

Henry C. Lee (Reconstructionist) — On Direct Examination

If you are lucky, you yourself will become a witness in this case—to the best forensics show money can buy. And you can bet it will be high-tech. (Not just charts and graphs drawn with magic markers, or blackboard drawings, or cute little plastic models. All that is passé.) Under the direction of Henry Lee, specialist in crime-scene reconstruction, you are likely to see the latest in computerized re-enactment razzle-dazzle. It will be virtual-reality stuff, like you are on the scene when the killings took place.

You may even see Nicole and Ron reacting to the vicious attacks, and finally falling into fetal positions on the ground. But rather than proving that O.J. is the killer (as you might think would be the result of such a realistic demonstration), the moral of the high-tech story is likely to be that the two victims could not possibly have been killed by one person. Look where the bodies were in relation to each other. Look at the positions of the bodies where they fell. Ron could not have been attempting to defend Nicole, as surely he would have, had there been a lone assailant.

And don't think it won't be a seductive scenario. It's amazing what can be done these days. Of course, Judge Ito may have something to say beforehand about the admissibility of these all-too-easily-manipulable demonstrations.

Henry Lee — On Cross-Examination

Like the judge, the prosecution will want to make sure that what is "real" is not just what is creatively imagined. Any part of the demonstration which hints even slightly at being beyond the facts in evidence will be grist for the prosecution's mill. Marcia Clark and her team are all too aware that a picture is worth a thousand words and a slanted video is worth an acquittal.

❧

Josephine Guarin (O.J.'s housekeeper) — On Direct Examination

It may seem insignificant on the surface, but a little tempest in a teapot might just boil over on behalf of the defense. The police have denied that they watched the "Frogmen" video while in O.J.'s house during a June 28th search of the premises. (And Marcia Clark put her own credibility on the line by denying it as well.) If on cross-examination of the investigating officers they have now testified under oath to that effect, then the defense will be able to attack their credibility by calling O.J.'s live-in housekeeper, Josephine Guarin.

Guarin will testify that she was fairly much quarantined in the kitchen during the search that afternoon, but that, at one point during their three-hour sweep of the house, the officers—about ten in number—asked that she come in and turn on O.J.'s videotape player so they could watch "Frogmen." Her testimony apparently will be a direct and unequivocal: "I know they watched 'Frogmen'." The defense will not only want to contradict the earlier testimony of the investigating officers (assuming they so testify), but will make much of what they will hope to show was a circus-like atmosphere, giving new meaning to the phrase, "search party."

Josephine Guarin — On Cross-Examination

The prosecution's best strategy may be to ignore the implications of a party-like atmosphere in the viewing of the video (if indeed there was a viewing), and perhaps ask Guarin if she knew that the video contained scenes where Simpson was holding a knife to a woman's throat. Even if Guarin says, "No," the point will once again be emphasized that Simpson, as an actor, had at least gone through the motions of threatening a woman with a knife.

Since Guarin is Simpson's live-in housekeeper, the prosecution may wish to also inquire about what she may know regarding bloody clothes, blood stains on the carpet, and even the events of the night in question. Did she see or hear anything unusual? Can she vouch for Simpson's whereabouts? (The latter is unlikely, or it probably would have been reported already by the media.) However, if the defense has not opened up this area of questioning on its direct examination, they could object to the prosecution's new line of questioning, saying that it is "outside the scope of direct." Such an objection would likely be sustained by Judge Ito. If so, the prosecution could call Guarin as their own witness in their rebuttal following the defense's case-in-chief.

❧

Dean Gilmour (Coroner's investigator) — On Direct Examination

In support of their attempts to embarrass the police for refusing to notify the coroner's office in time to have a tighter fix on the time of death, the defense could call to the stand Dean Gilmour (Captain of the Los Angeles County coroner's investigations division). He could be asked to read for the jury the California law that makes it a misdemeanor offense for a physician, funeral director, *"or other person"* not to immediately notify the coroner about violent and suspicious deaths, including murders.

Gilmour would presumably testify, as he has already been quoted as saying, that, although in most cases the police have been prompt in notifying the coroner's office of such deaths, the occasional exceptions have been worrisome to coroner's investigators.

The defense would do well to ask Gilmour about the history of the friction between the coroner's office and the LAPD, and how it prompted Police Chief Willie L. Williams to issue a special order, dated November 17, 1993. Gilmour may be asked to read the chief's order into the record:

> The investigating officer at the scene of a death...shall make notification immediately upon determining that the death falls within the purview of the coroner's office. If the coroner is not immediately needed at the scene, the investigating officer shall advise the coroner of an approximate time when the coroner's deputy can respond.

> When circumstances indicate that the investigation of the death requires the expertise of a specialized investigator (e.g., homicide detective, traffic collision investigator), immediate notification to the coroner shall be made by the concerned specialized investigator who responds to the scene of the incident.

In order to emphasize the unusual departure from this order in this case, Gilmour could be asked to indicate the coroner's log of events. He would testify that Nicole Simpson and Ronald Goldman were pronounced dead at 12:45 a.m., but that the coroner's office was not officially notified until 6:55 a.m. Even at that time, the police said, "Wait, we'll call you back when we're ready." It was not until shortly after 10:00 a.m. that the bodies were released to the coroner's office, and not until 12:20 that they could be transported to the morgue. That was some ten hours from the time the bodies were first discovered; eight hours from when Det. Fuhrman arrived on the scene, and six hours from when detectives Vannatter and Lange appeared.

The defense will want to nail down just how unusual this case is compared with other incidents of delay. Gilmour can testify that the LAPD delayed notification in only four other homicide cases that month, for periods of time ranging between three and five hours.

Dean Gilmour — On Cross-Examination

The prosecution will have been stung by Gilmour's testimony. Their questioning might follow somewhat along this line: "Is it not true that the investigating officers' first duty is to preserve the crime scene and collect evidence? Is there not a danger that close inspection of the bodies might disturb such evidence as fingerprints or bloodstains? When the cause of death is all-too-obvious, as in the case of a brutal stabbing, just how necessary is an immediate autopsy? Cannot the time of death be determined by occurrence witnesses, sometimes even better than a scientific guess made in the absence of known circumstantial evidence?"

Claudine Ratcliffe (Coroner's deputy) — On Direct Examination

Investigator Claudine Ratcliffe of the coroner's office may already have been called by the prosecution. If not, however, she would be an important witness for the defense. It was Ratcliffe who was called to the scene to retrieve the bodies. Ratcliffe will testify that she was sent to the scene when the police notified the coroner's office at 8:10 a.m. When she arrived at 9:05 a.m., she was told to wait until shortly after 10:00 a.m., at which time she finally was allowed to approach the bodies in order to perform the standard tests. Those tests would include taking the temperature of the victims' livers, determining the extent to which the blood had settled in the extremities, and the progression of rigor mortis. Her observations, later reported to Medical Examiner Golden, formed the basis for his own opinion that the deaths could have occurred anytime between 9:00 p.m. and 12:00 midnight.

Claudine Ratcliffe — On Cross-Examination

The prosecution will want to ask Ratcliffe if there was any lapse in police investigation between the time she arrived at the scene and when she was permitted to approach the bodies. That is, was there no activity such as fingerprinting, photographing, or collection of evidence near the bodies going on while she waited? The more activity she may have observed on the part of police investigators, the stronger the prosecution's argument that there was no *intentional* delay. Ratcliffe may be asked if she was aware of who the victims were, and, if so, whether that might explain why the police were taking extra pains (and, therefore, extra time) not to unduly disturb the physical evidence surrounding the bodies.

Battle of the Experts—Round Two

Already, you have heard the withering cross-examination of the prosecution's expert witnesses. But now the defense is able to call its own experts to do what damage they can to the People's case. They are likely to focus in on two primary areas: the DNA tests and the autopsy findings. Given the flow of testimony about conflicts between the police and the coroner's office, perhaps now would be a good time to bring in the big guns, the defense's forensic pathologist.

Michael Baden (Forensic pathologist) — On Direct Examination

In a way, Baden's role as a counter to Medical Examiner Irwin Golden is just too easy. His mustachioed, no-nonsense, authoritative presence is perfectly typecast in contrast to the mousey, fumbling figure one sees in Golden. And what a professional pedigree: former Chief Medical Examiner in New York City; experience with having re-examined forensic evidence in such high-profile cases as Martin Luther King and John F. Kennedy. This role is tailor-made for Baden!

Even the evidentiary target is too easy. What more need he say than that Golden didn't cut square corners? O.K., maybe nothing was *actually* lost along the way, despite the disposal of the stomach contents and the refusal to compare a particular knife with the particular wounds. Who knows? But Golden still didn't play it by the book, and that only opens up a gap of speculation that the defense can drive a Mack truck through.

Baden is also going to testify about the time delay, saying that the longer the wait from the time of death to the autopsy, the more inaccurate you become. He's going to verify the obvious—that the delay in this case would have prevented even a competent medical examiner from reliably estimating the time close enough to give O.J. a fair hearing on his alibi defense.

Michael Baden — On Cross-Examination

In this mismatch of personalities and experience, all that the prosecution can hope to do is ask a few "show questions," and move on. Why prolong the agony and give further credence to the defense's effort to distract the jury's attention from the obvious. The People already have strong evidence from occurrence witnesses fixing the time in which the homicides must surely have taken place. It was never in the cards for the autopsy to be a "Golden opportunity." So the prosecution will be well advised to cut their losses and run!

Unknown DNA Experts (Defense scientists) —
On Direct Examination

Whoever the defense brings in to talk about DNA, you know already what they are going to say: "DNA analysis is not the perfect science it is made out to be by the prosecution; the odds of unique identification of any one human being are far lower than the prosecution would have you believe; and, besides, none of the results are valid if the samples provided by inexperienced criminologists were improper samples."

It all comes down to those three criticisms. You saw it in cross-examination of the prosecution's DNA experts; you'll see it once again here with the defense's experts.

Unknown DNA Experts — On Cross-Examination

The district attorney's DNA deputies will be back at counsel table, intensively engaging in scientific jousting with the defense's experts. If the experts have overstepped the bounds of DNA knowledge even the slightest, these deputies will let you know. Their greatest success is likely to be in rehabilitating the process of DNA analysis itself. The uphill battle comes with fixing the odds. The prosecution will consider it a victory if, by the end of cross-examination, they have you thinking, not in terms of one in thousands, but one in millions.

❧

The Coolest O.J. in Town

Every defense counsel knows that you have to make your client look good. He's the good guy in the white hat, even if there is a smudge or two on the Stetson. So who can they bring in to make you feel good about O.J. in the face of blistering prosecution evidence against him? And what can they tell you that will defy the odds of DNA and a weak-at-best alibi?

❧

Craig Baumgarten (Golfing buddy) — On Direct Examination

Bringing movie producer Craig Baumgarten to the stand will start the day off right because it was Baumgarten, along with a couple of other golfing buddies, who saw the sun rise together with O.J. on that fateful mid-June day. It was 6:00 on a beautiful Sunday morning at the Riviera Country Club (near O.J.'s Brentwood home) when the foursome teed it up. Baumgarten may have to swallow his pride to tell the story, but he will admit that he blew a shot and quickly blamed O.J. for having distracted him. O.J., in turn, got mad and yelled back at

Baumgarten. But tempers just as quickly subsided and the round was completed in jocular good humor.

If you are wondering why the defense would want to show O.J. flaring in anger, the answer is that it shows he can get really mad without acting out his anger in violence. Baumgarten might well be asked, "Did O.J. get really mad?" Yes. "Did he take a swing at you with his club, or threaten you in any other way?" No.

More than that, the defense will want to have Baumgarten tell "the rest of the story." Following the round, the foursome had lunch together, then lounged in the club-house playing gin rummy. That's the relaxed O.J. the defense wants to show on the day that the prosecution claims he had nefariously schemed to kill Nicole. Does the golf-swinging, gin-rummy-playing O.J. fit the image of a maniacal cold-blooded killer? Or even someone who, by that evening, would be so upset with Nicole for who-knows-what that he would slash her body with the frenzy of a lion on the kill? Baumgarten's testimony will be several strokes under par.

Craig Baumgarten — On Cross-Examination

Does the prosecution dare chase the flaring incident, knowing how quickly it resolved itself? Probably not. Better to simply leave it with some suggestive questions, like, "Did you have any further contact with Simpson that day? Do you know if he talked at all with Nicole that day? Since you are one of his golfing buddies, did Simpson ever show you a stiletto that he had bought, or perhaps talk about it?"

❧

Traci Adell (Playmate) — On Direct Examination

Just how cool is O.J. on the afternoon before the evening of the homicides? So cool that he called *Playboy* magazine's Playmate for July, twenty-four-year-old Traci Adell, back in Maryland where she was doing a movie called *Life 101*. Although they had never met, Traci welcomed O.J.'s call and they talked for about 45 minutes. Or she *listened*, as O.J. talked about his ex-wives and how he was on the prowl for someone else. Tongue in cheek, O.J. mentioned that blondes hadn't exactly worked out for him.

Did that comment sound manic? Or glum? Or revengeful? "Miss July" will probably say, "No, just the opposite." O.J. told her that he'd had enough. "I've lived my life. I've done things most people couldn't do in a hundred lifetimes," said O.J.

It was an upbeat O.J. who hung up the phone that afternoon, Traci will tell you. Certainly no indication of a man who nervously awaits the premeditated hour of Nicole's execution. Nor a man who is sullen and angry, just waiting to explode.

Traci Adell — On Cross-Examination

Will the prosecution think that Ms. Adell is a good witness for its side? Will they want to explore the theory that O.J. was already checking out Nicole's replacement? That would *indeed* be a "cold-blooded" O.J. Simpson!

❧

Arnelle Simpson (Daughter) — On Direct Examination

She has testified once before in aid of the defense as they were trying to exclude evidence taken from the Brentwood estate where she has been living in the guest quarters. O.J.'s twenty-five-year-old daughter by his first wife (Marguerite Whitley) may well testify again here at the trial. Arnelle, who had arrived home at 1:00 in the morning, was awakened by the police at 5:00 a.m. Some 45 minutes later, she helped the police contact O.J.'s assistant, Cathy Randa, who in turn led them to call O.J. at his Chicago hotel.

Arnelle will probably bring a touching moment to the proceedings when she tells of picking up Sydney and Justin at the police station around 7:00 a.m. After returning home, it becomes her grim duty to notify Juditha Brown of her daughter's death. Again, it will be Kleenex time when Arnelle tells the jury that she broke down and had to hand the phone to a police officer.

Did Arnelle talk to her father when the police called him in Chicago? If so, defense counsel will surely want to know how he reacted to the news of Nicole's death. You can bet that, guilty or not guilty, O.J. was not jumping for joy at that moment. His reaction will undoubtedly reflect shock and dismay, whether truly from absolute, innocent surprise, or from the finger of deserved guilt so soon being pointed his way. The good news for the defense is that Arnelle will put whatever reaction her father had in the best possible light.

Arnelle Simpson — On Cross-Examination

It's time to be super sensitive. How do you dare cross-examine the daughter of the accused? It may be another time to ask some tangential suggestive questions and move on. Were you home between 9:45 p.m. and 11:00 p.m.? Do you know where your father was during that time? Can you vouch for his whereabouts? Had you noticed any blood in the driveway of the house before that night? Did you, by any chance, drop any blood on the driveway as you came home? Thank you.

❧

Cathy Randa (O.J.'s assistant) — On Direct Examination

For twenty years, Cathy Randa, 47, has served O.J. as a faithful administrative assistant. It was she who knew that O.J. was staying at the O'Hare Plaza in Chicago. How else could Randa characterize her boss but as a man who has treated her well for over two decades? Could O.J. possibly be a murderer? Not according to this loyal employee and personal friend.

Cathy Randa — On Cross-Examination

If the defense doesn't get to it first, the prosecution will want to paint Ms. Randa as a biased witness—not just your normal biased employee and friend, but one who has demonstrated *special* bias in this particular case. While police were waiting to obtain a search warrant of Simpson's office, a detective spotted Randa shredding documents. The prosecution will want to press Randa about her explanation that the documents were pamphlets on domestic violence that Simpson had received back in 1989 when he had pleaded "no contest" to battering Nicole. Randa might not turn out to be the best witness for Simpson.

Mark Partridge (Passenger) — On Direct Examination

Mark Partridge, a Chicago attorney who sat next to O.J. on his return flight to L.A., may be one of several witnesses (whether passengers or airline personnel) whom the defense will want to call to show how calm O.J. was on the flight out to Chicago, and how deeply disturbed he was on the flight back home.

Partridge himself would be in a position to testify that his neighbor in coach class ordered mineral water and made a number of calls on the airphone to friends and advisors. Through Partridge, you may learn of the substance of those calls. It will put O.J. in a good light if Partridge testifies to what he told one reporter: "It was evident from the phone calls he was making and the comments he made during the flight that a great tragedy was affecting his life and the lives of his children....I remember feeling very sorry for him."

Mark Partridge — On Cross-Examination

Was Simpson's attorney, Howard Weitzman, among those called from the less-than-friendly skies that morning? (Weitzman *did* meet Simpson at the Brentwood estate upon Simpson's return.) If so, the prosecution will wonder aloud through Partridge's testimony as to whether legal counsel would have been indicated simply on the strength of one's ex-wife having been killed. Or, indeed, did Simpson indicate to anyone over the phone that he had already become a suspect? Partridge promises to be a most interesting witness all around. And will his testimony take on any unusual flavor by virtue of the fact that he, himself, is a lawyer?

❧

What to Do With the Low-Speed Chase?

Can the defense afford to talk about the low-speed freeway chase? Can they afford *not* to? Even if there were not one shred of evidence to link O.J. to the homicides, his actions were not that of a falsely-accused, innocent, "absolutely 100% not guilty" man. Yes! The defense *must* talk about it.

Al Cowlings (Best friend) — On Direct Examination

He doesn't need an introduction to the jury. By now everybody knows Al Cowlings is O.J.'s best friend—a lifelong friend who made his way with O.J. out of the tough Potrero Hill district of San Francisco where they had grown up. O.J. has pretty much carried Al with him wherever he went, from Galileo High School, to San Francisco City College, to the USC Trojans, the Buffalo Bills, and the San Francisco 49ers. Apart from being a friend and bodyguard for O.J., Al has played pretty much a minor league role as bit-part actor and sometimes bartender.

As everyone knows, O.J.'s friendship and loyalty could hardly be more closely entwined than with Al Cowlings. If the defense team decides to call Al on O.J.'s behalf, that mutual friendship and loyalty could turn out to be either an asset or a liability. Unquestionably, having Al testify is a gamble. Maybe O.J. himself will make the call. After all, he and Al have done everything else together. Maybe this isn't the time to break up a winning combination.

But to what would Al testify? To their friendship. To the good friend O.J. has always been to him. To the man he knows probably better than anyone on the face of the earth, including O.J.'s own mother. To the man who could not possibly have been capable of killing the mother of his two children. To the man who was so distraught at being accused of murder that he turned into another man whom Al had never seen before. A strong man who, for the first time, went weak on him. A man who, this time, needed Al's help—not the other way around. And, of course, he helped him. How could he have done otherwise? What else would be expected from a best friend, but to save his life and allow O.J. to retain the last shred of dignity that he had after seeing his whole career go down the tubes?

Sure, there was a bundle of money in Al's Bronco, but it was for O.J.'s children. And sure, there was a fake beard and mustache, but those were for a trip to Disneyland. There were many times that he and O.J. wanted to do normal kinds of things that everyone else does, but had to resort to disguise in order not to be hounded by fans.

What about the prosecution's belief that you and O.J. were trying to escape to Mexico? No way. O.J. simply wanted to visit Nicole's grave. What was a friend to do? And how could any friend let the police approach O.J. while he was holding a gun to his head. The best thing to do was drive slowly back to O.J.'s house and work something out with the police so that O.J. didn't do what everyone thought he was going to do.

O.J.'s best friend just might be a good defense witness after all. He's run interference for O.J. before. He knows what it is like to lead the way for O.J.

Al Cowlings — On Cross-Examination

If Cowlings is able to make an opening for Simpson, the prosecution is going to pounce like a hungry linebacker on all those convenient explanations. Why *cash* for the children? When was the fun Disneyland trip supposed to take place? During a time when Simpson should have been in mourning? And if the only thing that was happening when they were first spotted by the police was a visit to Nicole's grave, then why not stop and tell the police?

And how about the picture of a suicidal Simpson? Was he *really* suicidal? (That's not the sign of an innocent man.) Or was he just faking it to keep the police at bay? (A worse scenario yet.)

And could you find a more biased witness? Wouldn't Al Cowlings say anything on the stand to protect the man he loves so? As you can appreciate, it really is a gamble for the defense to call on Al Cowlings.

꩜

Robert Kardashian (Devoted friend) — On Direct Examination

He'd be a much better witness than Al Cowlings, but there are many similarities. Robert Kardashian is also a devoted friend of some twenty-five years—not so much a buddy, but more of a close advisor. His was the house that O.J. and Al left at the start of their freeway meanderings. His was the voice that a bewildered nation listened to as he read that incredibly strange farewell note from O.J. His, too, was the voice that had tried to calm O.J. by a cellular-phone call to the infamous white Bronco.

Could Kardashian gain the sympathy of the jury for O.J.? Would *you* be susceptible to such sympathy? Is there any way that you could *not* be touched by the sadness of it all? As the trial winds down, maybe this is just what the defense needs—a touch of sympathy, and wonder, and...all those questions we were all asking that extraordinary June 17th day. Questions—any questions—translate into doubts, and doubts into acquittals.

Yes, this could just be the ticket.

Robert Kardashian — On Cross-Examination

No time for sympathy on the part of the prosecution. Quick—ask some very perfunctory questions. When did you first meet Simpson? What were the circumstances? Did you ever see Simpson drunk? Did you ever see him angry? Were you aware of Nicole's 911 call before this case came to light? Were you surprised that the man you knew so well could be capable of those kinds of threats and violence?

With any luck, from the prosecution's standpoint, the sympathy recedes ever so slightly. If even his best friends are surprised at the 911 call, maybe none of us knows O.J. Simpson as well as we thought we did.

The Biggest Gamble of All

In the movies, the plot inevitably builds to a climax and the hero is faced with his greatest crisis, the moment of truth. Will he survive the test or won't he? In the movies, at least, you are pretty sure that he will.

The stage is set now in the trial of the century for what could be the most dramatic moment of all—when O.J. himself walks to the witness stand, swears to tell the whole truth, and slowly begins to tell us what that truth is. But not so fast. Maybe we're talking movies again. This is a trial—not a cinematic happening, but a real trial. And the hero of this ordeal might not just walk away from the set when the lights go down and the cameras stop rolling.

Will O.J. testify in his own behalf? The Fifth Amendment to the Constitution says he doesn't have to testify either for or against himself. As everyone who has ever heard of the *Miranda* warnings knows, O.J. has a right to remain silent.

Or is it possible that—the Constitution notwithstanding—O.J. Simpson is the lone exception, and does *not* have the right to remain silent? Will a bewildered nation and millions of loyal fans allow their friend O.J. to let the trial close with not a word from his lips? Would that in itself be an act of betrayal? The defense team, naturally enough, is divided as to whether they should put O.J. on the stand. Without question, it goes against their defense lawyer instincts. Something about, well, better to be thought a fool than to open your mouth and remove all doubt.

But what are you going to think if O.J. refuses to speak on his own behalf? In spite of Judge Ito's warning that you are not to consider his silence as an admission of guilt, could you really get it out of your mind? Wouldn't you simply *have* to wonder what he has to hide if he is truly innocent? Wouldn't someone who is falsely accused desperately *want* to have you hear his side of the story? Trying to keep tainted evidence from coming to your attention is one thing; being unwilling to risk cross-examination is quite another.

The decision, of course, might have been a lot easier if O.J. hadn't already talked to the police. What did he say to them on the morning after the killings? Can O.J. *remember* what he told them—*in every detail?* That factor will be absolutely crucial because the slightest misstep here and the prosecution, looking at its transcript of that conversation, will pounce on the slightest deviation as being a prior inconsistent statement. If O.J. sticks to his original story, he risks not matching up with facts which have now been proven in the trial. If he changes his story even the slightest, then he will risk the conclusion that he is fabricating his alibi to suit what he has heard in the courtroom.

It is pretty much a lose-lose situation. Perhaps the only glimmer of hope is that, if Marcia Clark tears into O.J. on cross-examination (even with evidentiary justification), the jury and the watching world may identify with O.J. all the more. He then would become the helpless victim standing alone against a ruthless accuser. That might work. Might.

So you see, it is not the easy call that anyone on the defense team would like it to be. The good news is that if O.J. decides to testify (and it may well come down to his own decision), you couldn't ask for a better client to do such a fool thing. He's bright, quick, personable, and polished. He's used to the lights, the pressure, the sound bite. And he's an actor who will know his lines perfectly.

Maybe it is O.J.'s running instincts that will protect him most. After juking here, and side-stepping there on his way to record-breaking fame, surely Marcia Clark represents nothing so threatening. Or is it Marcia Clark who he is running from? What if it is the truth out of whose tenacious grasp he is trying to get free? Sometimes the truth hits you behind the line. Sometimes it hits you with a flying tackle that knocks your very breath out.

But that is only if the truth is your opponent. If truth is on your side, you can be unstoppable. Everybody knows that when truth is running interference, no one can stand in its path. So if O.J. knows he has truth on his side, what is there to fear? He'll testify. It wouldn't be like O.J. *not* to. He's always been up front with us, and now, in his moment of greatest crisis, he will be up front with us once again.

And we will *want* to believe him.

And we will give him *every* benefit of the doubt.

And we will...never forgive him if he lets us down.

Time for the Defense to Rest

Only now will you know whether O.J. took the stand in his own defense, and, if so, what he said. Only now will you know whether he acquitted himself in the face of a withering cross-examination. Only now will you and Paul Harvey really know "the rest of the story."

If O.J. does *not* testify, you can be sure that the defense already has every confidence in how you will vote. It will be their belief that they have created sufficient doubt that putting O.J. on the stand could only hurt his chances. Better to get an acquittal and let the world think what it might than to do anything which would put that acquittal at risk. There will be plenty of time afterwards for an army of public relations folks to airbrush away whatever blemishes we've discovered in our All-American hero. Unlike anyone else in the whole world in the same boat, he may even be hotter property after the trial than before.

For now, however, the defense team must place O.J.'s future squarely in your hands. From the evidence that they have presented in their case-in-chief, the doubts are there. All you have to do is act on them.

"Your Honor, the defense rests."

Another Moment to Reflect

Now that you have heard the defense's case-in-chief, what surprises or disappointments were there for you?

....

....

....

....

Do you think the defense succeeded in raising doubts about O.J.'s guilt?

....

If so, which?

....

....

....

What still bothers you about the defense's case?

Have you changed your mind in any way now that you have heard the defense's own DNA experts?

How much damage did the prosecution do on cross-examination?

If O.J. has testified on his own behalf, what is your reaction to his testimony?

Is there any defense tactic or strategy that you would question?

....

....

....

....

If you had to decide the outcome of the case at this point in the trial, what would be your verdict?

....

❧

It's Time To Sum it Up

It is altogether possible that more witnesses for both sides could be called by way of rebuttal. Any testimony elicited at this point by either side would be strictly within the confines of that which was brought out in the cases-in-chief. But, for our purposes, we will assume that each side is satisfied with its case and is prepared to proceed toward the conclusion of the trial.

Undoubtedly at this point, Judge Ito will declare yet another recess—and by now you must be hoping for one. The action has been non-stop. But before you and your fellow jurors deliberate on your verdicts, each side will have an opportunity to summarize the evidence as they see it and make the arguments they hope will convince you of the rightness of their cause. Who knows whether counsels' arguments really persuade a jury? After all, it is the evidence that counts, and that is already in. But no trial would be complete without the stuff of which good lawyer dramas are made—the closing arguments.

Because the prosecution is the plaintiff in this case, it will be given an opening argument and a closing argument. Sandwiched in between will be the defense's one final argument. There is one thing you can count on: no more boredom or tedious questioning. What you are about to hear is top-class excitement—something in the nature of a debate, something not unlike an unfolding drama. Done well, the closing argument can be a work of art, a thing of beauty to behold. Engaging. Mesmerizing. Bewitching. Hopefully even convincing.

That is particularly true of the defense. While the prosecution will appeal to your mind, the defense will appeal to your heart. You'll see it as the two styles come your way—each with its own strength, each with its own moral force.

Are you ready for the showdown? Here comes Marcia Clark.

9

Don't Forget
What You've Heard

❧

Prosecution's Opening Argument

I was with you, Mr. Scott—'til I heard your argument.

—Lord Thurlow
Life of Lord Eldon

With the close of the defense's case-in-chief (and any possible rebuttal from either side), the time comes for counsel to summarize the evidence which you have heard. More than a summation, of course, this is high-level argumentation. But in the process of making their arguments, counsel will want to re-package the testimony which you have heard in scattered bits and pieces over these many weeks of the trial.

By now you must realize that at times the presentation of the evidence has been necessarily overlong and indirect. The reason, in many instances, is that prior foundations had to be laid before certain testimony or other evidence could be admitted. So now is the time for counsel to succinctly organize what otherwise has too often been a crazy-quilt presentation.

In the prosecution's opening argument, Marcia Clark and her team will want to reduce weeks of garbled testimony to a few well-defined, clearly-articulated points that will stick in your minds as you participate in your deliberations. Since you have already read the details of the "article," as it were, the prosecution will work in reverse order to imprint on your minds the most catchy and grabbing "headlines" which they wish to leave with you.

For example, Clark could organize her argument around the following five *checkout-counter type headlines*:

1. "Reasons for O.J. Killings Revealed!"

2. "DNA Gives O.J. an Identity Crisis"

3. "O.J. Caught When Window of Opportunity Slams on Him"

4. "Mystery Witness May Have Seen O.J. Killings"

5. "O.J. May Run, But He Can't Hide"

By use of these dramatic "headlines" (especially if they were creatively incorporated into an exhibit perhaps depicting real newspaper pages), Clark could grab your attention and lead you to the heart, soul, and essence of the prosecution's case.

❧

"Reasons for O.J. Killings Revealed"

One of the grand ironies of this case is that about the only thing the prosecution is *not* required to prove—*motive*—is that which the prosecution has most readily available. And in some respects (due to the uniqueness of this particular defendant), it is *motive* that most intrigues a watching world. ("If O.J. really did kill Nicole and Ron, what could possibly have driven him to do such a shocking thing?") So it would not be at all surprising if motive turns out to be the headline on the front page.

The story beneath the headline will recap for you the dates and events which show O.J. Simpson to have been guilty of spousal abuse—a first cousin to wife-killing, and more especially *ex-wife* killing.

"Don't forget the 1985 incident in which Simpson angrily smashed the window of Nicole's car. Or the 1989 beating that sent Nicole to the hospital (a battery to which Simpson pleaded 'no contest'). And how could anyone ever forget the terror in Nicole's voice—or the rage in Simpson's own voice—that we have all heard on the 911 tapes?"

Surely, too, Marcia Clark will replay another "tape" for you—the testimony of several witnesses who told you about the stormy relationship between Simpson and Nicole; and about Simpson's jealousy and possessiveness; and even about his threats to her life because of her decision to break off their relationship forever.

"It is this 'tape,' too, so well known by her family and friends, which tells the horrible story of what happened on the night of June 12. Given Simpson's history of violence and abuse, it was always only a matter of time before Nicole's body would be discovered lying dead in a fetal position, as if involuntarily seeking the protected safety of death's womb."

❧

"DNA Gives O.J. an Identity Crisis"

"It is one thing to have a motive to kill; another altogether to actually take a person's life. So the important question is, did Simpson do it? This story may be the most controversial, but it was also the easiest to write. All the facts were there, written in blood red. Not just anybody's blood, but Simpson's blood, and Nicole's blood, and Ronald Lyle Goldman's blood. It was mixed and mingled in a lethal cocktail of guilt—at Nicole's condo, in Simpson's Bronco, and all over the Brentwood compound.

"Don't forget what you heard from the lab experts who testified regarding the blood samples. The trail of blood leads to none other than Simpson—*and to literally no one else!* It is as if the DNA analysis were an unbiased, uncoached eyewitness to the killing, and even now it sits with you as a thirteenth juror. As you deliberate, it will be constantly reminding you that Simpson can never wash his hands of the blood. Like his Bronco, his driveway, his foyer, his bathroom, and—most of all—his gloves, O.J.'s hands will forever bear the stains of his guilt.

"You know sometimes, ladies and gentlemen, truth comes so conveniently packaged that it seems as if a gift from On High. In this case, we find truth handed to us in the simple form of two matching gloves—an exact pair of brown leather gloves, each stained with blood. Discovered in two different locations, they bring together, hand in hand, the condo and the compound; the crime scene and the criminal; the victims and their killer. The gloves do more than point the finger of guilt at Simpson; they point *all ten fingers* at him!

"You've seen for yourself how the gloves match. It doesn't take some DNA or other crime lab expert to make that comparison. This is a case that could be decided on the basis of two matching gloves alone. If there were not a single clue or other item of evidence available of any kind, still, the two matching bloodstained gloves would grasp O.J. Simpson in an inescapable chokehold."

❧

"O.J. Caught When Window of Opportunity Slams on Him"

"What can Simpson say to all of this, but 'I couldn't possibly have done it. I wasn't at the scene and *couldn't* have been there when the killings occurred.' That, of course, is Simpson's attempt at an alibi. But just how airtight is his story?

"Let's first set the outer parameters of Simpson's true alibi possibilities. This is the easy part. We know for a fact that Simpson was on a McDonald's run with 'Kato' Kaelin until around 9:45 p.m. on the night of June 12. We also know for a fact that there was no known conversation with Simpson until the limo driver, Allan Park, talked to him over the Brentwood estate intercom at 10:56 p.m. From that time forward, Simpson was being driven to LAX and flying out of town to Chicago. So if Nicole and Ron were killed anytime *before* 9:45 p.m. or *after* 10:56 p.m., then Simpson has a perfect alibi. There would be witnesses who could corroborate his whereabouts, and O.J. Simpson would simply never have been a suspect.

"But it is that 'window of opportunity'—of something over an hour—that causes such a big problem for Simpson. As you heard from a number of witnesses, it only takes a few minutes to drive each way between Simpson's house and Nicole's condo. That leaves an hour in which the killings could have taken place. And that is precisely the hour in which Nicole and Ron were brutally slain.

"How do we know? Remember what Nicole's mother told you about their final phone conversation? It began at 9:40 p.m. and lasted until about 10:00 p.m. That means Nicole was definitely alive up until 10 o'clock. Meanwhile, Simpson would have had plenty of time to prepare himself, leave his house, and drive to Nicole's condo by the time Nicole hung up the phone. Again, that would easily put Simpson at Nicole's condo at 10:00 p.m. or shortly thereafter.

"That opens the window on the front end. Now let's work backward in time. We know for a fact that the bodies were discovered at 12:00 midnight by Sukru Boztepe and his wife. But it was earlier, at approximately 11:40 p.m., that Boztepe had arrived home and talked with his neighbor, Steven Schwab, about the dog that Schwab had taken under his care. It was the white Akita which eventually led Boztepe to Nicole's condo.

"Backing up still further, you heard Steven Schwab tell you that his attention had been drawn to the dog because of its incessant barking and its bloody paws. Conceivably, incessant barking might be explained by something other than the violent death of a dog's owner. Conceivably. But focus on the bloody paws. The bloody paws tell you that the Akita had stepped in the victims' blood at some point in time before Steven Schwab found the dog. And that is where it gets *very* interesting.

"When did Steven Schwab tell you he found the dog? Shortly after 10:35 p.m. Maybe as late as 10:45 p.m. And how does he remember those times so clearly? It's a dead cinch: He left the house just after *The Dick Van Dyke Show* had ended—at 10:30 p.m.—and that would have put him with the white Akita no later than 10:45. Ladies and gentlemen, the murders had to have occurred before 10:45 p.m. at the very latest. And they probably occurred even earlier than that. It appears that the Akita was running around loose for some time before Steven Schwab found it.

"I confess it is a bit eerie to think about it this way, but you may even have heard the death wail of Nicole Simpson and Ronald Goldman at almost the very moment they died. Through the testimony of Pablo Fenjves, you can almost hear a dog's "plaintive wail" at the moment of death. You'll remember what Fenjves told you—that he heard such a wail around 10:15 p.m. If that was the white Akita, as Fenjves believes it was, then we know almost the precise minute that Nicole and Ron took their last dying breaths. It would have been 10:15 p.m. on June 12, 1994.

"Whether it was at that precise moment, or a few minutes either way, the one thing we do know—beyond all reasonable doubt—is that their deaths could not have been later than 10:45, and probably not later than 10:35.

"Now, what was Simpson doing during this time frame? If the defense is right, Simpson called Paula Barbieri at 10:05 p.m. But don't forget that it was a call made from Simpson's *cellular* phone—a likely indication that he was not calling from his house, but from some place where he did not have access to a fixed phone. Somewhere like his Bronco. Parked outside Nicole's condo, most likely.

"So, not only would the alleged phone call still allow plenty of time between 10:05 and 10:35 for Simpson to have committed the murders, but it might be telling us something even more important. Perhaps, that the phone call to Barbieri was an intentional attempt at providing an alibi, just moments before Simpson got out of his Bronco, lured Nicole outside the condo, and then and there viciously slashed her throat.

"Does Simpson have an alibi in this case? Not on Nicole's life! Don't forget what 'Kato' Kaelin told you as to when he heard the three loud thumps outside his room. It was around 10:40 p.m.—perfect timing for Simpson to be outside trying to quickly get rid of the evidence, including the bloody glove.

"And don't forget what the limo driver, Allan Park, told you about seeing a black person cross the lawn and enter the house. Who else in the whole world might that have been, if not Simpson? And here again it makes perfect sense for Simpson to have come from the back of the estate to the front of the house at that precise time.

"Given all of that evidence, do you believe for one moment that O.J. Simpson was inside the house, as he claims, from 9:45 p.m. until 11:00 p.m.? Is there a chance in the world that the time of death was later than 10:45 p.m., when

Steven Schwab found the bloody-pawed Akita?

"No, O.J. Simpson was not home during the crucial hour of death. Nor was he on a jet plane when the deaths occurred. The only finding you can possibly make is that Simpson is trying desperately to wiggle his way out of the 'window of opportunity.' Unfortunately for him, the 'window of opportunity' has just slammed shut on his lies. And if he would lie to you about his whereabouts, would he not have even more reason to lie to you about the murders?"

❧

"Mystery Witness May Have Seen O.J. Killings"

At some time along the way, both the prosecution and the defense must present you with their *theory of the case*. It is not enough for them to throw a bunch of times and places and events your way. They must make up their own minds about exactly how the homicides occurred. If *they* can't do that, then they can hardly expect *you* to. Let's see what the prosecution's theory of the case might be.

"Ladies and gentlemen, you have heard the defense attempting to paint the picture of a man who was nothing but 'Mr. Cool' throughout the day of June 12th. And we agree, if perhaps for different reasons. The defense would have you believe that a calm, collected, normal O.J. Simpson could not have so casually gone through a day of golfing, card playing, telephone 'dating,' and a routine McDonald's run with Kaelin—knowing all along that he was going to kill Nicole that night.

"Of course, that particular defense strategy is intended to rebut only one possible scenario of premeditated killing—that Simpson had been meticulously planning, perhaps for weeks, that at 10:15 p.m. on the night of June 12th he would kill his ex-wife. And certainly that is a possibility, suggested in part by the log of Nicole's normal routine [if admitted into evidence] and the narrow 'window of opportunity' Simpson might have intentionally created in order to make it appear that he couldn't possibly have done the killing (even though there was, in fact, more than sufficient time for him to have accomplished his purpose).

"That scenario would account for the advance purchase of a knife, the purposeful 'alibi' phone call to Paula Barbieri immediately before the killing, and the convenience of flying out on an intentionally-scheduled business trip immediately thereafter. If someone is cool enough to do all of that planning, they are cool enough to make sure they *look cool* to lots of people. Under those circumstances, it's all part of the carefully planned cover!

"But one can premeditate a murder in other, less specifically planned ways, as when a person says, 'One day she is going to press me too far, and when that day comes I'm going to kill her!' It's not a matter of some 'heat of passion' stirred up in the cauldron of the moment. The killing is premeditated as to everything but the exact timing. The killing is considered in cold blood...and then reconsidered. A lot of thought is given to it over a period of weeks or perhaps months. You even buy a knife...for whenever the moment comes. And there are gloves...just in case.

"With this kind of premeditation, the killer is just biding his time, hoping against hope that he'll eventually get what he wants. But at some point it becomes clear that he will never have that which he wants so badly he is willing to kill for, if necessary. It is at that moment in time—whenever and wherever it happens to be—that the contingency plan is brought swiftly into play.

"That brings us to O.J. Simpson, a man who has everything he wants—everything, but the woman he can't live without. No one says 'No' to O.J. Simpson and gets away with it. Especially not Nicole, whom Simpson has repeatedly threatened to kill if she ever completely turned her back on him. And now we remember the brief conversation in the school parking lot. Was Nicole telling him for one last time that she was not going back with him?

"And there is the family dinner to which Simpson is specifically *uninvited.* (Nicole's resolve not to reconcile with Simpson is shown in her conversation over dinner. The talk is all about her new life as a single woman, and her plans for travel and possibly opening a restaurant. Simpson doesn't figure at all in her future.)

"Was that family dinner invitation, which he never got, responded to by Simpson with a deadly R.S.V.P.? Was he brooding about not having rigatoni with Nicole while he was having, instead, a Quarter Pounder and fries with Kaelin? So they get home and Simpson is still brooding. He's got a flight to Chicago at 11:40, but he's got time to kill. So he drives over to Nicole's condo, just as he has done many times before. Just checking her out. Just seeing what she is up to. Other people might call it *stalking*.

"Sitting there in the car, he can't stand it any more. He knows he needs 'an outlet pass,' something to get his mind off what he's thinking. So he calls Barbieri but she's not home. He's all alone with his thoughts. He thinks about Nicole's final rejection and broods about it. The more he thinks about it, the angrier he gets. Finally, he reaches into the glove compartment for what else? Gloves. And the knife. They're both there. They've both *been* there, just waiting for this very moment. He moves the Bronco to the back alley, gets out of the car, and walks to the front door. With hardly a moment's hesitation, he rings the door bell.

"Nicole, who has put the children to bed and just gotten off the phone with her mother, is in the bathroom, where she has lit some scented candles. It's a relaxing nightly reverie for her. She hasn't yet taken her black cocktail dress off for the night because she is expecting Ron to come by with her mother's glasses. The door bell rings. Nicole descends the stairs and peers through the view-finder expecting to see Ron. To her great dismay, she sees Simpson instead. Hadn't she told him not to stop by tonight? Hadn't she told him to leave her alone, once and for all?

"As Nicole reluctantly opens the door, words are exchanged and Simpson grabs her and pulls her away from the house. There are more words, a moment of sensing danger, and, as Nicole heads back for the door, Simpson grabs her from behind in a chokehold. And suddenly there is the knife. Too terrified to even scream, Nicole raises her arms and hands in a protective position. The knife lashes at her over and over, and finally goes for her throat. With a horrific slash, it cuts her from ear to ear, and with that blow, Nicole Brown Simpson drops to the ground mortally wounded.

"But what about Ronald Lyle Goldman? Where does he fit into this picture? It's all a matter of timing. In his case, *tragic* timing. There is a single, almost obscure clue that tells us about Ron Goldman. It's the envelope with the glasses that were found by his body. If Ron had arrived prior to the killing of Nicole, surely the glasses would not have been where they were found. Rather, Ron would have rung the doorbell, probably been invited in at least for a moment, and handed the envelope and glasses over to Nicole. After all, that is why he was there that evening—to return the glasses.

"But Ron Goldman never makes it to the front door. As he approaches the door through the gate from the front sidewalk, Ron encounters a bloodied Nicole and her killer, O.J. Simpson, still standing over her. Before Ron can think twice, Simpson looks up, stares him in the eyes, and slashes at him with the knife. A terrible struggle takes place, with the envelope and glasses falling to the ground. Within seconds, Simpson overpowers Ron and slashes his throat just as he had done with Nicole. Succumbing to his wounds, Ronald Lyle Goldman joins Nicole in death as he also drops to the ground mortally wounded.

"Ladies and gentlemen, I remind you that what I have envisioned for you, while speculative in detail, is the theory most consistent with all the evidence which you have before you. As for the details, there was no eyewitness to the killing. Or was there...?

"Is it possible that, in all the testimony, we never heard from an actual eyewitness to the murders? Once again, there are clues which suggest that someone wanted you to know what he saw that night. And particularly *who* he saw that night. That eyewitness may well be Kato—no, not 'Kato' Kaelin, but Kato, Nicole's white Akita.

"Think about it. When Pablo Fenjves told you that he heard the sound of a dog around 10:15 p.m., it was not a dog's 'furious barking' that he heard, but a 'plaintive wail.' A 'plaintive wail' is not the sound you would expect from a dog who is fearful of a strange intruder. What Kato the Akita wants you to know is that whoever it was that came to the door that night and took Nicole's life was no stranger.

"There is, perhaps, yet another clue related to the brutal killings. Remember Steven Schwab told you that when he found Kato, the dog's tags were missing? Now why would that be? Let's assume that Kato was in the house when the assailant came to the front door. When Nicole went outside with her killer, the front door was left standing ajar. This means that Kato was free to walk outside, which, evidenced by the bloody paws, is exactly what he did. Is it likely that a stranger could have treated Nicole so violently without getting a challenge from Kato? Not likely. But put Simpson in the assailant's shoes and you can understand why Kato gives him more latitude for a violent encounter.

"When Simpson realizes that Kato is an eyewitness of sorts, he uses the same knife with which he had killed Nicole and Ron and cuts off Kato's tags, then opens the gate to let Kato roam free. Simpson has nothing against the dog, and, in fact, probably likes the dog very much. But it undoubtedly crosses Simpson's mind that Kato's bloody paws could spell trouble ahead. He's hoping that the dog—like the blood-laden lamb of atonement driven out into the wilderness carrying the sins of the people—will run away, never to be seen again.

"The bottom line is that the white Akita's reactions that night were consistent with the scenario which I outlined for you earlier. O.J. Simpson—by no means a stranger to the dog—was allowed to do what no stranger could have gotten away with. "In stark contrast, Kato's plaintive wail tells us poignantly what the aftermath of Nicole's death was like for her canine companion. Simpson may have been no stranger to Kato, but he was now no friend, either."

∝

"O.J. May Run, But He Can't Hide"

"Ladies and gentlemen, suppose I were to tell you that a crime had taken place, but that you knew absolutely nothing about the facts surrounding the crime itself. And then suppose I told you that one of two suspects to the crime had left town in a hurry. Which one of the two suspects would you tend to think did the crime?

"Unless I'm terribly mistaken, you all chose the suspect who left town in a hurry. Why do we almost automatically associate 'flight' with guilt? There is just something in us, isn't there, that tries to escape the consequences of whatever it is—big or little—that we've done wrong? It's just human nature to evade guilt if at all possible. So it is not surprising that 'flight' raises the specter of guilt.

"Now consider this: Suppose you didn't know anything about the circumstances surrounding the murders of Nicole Brown Simpson and Ronald Lyle Goldman. Nothing at all. All you know is that there is a suspect, and that the suspect has evaded arrest and led police on a fifty-mile freeway pursuit. When finally stopped, the vehicle is found to contain up to $8,000 in cash, a gun, a disguise, and a passport. What else are you *supposed* to think? Is that the act of an innocent man?

"And what are we to think if during the freeway pursuit the suspect is said to have been holding a gun to his head? Again, is that the act of an innocent man? Why should someone even think about suicide if he is 'absolutely 100% not guilty'? Does that make any sense at all?

"Ladies and gentlemen, when a suspect to a crime threatens to kill himself and eludes police arrest, there is simply no escaping the conclusion: He is a guilty man.

"In this case, that guilty man is Orenthal James Simpson. Just read the newspaper. It's in all the headlines. [Marcia Clark now points to the newspaper exhibit and slowly reads headline by headline...]

'Reasons for O.J. Killings Revealed!'

"How could we ever forget Nicole's frantic 911 calls or the injuries that caused her to be hospitalized?

'DNA Gives O.J. an Identity Crisis'

"The story is in the blood. The accused can be expected to lie, but DNA never does.

'O.J. Caught When Window of Opportunity Slams on Him'

"Simpson wouldn't be here today if he, too, had stayed home and watched *The Dick Van Dyke Show* to its 10:30 conclusion.

'Mystery Witness May Have Seen O.J. Killings'

"View the terror of the murder in slow motion through the eyes of a bewildered white Akita. No stranger could have gotten away with such a brutal, premeditated killing.

'O.J. May Run, But He Can't Hide'

"If you really are 'absolutely 100% not guilty,' what reason is there to run?"

"Ladies and gentlemen, from the headlines to the fine print, the evidence is simply overwhelming. Beyond any reasonable doubt, Orenthal James Simpson is absolutely 100% *guilty* as charged. In the interest of justice, therefore, the People of California ask you to find the defendant guilty of murder in the first degree in the deaths of Nicole Brown Simpson and Ronald Lyle Goldman."

How Do You Feel At This Point?

After listening to Marcia Clark's own opening argument, how would you evaluate her style and presentation?

....

....

....

....

How well did she succeed in logically pulling together the many weeks of confusing testimony?

....

....

....

....

What "headlines" did she use to help organize her main points?

....

....

....

....

....

What were the prosecution's strongest arguments?

....

....

....

....

....

What were the prosecution's weakest arguments?

....

....

....

....

....

Are there any arguments you would have made in favor of the prosecution that were not made?

....

....

....

....

How convincing is the prosecution's case at this point?

....

....

....

....

....

10

Surely You Must Have Doubts

❧

Defense's Summation and Argument

Among attorneys in Tennessee the saying is:
When you have the facts on your side, argue the facts.
When you have the law on your side, argue the law.
When you have neither, holler.

—Al Gore

By this point in the actual trial, you will have a much better idea of what you might anticipate from the defense in its closing argument than can possibly be known in advance of the trial. The biggest "unknown" prior to trial was whether O.J. himself would testify, and, if so, what he would say. By now, that mystery will have been revealed. For reasons given earlier, we can only presume that O.J. *will* have chosen to testify, despite the fact that almost no other defendant in similar circumstances would ever have gotten the green light from his lawyers.

Without knowing in advance what O.J.'s story turned out to be, it is a safe bet to assume that he maintained his pre-trial posture—that he was at home during the time when the prosecution claims the homicides took place, and that his bizarre post-arrest actions were the actions of a man greatly upset at the death of his ex-wife and the mother of his two children, a death for which he was not responsible. If O.J. sticks to those two positions, then his attorneys are pretty much bound within those factual parameters.

❧

Your Basic Defense Arguments

Although we are more than slightly handicapped by not knowing what testimony will have been given by the time of closing arguments, it is possible to anticipate with some certainty that the defense will make the standard arguments that all defense counsel make. For example, the defense will want to remind you that the prosecution has the burden of proof in this case. What that means is that O.J. need prove nothing. Absolutely nothing. If through its presentation of the evidence the prosecution has failed to prove its own case, then you must return a not guilty verdict, regardless of how weak you might happen to believe the defense's own case is.

Next, you will undoubtedly be reminded that it is the prosecution's burden to prove its case *beyond a reasonable doubt*. (The defense may even be tempted to use phrases such as *beyond any shadow of a doubt*, though that exceeds what the law demands.) They will want to make sure that, if any of you have ever served on the trial of a civil case, there is no confusion in your minds about the two very different types of burdens of proof. In civil cases, the moving party need only prove the case by a preponderance of the evidence—that is, the scales of justice need only be slightly tilted in their favor in order to win. By contrast, the burden of proof in criminal cases must reach the lofty level of *a moral certainty*. That, obviously, is an *extremely* high degree of certainty.

You may recall what Johnnie Cochran told you in voir dire when you were first being considered as a juror. "You should vote your conscience," he said, "even if it means failing to reach a verdict." Even then, he was priming the pump for a hung jury, if necessary, in the event that an outright not-guilty verdict is unattainable. Here again at the close of the trial, you can be sure that you will hear his admonition repeated. (You will also have heard the prosecution urge you to listen to each other during the deliberations and be willing to reconsider your opinions if your fellow jurors make compelling arguments.)

Following along in the same vein, defense counsel will drive home one more time the fact that, by law, O.J. is presumed to be innocent. You will be asked to ignore the fact that formal charges have been brought against O.J. Perhaps you recall that during voir dire Johnnie Cochran pressed this very point, asking one of the prospective jurors, "You won't subscribe to the old adage that 'Where there's smoke, there's fire,' will you?" In some form or another, you'll hear the defense ask you that same question again.

❧

Responding to the Prosecution's Argument

As counsel moves beyond the standard defense admonitions, you will undoubtedly hear his rebuttal to the prosecution's case, as was articulated in the People's opening argument. One can already see that Ms. Clark [as depicted in the previous chapter] has given the defense a perfect opportunity for an effective opening barrage. Will Johnnie Cochran be the one to deliver that barrage?

"Ladies and gentlemen, in her opening argument, Ms. Clark read the papers for you. Or was it the tabloids? As you and I both know, you can never trust the tabloids. [Broad smile.] And surely you will agree with me when I say that headlines can be misleading. In fact, let me share one headline with you that pertains to this very case. It was even the subject of much discussion while you were in the jury selection process. The headline read: 'DNA Ties Nicole's Blood to O.J.'s Socks.' Remember?

"But by this time, you and I—and even the prosecution—know that there was no truth to the headline, or even to the story beneath it. It was all the figment of someone's imagination—a rumor—just like all of Ms. Clark's cute little 'headlines.' As I am set to demonstrate to you, her 'headlines' are about as reliable as the one I saw at the checkout counter yesterday: 'Elvis sighted at Michael Jackson Concert!' But if she insists that you read such trash, then let's take a magnifying glass to it."

✺

Motive? What Motive?

"First of all, she wants you to believe the rumor that O.J. is mean. That's right, *mean*. And that he is so mean he is even capable of murder. But just ask yourself, 'Is someone who is capable of being mean necessarily capable of *killing* someone?' Take 'Mean' Joe Green, for example. Of course, he's retired now, but when he played for the Pittsburgh Steelers, there wasn't anyone who was tougher, stronger, or meaner on the field than Joe Green. That's how he earned his nickname, 'Mean' Joe Green. But the prosecution is asking you to believe, in effect, that Joe Green is capable of murder just because he was a terror to the opposition whenever he was on the gridiron. Does that make sense? Is all meanness the same kind of meanness?

"When you hear the stories about O.J. smashing Nicole's windshield, and sending her to the hospital—or even the 911 call—you have to ask yourself, 'What could make a nice guy like O.J. do such crazy things?' Think back to that New Year's Eve morning when O.J. let his anger get the best of him—and Nicole. It wasn't just possessiveness, or jealousy, or rejection. It was too much to drink, that's what! It doesn't justify it for a minute, but the truth is that lots of people get a little bit crazy when alcohol starts working overtime on the brain.

"Now look where that leads us in this case. On the night of June 12, there was no evidence that O.J. had been on a drinking binge. 'Kato' Kaelin testified that O.J. was normal in every way when they made their McDonald's run. And Allan Parks, the limo driver, never said a word about a 'drunken O.J.' So there's simply no reason to expect that any past drink-related violence would have surfaced again that night. O.J. may have been a *mean drunk* on occasion (when he'd been drinking), but he is not *generally* mean (when he *hasn't* been drinking).

"Didn't you agree a moment ago that not all meanness is the same meanness? You *know* it's true. And just how low are they willing to go to subtly imply that O.J.'s ability to be tough, and strong, and mean in a football game somehow suggests that he is mean enough to kill the mother of his two children? Heaven help 'Mean' Joe Green if, God forbid, something violent should happen to someone *he* loves!

"Don't forget what O.J. himself told you. He sat right there in that witness chair and bared his very soul. He admitted to you right up front that he had been a terrible husband to Nicole—that he had yelled at her, threatened her, and, yes, even beaten her. O.J. Simpson never even got close to being a hall-of-fame husband. And he admits it. But that doesn't automatically tell us that O.J. Simpson *killed* Nicole.

"Here's a thought for you. If we had been fortunate enough to have an eyewitness who saw the real killers, would we still want to pin the killings on O.J. just because he has a history of being a lousy, even violent husband? So why is it when we *don't* have an eyewitness that the police and the prosecution are jumping all over themselves to pin the killings on O.J.? Is O.J. to be penalized simply because there is no instant replay available to show who it was that committed the personal foul?

"There's something else. The picture which the prosecution paints of a crazed, knife-wielding O.J. threatening Nicole is anything but the picture which the witnesses painted of O.J. on the night Nicole was killed. He's not mad. He's not brooding. He's not *anything*. He's just O.J., havin' a Quarter Pounder and fries before catching a red-eye to Chicago to play a little golf. What could be more 'O.J.'?

"And no one confirms that fact more clearly than Nicole herself. As seen through every single witness who testified about Nicole's demeanor on the night of her death, there is nothing but calm in her voice; nothing but a relaxed expectancy of a bright future ahead. Remember how her own sister, Denise, described her? No worry. No fear. No concern. Whatever she and O.J. talked about briefly after their daughter's dance recital, it didn't send Nicole reeling into some kind of terrified spin.

"So if O.J. was cool as a cucumber, and if Nicole was too, how in the world does the prosecution expect you to believe some wild fantasy of theirs in which O.J. sits in his car outside her house for a few minutes, gets into some kind of a 'brood mood,' and suddenly goes ballistic? In order to believe that, you've got to give more credence to mere speculation than proven facts. And the facts are that nothing in O.J.'s troubled history with Nicole fits anything at all that happened between them the day and night of June 12th. The prosecution wants you to put two and two together and come up with five! The premise of a stormy relationship may be clear enough, but, on that night, the conclusion just doesn't add up.

"Motive? What motive?"

❧

A Broken Window of Opportunity

"Now ladies and gentlemen, you have heard the prosecutor make much of the so-called 'window of opportunity' which she claims has slammed shut on O.J. I'm afraid that in her house of cards the window she is speaking of has at least four broken panes.

"The first 'broken pane' ought to be a great source of embarrassment to the prosecution. More than that, in the interest of justice it should have brought a swift dismissal of this case from the word 'go.' In violation of state law, in breach of clear LAPD guidelines, and contrary to standard police practice, the police purposely, wilfully, and intentionally kept the bodies of the victims from the coroner's investigators for a full ten hours! Just long enough, of course, to prevent any scientific determination of the time of death.

"Wouldn't you think that time of death would be important for the police to know if they wanted to catch the real killers? Don't you have to ask yourself why the police were so intent on keeping this information from being known? What did they have to hide?

"Then there is the second 'broken pane.' And this one is just totally inexcusable. After ten hours from the time they are first discovered, the victims' bodies are finally brought to the morgue for autopsies. And then what happens? The crack coroner destroys the only evidence that could have verified O.J.'s alibi! Can you believe it?

"There are only two reasons to do an autopsy: first, to determine *cause* of death; and, second, to determine *time* of death. In this case, it wouldn't have taken even a marginally-qualified deputy medical examiner like Irwin Golden to figure out the cause of death. That, tragically, was the easy part. But when it comes to the really important part of the autopsy—*time* of death—Golden casually tosses out the contents of Nicole's stomach, the best clue we would have had as to when she died.

"So what does Golden say about the 'window of opportunity'? Taking only a wild guess, Golden says the homicides could have occurred over a period of three hours, between 9:00 p.m. and 12:00 midnight. Of course, that is good news/bad news for O.J. On one hand, it suggests that Nicole and Ronald might have been killed even after O.J. was flying at 37,000 feet on his way to Chicago. And that, of itself, ought to create enough doubt in your minds to find O.J. not guilty.

"The bad news, unfortunately, is that if they *were* killed after O.J. left for the airport or was already in the air, he now has no way to prove it. Thanks to Golden's speculative and unverifiable three-hour time frame, O.J.'s alibi evidence was tossed right out of the proverbial 'window of opportunity.' Can that be fair? Should O.J. be convicted solely on the basis of Irwin Golden's incompetence?

"The third 'broken pane' reflects just the opposite problem. If Golden's three-hour window is too wide, the window presented by the prosecution's occurrence witnesses is simply too narrow. Think back on the testimony. Juditha Brown says her phone call with Nicole ended at about 10 o'clock. But she didn't look at her watch as she hung up, so maybe it was later. And, in any event, we know that O.J. made a call to Paula Barbieri at 10:05.

"The prosecution, of course, was more than pleased to tell you that Steven Schwab found Kato the dog shortly after Schwab left his house at 10:35 p.m. That probably means Kato had been wandering around for at least five or ten minutes. Schwab certainly doesn't sense anything amiss in the neighborhood. So that backs us up to, say, 10:30 p.m. What that leaves us with, ladies and gentlemen, is not a 75-minute window, as the prosecution would have you believe, but a 20-25-minute window.

"Give that some thought, especially as you think back on the prosecution's dramatic scenario. According to Ms. Clark, O.J. pulls up outside Nicole's condo and gets restless. He calls Paula Barbieri to calm himself down, but she's not home so he starts brooding. How long does it take to brood? A minute? Two minutes? Surely, brooding is something that happens over a significant time period.

"Are we really supposed to believe the prosecution's nice bit of fiction that, for no apparent immediate reason, O.J. goes from being as cool as a cucumber, to brooding, to angry, to *maniacal* within just a few short minutes? With this narrow a window, that's all he's got. Don't forget, if the prosecution is to be believed, O.J. has to move his car to the alleyway, put on his gloves and get his knife ready, walk to the front door, wait for Nicole to get downstairs, become embroiled in some kind of angry confrontation with her, stab her repeatedly, stand over her body, look up and see Ron Goldman enter through the gate, engage in a violent struggle with him before knifing him to death, cut the tags off Kato, send Kato out through the gate, make his way back to the alleyway, and drive away to his Brentwood estate, which—although it's in the same area of town—is not exactly next door. And all of that within a half hour or less? Wow!

"Even if a person could physically do all of that in a race against the clock, does it make sense that it would have given O.J. enough time to be transformed from a cool dude into a homicidal nightstalker? *Does it?*

"The last 'broken pane' is one of those pieces of the puzzle that falls to the floor and gets lost in the cracks. Ladies and gentlemen, we need to talk about Ronald Goldman. According to Karen Crawford, the bar manager at Mezzaluna, Goldman clocked out at 9:33 p.m., changed his clothes and left Mezzaluna about 9:45 p.m. You've heard testimony that the restaurant, on San Vicente Boulevard, is just a short distance from Nicole's condo on South Bundy Drive.

"Can it take even fifteen minutes for Goldman to arrive at Nicole's? We already know that Juditha Brown can't be sure of the time when her phone conversation with Nicole ended. Maybe it was a few minutes *after* 10:00 or *before.* Let's say, *before.* That puts Goldman at Nicole's house close to the top of the hour, at which time they are viciously attacked by who knows who?

"What's important to remember here is that 'Kato' Kaelin says he and O.J. returned to the Brentwood estate at 9:45 p.m., which is exactly the same time that Goldman left Mezzaluna for Nicole's condo. Now, even supposing O.J. had left his house immediately after dropping Kaelin off, which one of them would have gotten to Nicole's place sooner—O.J. or Goldman? Goldman, of course. Given the comparative distances they would have had to travel, it's not even a close race.

"There is not a chance in the world that O.J. could have been at Nicole's place by the time Goldman arrived. So much for the prosecution's slam-dunk 'window of opportunity'!"

❧

Blood, Hair, Gloves, and Other Myths

"Ladies and gentlemen, does it make you uncomfortable knowing that the prosecution's case is wholly circumstantial? It ought to—especially when you view the blur of circumstances in stop-action slow motion. I suspect you may have wearied of what surely seemed to you an endless process of nitpicking on our part as we challenged the prosecution's physical evidence item by item. And I apologize for having to put you through that. But unless you slow down and smell the dandelions, you can't appreciate that they are not the blood red roses the prosecution would have you believe.

"Was there blood at the scene of the homicides? Of course. Plenty of it. Tragically, too much of it. Would it have been Nicole's blood? Absolutely. Ron Goldman's blood? No question about it. No one needs a DNA test to figure that out. The only question is, was O.J.'s blood there as well? Or maybe a hair from O.J.?

"To hear the prosecution, you'd have to be some kind of a fool to dare question the DNA analysis which their experts say points the finger *exclusively* at O.J. Like it's supposed to be some infallible test. Mind you, the test itself is not the basic problem. Remember what we asked you to keep in mind when we made our opening statement? We've said it several times, and you need to say it over and over again to yourself, because it's worth remembering: *Scientific tests are only as good as the people who use them.*

"Or to put it another way—garbage in, garbage out. The question is not whether tests are available to identify a person's genetic characteristics. We *would* be fools to deny that. The question you must ask is, what is it that is being tested? What's the sample?

"And there are other questions as well. From where was the sample taken? How was it collected? By whom was it taken, and did they know what they were doing? Was there a possibility that the sample could have been contaminated? Can we be assured that the scores of samples weren't mishandled or mislabeled during the chain of custody?

"As you will recall, we meticulously asked all of those questions of the police, the criminologists on the scene, and the scientists at the crime lab. As you will also recall, we repeatedly turned up mistake after mistake, problem after problem, doubt upon doubt. There were time delays and opportunities for contamination. There was shocking inexperience on the part of the criminologists, some of whom had been assigned to do what—in a case of this magnitude—clearly should have been done by more experienced personnel.

"Some might call it sloppy police work. But with a person's freedom on the line, you should recognize it for what it is—a miscarriage of justice. If the sword of justice is double-edged, so is the miscarriage. With a single misguided thrust, we have unreliable evidence which could end up wrongfully convicting an innocent man, while at the same time there is now no way to determine who the real killers were.

"When it comes to DNA analysis, ladies and gentlemen, maybe you are like I am. Frankly, if I never heard another DNA expert testifying—for either side—I don't think I'd miss it. All the talk about population genetics and calculated odds into the hundreds of thousands, or maybe even millions, takes my simple mind off into some pretty rarefied atmosphere. All I know is that *they* don't seem to know, or at least agree, on what it's all supposed to mean. And if *the experts* can't agree, how do they expect you and me to decide what the odds ought to be?

"Or is this one of those places where the law tells us which way to jump? Isn't this one of those issues where the law tells us to give the defendant the benefit of the doubt? If so, we have to go with the *lower* odds, the odds like one in 4,000 people, or even just one in 800 people. And that's fair isn't it? It says that O.J. *could have been* there at the scene sometime, but it also lets us know that we can't go to the bank with it; that we need other evidence of guilt before we can convict O.J. and still sleep well at night.

"Do you want to know what the DNA analysis really says? It says that *whoever it was* that killed Nicole and Ron, they were *African-American*. That fact is no longer in question. The odds of their being anything other than African-American is like one in a zillion. But *which* African-American persons did the killing is very much up for grabs. What you now know from the evidence most favorable to O.J.—which is the evidence the law compels you to consider—is that O.J., along with one in 800 to 4,000 other African-Americans, could have done it. Given the millions of African-Americans in the Los Angeles area, and the many millions more who may live elsewhere but who could easily have been in L.A. on the night of the killing, there is wide latitude for the possibility that the killer was some African-American person or persons *other* than O.J.

"Far from being the open-and-shut case the prosecution would have you believe, DNA is just one other factor to consider along with all of the other evidence. Just one of *many* factors. And if we already know for certain that O.J. could not possibly have been at Nicole's before Goldman arrived, then the prosecution's own theory about how the killings took place nullifies any so-called 'conclusive' DNA identification of O.J. All it tells us is that the prosecution has the wrong African-American in their sights.

"And that is precisely what you need to consider next: that the wrong *African-American* has been in their sights. You see, ladies and gentlemen, from the very beginning of this case we have had a seething racial undertone at work. As we demonstrated in our cross-examination of Det. Mark Fuhrman, here is a public servant who, when suing for a stress-related discharge and pension back in 1983, was not the least bit embarrassed to make anti-black references.

"Now I recognize that this is a sensitive issue, and that some folks in the media have suggested that we are wrongfully injecting the issue of race into this case. But don't forget, ladies and gentlemen, that it was Fuhrman himself—through the statements that he made while acting as a public servant—who injected the race issue.

"What is so very disturbing about this aspect of the case is that such anti-black sentiment naturally raises a question about how objectively Fuhrman may have conducted his investigation on the night of the killing. Was it O.J.'s status as a successful black athlete and media personality that galled Fuhrman, or perhaps O.J.'s and Nicole's interracial marriage? What else can account for what looks suspiciously like a piece of planted evidence that only Det. Fuhrman could have planted?

"Here, of course, we are talking about that brown leather right-hand glove which Fuhrman claims to have discovered on O.J.'s estate. Speaking of long odds, what are the odds that, had O.J. done the killings as alleged, he would have accidentally dropped one glove at the scene of the homicides, and then accidentally dropped another one in his own back yard as he was running back into his house? Just how do you *accidentally* have leather gloves fall off your hands in the first place?

"Something very strange has to be going on here folks, and I, for one, smell a rat. How about you?"

❧❧❧

Holes in Prosecutor's Theory

"Now, ladies and gentlemen, we've all heard this dramatic piece of fiction which Ms. Clark has presented to us that is supposed to explain exactly how O.J. did the killings. I don't mean to be cruel, but if Ms. Clark aspires to being a famous author of suspense thrillers after this trial is over, my advice to her would be, 'Don't give up your day job!' For a suspense thriller to work, it's got to be at least halfway believable.

"Don't forget that Ms. Clark is trying desperately to convince you that this is a cold-blooded, premeditated killing. But just think about that for a minute. If O.J. intended all along that one day he would kill Nicole, why on earth would he choose to kill her by slashing her with a knife? Is that the method-of-choice for a cold-blooded killer? Would a gun not have suited his purposes far better? It's clean, efficient, and less personal. But a *knife*?

"On the other hand, Ms. Clark hedges her bets by making O.J.'s final decision to kill to be something that takes place on the spur of the moment, when his anger and brooding finally explode into a homicidal rage. But if that's the case, what explains the gloves? Are we supposed to believe that someone in the heat of flaring rage and emotion is going to think logically enough, or even long enough, to pull out a pair of gloves and put them on?

"When you hear the prosecution talk about alleged matches between gloves and blood drops, don't forget that there are other matches which also count. *Gloves* go hand in hand with *premeditated killings*, and *knives* with *heat of passion killings*—not the other way 'round. Listen carefully to what particular evidence is supposed to match which particular theory. Every good fiction writer knows that specific items of evidence and particular scenarios of a killing are not necessarily interchangeable. So beware. If neither theory of the killings is supported by the right evidence, then neither theory of the killing is a right theory.

"Ms. Clark's attempt at writing a thriller for us is, well—to put it as kindly as I can—stranger than fiction. But I must admit that the bit part she gave the white Akita was very creative. Having a dog testify is certainly a novel idea. More than anything, I suppose it tells us just how desperate the prosecution must be to have to subpoena a dog!

"As for Kato's supposedly telling us that the killer was no stranger, it's worse than hearsay upon hearsay. Not having the slightest clue about the dog's disposition—whether it barks and snarls at strangers, or whether it rolls over and begs—all we have to go on is speculation upon speculation. Is wild speculation the kind of evidence which the prosecution would have you believe *beyond a reasonable doubt?*

"Perhaps you are saying to yourself, 'If the prosecution's scenario is not to be believed, then what is the defense's theory of how the killings took place?' I'm going to be very frank with you, ladies and gentlemen. As you can imagine, we on the defense team have spent literally hundreds of hours trying to reconstruct and piece together what happened at Nicole's condo on the night of June 12th. Some of us have speculated one scenario; some of us another; and still others admit to being as clueless as when we began. As you yourselves know, the facts just haven't presented themselves in a convenient package. If they had—either way—none of us would be here today.

"I say all of that simply to show that the Deputy District Attorney's glib attempts to paint in technicolor the last tragic moments in the lives of Nicole Brown Simpson and Ronald Lyle Goldman are just too easy, and too self-serving to her case for you to base your decision on it. When no one truly knows what really happened that night, then it's best that we leave speculation as far behind as possible and stick with what we know. And what we know is that O.J. Simpson couldn't have done any of the things that Ms. Clark attributed to him because he was never there that night. *That* is not some wild, imaginative piece of fiction. *That* is what we know!"

"Among the matters of law about which I anticipate that the Judge will soon instruct you, there is one instruction in particular which I want you to carefully consider. It says, in effect, that if the circumstantial evidence is susceptible of two reasonable interpretations, one of which points to the defendant's guilt and the other to his innocence, then as a matter of law you must adopt that interpretation which points to the defendant's innocence, and reject that interpretation which points to his guilt.

"So if you think Ms. Clark's story is somewhat reasonable, but that O.J.'s own version of events that night is also somewhat reasonable, then as a matter of law you *must* find in O.J.'s favor. Are you willing to follow the judge's instructions in this regard?"

Chasing Away the Flight

"Ladies and gentlemen, Ms. Clark's final headline read, 'O.J. May Run, But He Can't Hide.' Like the Information of felony which has been charged in this case, that headline is also wrong on both counts. O.J. neither ran nor attempted to hide. The very fact that he chose to testify in this trial shows that O.J. Simpson has nothing to hide. I don't know whether you fully appreciate what a personal risk he took in taking that stand when he had a Constitutional right not to. Even when you are absolutely 100% innocent, it is no easy job to take on a bunch of trained lawyers who know how to eat witnesses for breakfast.

"As for 'running,' O.J. Simpson never ran toward the wrong end zone in his life! For all the drama of the low-speed freeway chase, don't forget that when the police first saw O.J., the white Bronco was headed *north* on Interstate 5. There's no way that O.J. was goin' south on us. O.J. was headed *home*, not to Mexico or Canada or who knows where?

"Did you, along with the rest of us, watch the so-called chase on television? From the questions we asked you on voir dire, I know that most of you did. If so, what strikes you about that 'chase'? Was it like any police chase you've ever seen before, either in the movies or in real life? Did the bad guys try to outrun the cops, or race at high speeds down the freeway, or ram their Bronco into squad cars in an effort to escape? You know they didn't. To that part of this case you yourselves were eyewitnesses.

"So what is all this talk about 'flight,' as if somehow it is automatically to be equated with guilt? If it truly *had* been 'flight,' well, maybe so. But if that is what the prosecution wants us to call 'flight,' then they must have a new definition for the word that the rest of us don't have.

"Of course, the prosecution knows that they are stretching this 'flight' thing so far that it's got stretch marks! In fact, they even had to come up with a new name for it—a *low-speed* chase. Now, that's an oxymoron if ever I've heard one! No wonder they hurriedly started talking about what they found inside the Bronco—the cash, the passport, and the funny disguise—as if those items could magically change the basic nature of the ride back to O.J.'s place where he turned himself over to the police.

"O.J. has told you what all of those items were for: cash for his kids; the disguise for keeping the media away while at Disneyland; and so forth. And all of that is just as reasonable an explanation as the prosecution's theory of a 'flight' so slow that the word *chase* had to be ridiculously re-named! So, once again, there is circumstantial evidence which—since it could be seen as reasonable in either direction—must be decided in O.J.'s favor.

"After awhile, what you have to ask yourself is, 'Does the prosecution just not care in the least about the *person* behind the *persona* of O.J. Simpson? Are they willing to do whatever it takes to convict him, even if it means compounding his own personal tragedy?' It's the suicide issue I'm talking about here. If the prosecution is to be believed, O.J. is guilty of murder simply because he became distraught over the death of his ex-wife and being falsely accused of her murder.

"Who's kidding who, here? Surely, it doesn't take much imagination to figure out how *you or I* would feel under similar circumstances. And look how hypocritical the prosecution is on this point. On one hand, O.J. is supposed to have this inextinguishable flame of passion still burning for Nicole; and yet, on the other hand, he can't become distraught over her death without risking some inference of guilt for displaying such a predictable mental state!

"Just the other day, you listened as O.J. confessed to you that he definitely was 'in a state,' as he called it, during the drive back to his home. He's so open about it all that, at a bail hearing last October, we could hardly restrain him from talking. As you know, we lawyers get real nervous when our clients want to do the talking instead of letting us do it for them. We see it as our job to protect them against themselves. But O.J. doesn't want us to run interference for him. Whatever the risk, he wants to tell it like it is. He wants you to know just exactly how distraught he really was—not because he was guilty, but precisely because he knew he was *not* guilty.

"Let me read back just this much of what he told you the other day. It's worth hearing again:

> Ms. Clark said I was trying to run. Everyone knows that I called
> my father-in-law. I was not in a frame of mind. I admit that I
> was not in the right frame of mind at the time I was trying to get
> to my wife...I was headed back home.

I don't know about you, folks, but that doesn't sound like the voice of guilt to me. It sounds like the voice of a man whose world was crumbling around him through no fault of his own. A man who had just lost everything in the world that was precious to him—his Nicole, the companionship of his two children, his reputation, and, of course, his freedom.

"Can any of us say for sure that we would never have reacted the same way as O.J.? The O.J. we all know and love may have gone a little bit crazy on us during that stressful time, but of two things you can be absolutely certain: O.J. did not run. And he did not hide."

❧

A Final Appeal

"Ladies and gentlemen, this is our last opportunity to talk with you about this case. You will soon hear a rebuttal from the prosecution to which we will not have the opportunity to respond. We must, therefore, leave it with you to ask the hard questions of the prosecution which we will not be able to ask.

"For sure, don't let them paint any more fanciful pictures for you. The only colors they know are the black and white of prejudice—and the blood red of contaminated DNA samples. Buy *their* picture and it won't be just some figment of their imagination that ends up getting framed.

"Above all, keep remembering the multitude of reasonable doubts in this case. Keep asking yourself:

If O.J. knew he was going to kill Nicole that night, why is it that no one detected anything unusual about his demeanor throughout the day?

If O.J. was really such a threat to Nicole that night, why didn't Nicole sense it and guard against it?

How could the prosecution's theory of the killing be correct if O.J. could not possibly have gotten to Nicole's condo before Ron Goldman?

How can you trust any of the scientific evidence after it was collected in such a sloppy and unprofessional manner?

Do we have any assurance at all that the bloody glove was not planted by Det. Fuhrman?

Does it make any sense at all that O.J. would have used a knife instead of a gun if he had really wanted to get rid of Nicole in a fast, efficient pre-planned murder?

Is it even remotely possible that a killing of this brutality could have been committed by the decent man all of us know simply as O.J.?

"Folks, there is as much doubt in this case as there is blood. And that reasonable doubt is a perfect laboratory match with the good character of O.J. Simpson—a man who never claimed to be perfect, especially in his relationship with Nicole, but a man that all of America trusts. Have we been so wrong about O.J. Simpson all these years? Surely, not.

"But ladies and gentlemen, O.J. Simpson wants to be right up front with you about your verdict. The last thing he wants is a sympathy vote. He does not want you to acquit him because he is O.J.; or because you loved to watch 'Number 32' run with such elegance up the field; or see him jump over suitcases in airports; or because you were a devoted fan of the man in the booth on Monday Night Football. He wants you to acquit him because, as he said when he entered his plea, he is 'absolutely 100% not guilty.'

"The time has come for you to decide, and the choice may not be nearly as difficult as you might think. For if you are not absolutely 100% sure that O.J.

is *guilty* (and how *can* you be?), then you must do the right thing and find him *not guilty*."

Now, How Do You Feel?

After listening to defense counsel's summation and argument in the actual case, how would you evaluate his style and presentation?

_____

_____

_____

_____

_____

How well did he succeed in logically pulling together the many weeks of confusing testimony?

_____

_____

_____

What "hooks" did he use to help organize his main points?

_____

_____

_____

_____

What were the defense's strongest arguments?

_____

_____

_____

What were the defense's weakest arguments?

....

....

....

....

....

Are there any arguments you would have made in favor of the defense that were not made?

....

....

....

....

....

How convincing is the case for the defense at this point?

....

....

....

....

....

11

It Is Your Duty to Convict

Prosecution's Closing Argument

*The trial lawyer does what Socrates was executed
for: making the worse argument appear the stronger.*

—Irving R. Kaufman

As the defense counsel turns from the jury box and takes his seat, Judge Ito will nod toward the prosecution's table, indicating that Marcia Clark, or her designee, may proceed with the People's closing argument to the jury. Closing argument is a time to rebut any points brought up by the defense that may not already have been addressed in the opening argument, or which appear to be particularly damaging and in need of further buttressing.

Without knowing in advance of the trial exactly what approach the defense will have taken in the case (and especially what they may have just argued), it is virtually impossible to anticipate what issues will need to be covered by the prosecution in its rebuttal. Like us, Marcia Clark and the prosecution team undoubtedly find themselves in a similar situation. In the first part of the People's closing argument, they will be reacting on the spot to what they have just heard from the defense.

A Final Rebuttal

Responding to the defense's summation and argument, you might possibly hear someone from the prosecution team cover the following points by way of rebuttal.

"Ladies and gentlemen, you have heard defense counsel suggest that the defendant was mean and violent only when he had been drinking. That is nothing more than an assumption based upon the fact that in the 1989 New Year's Day assault there apparently had been some heavy partying going on. Of course, that is not to be unexpected, given the occasion. However, there is no evidence whatsoever that alcohol was involved in the later 911 call. The defense's argument that Simpson could not have turned violent on the night of June 12th because he had not been drinking simply won't wash.

"'Motive? What motive?' counsel asked cynically with reference to Mr. Simpson. But that is exactly what you should ask yourself about any alternative scenario for the double-murder. From the beginning of the trial to the very end, the defense kept suggesting that someone else acting alone, or even two or more persons acting in concert, had done the killing. But if so, what motive would they have had? Robbery? Larceny? Nothing was taken, not even with the front door of the condo left open. Rape? There is no hint of it.

"Ladies and gentlemen, this was not some drive-by stabbing! Whoever killed Nicole Simpson had specifically targeted her that night. And who, but O.J. Simpson, had the kind of stormy relationship with her that could even possibly explain such a murder?

"As for the defense's theory that Simpson could not possibly have arrived at Nicole's condo before Ron Goldman, it assumes that Goldman proceeded directly from Mezzaluna to Nicole's. Is there any reason Goldman might not have stopped off somewhere on the way? Maybe he needed to fill his car with gas. Maybe he stopped by a drug store. There are any number of possible reasons why Goldman might have been delayed, but since the defense counsel has chided the prosecution for being speculative, we won't indulge in speculation. What we do know is that the tell-tale glasses indicate Goldman never made it to the front door before Mr. Simpson cut him down.

"That very confrontation also accounts for the brown leather left-hand glove which was found at Goldman's feet. When counsel asked suggestively how a leather glove accidentally slips off the hand, the answer is that it *doesn't*. The glove found there at the condo didn't just *slip off*. It was obviously *pulled off* during the ferocious struggle which took place that night between Simpson and Goldman.

"In his panic to get away from the scene, Simpson obviously didn't notice that one glove was missing. In fact, he didn't notice it until he was back at his estate trying to hide whatever evidence he could behind the guest quarters. If I were a betting person, I would bet that his discovery of the missing glove had something to do with the three loud thumps which 'Kato' Kaelin heard.

"Just imagine what must have been going through Simpson's mind as he tried to rid himself of anything incriminating. He realizes now in the aftermath of the murders that he has actually done the unthinkable and killed Nicole. And why did that jerk, Ron, have to come along just when he was about to get away? Ron was never in the original game plan! And then there is that moment of panic when Simpson realizes that there is only one glove. Where is the other glove? Where is it?

"When Simpson finally realizes that he has left the other glove at the murder scene, he knows he is in deep trouble. It is at that moment you can almost see Simpson double up his fist and pound away at some convenient 'punching bag' nearby with not one, not two, but three anger-releasing jabs. Stupid! Stupid! *Stupid!*

"And if you think any or all of that is just speculation, what would you call the defense's efforts to make you believe that an LAPD detective is so racially biased that he would risk his career to nail Simpson by picking up a second glove at the murder scene, carefully concealing it from his fellow officers, and—at some moment when no one else is around at Simpson's residence—suddenly announcing his 'discovery' of the glove?

"The best way to see through this obvious, cynical ploy is to ask a similar question to the one posed by the defense themselves. Is it likely that whoever did the killing would have either purposely or accidentally left *two* gloves at the murder scene? In order for Det. Fuhrman to have taken and planted *one* glove, *both* gloves would had to have been left behind in the first place.

"The only manufactured evidence in this case, ladies and gentlemen, is a completely fantasized racial bias and an unworthy allegation of outright deception on the part of the police.

"But let me just say this. If by any chance the defense has managed to persuade you that Det. Fuhrman is not to be trusted, and that, against all odds, he planted the glove at Simpson's estate, then feel free to ignore that one item of evidence. Given the overwhelming evidence otherwise, the glove isn't even needed for proof of guilt in this case. No one has even remotely suggested that Det. Fuhrman or any other LAPD officer might have dummied up all the blood samples taken from the driveway and from inside Simpson's house. And the DNA results from those samples tie the whole plot together beyond any reasonable doubt whatsoever.

"Whatever you do, ladies and gentlemen, don't fall for the oldest trick in the world—pointing the finger of blame at someone else. It didn't work for Adam. It didn't work for Eve. And it surely isn't going to work for O.J. Simpson."

Moving from the Mind to the Heart

The remainder of the prosecution's closing argument will have been thoroughly considered beforehand and carefully scripted. It will have been designed, not so much for the mind—as in the opening argument—but for the heart. Even if the evidence of guilt is overwhelming and intellectually convincing beyond a reasonable doubt, the problem remains: how do you get twelve people to actually convict O.J. Simpson of murder? Somehow, there's got to be a hook—something that will allow you to convict O.J. against all your instincts to the contrary.

Who knows what that hook will be, but the following closing argument will give you some idea of what it *could* be.

How Do You Convict an O.J. Simpson?

"Ladies and gentlemen, now that you have heard all of the evidence in the case of People v. Orenthal James Simpson, the time has come for you to render your verdicts. In my opening statement, I promised you that the People would prove beyond a reasonable doubt that, as alleged in the formal charges against him, O.J. Simpson maliciously and premeditatedly killed Nicole Brown Simpson and Ronald Lyle Goldman on June 12, 1994. I believe we have honored that promise.

"You, in turn, promised me that if the People met its burden of proof you would render a guilty verdict just as the law demands—a verdict of murder in the first degree on both counts. The time has now come for you to honor your promise.

"In all candor, I think it would be foolish for anyone to believe that it is a verdict any of you would wish to return. This indeed is a most unusual case involving a most unique defendant. But sympathy is not to be a deciding factor in a court of justice. If it were, the sympathy which one might wish to bestow on the defendant is far outweighed by the sympathy which must be felt on behalf of the two victims of this brutal murder, not to mention their families and many friends who have been cruelly deprived of those they dearly love. In the court of sympathy, a killer must never win out over his innocent victims.

"And that is what you must keep uppermost in your minds—that what we are dealing with here are two extremely vicious, almost unbelievably savage slayings, the obvious result of deep-seated hatred and revenge. The very manner in which these two victims met their deaths rules out any chance that some rogue street hoodlums might have done the deed, as the defense has repeatedly tried to suggest. Not even rogue hoodlums kill their victims so savagely. They have no personal score to settle; no love-hate relationship which hates with as much intensity as it once loved.

"No, this killing is the work of a man who could not contain his possessiveness—a man who could not handle rejection by a woman whose only crime had been to tolerate time and time again his verbal and physical abuse. O.J. Simpson was that man.

"There's no question about it: O.J. Simpson is a football hero, a talented actor, and a likeable media personality. All that and more. Unfortunately, the 'more' part of O.J. Simpson bears no resemblance to the affable, gentle-looking figure of a man who sits before you today. There is another person inside O.J. Simpson who is cruel, and mean, and violent. None of us wanted to believe it, but what else can we conclude when we hear about his smashing the windshield of Nicole's car in the first year of their marriage? What else are we to think when he beats Nicole so severely that she has to be hospitalized? Let me repeat that. She had to be *hospitalized.*

"The sad irony is that, but for the grace of God, this trial could easily have taken place in 1989. And maybe it *should* have. Maybe, just maybe, if—as he should have been—O.J. Simpson had been publicly tried for cruelly beating his wife, Nicole would still be alive today. But he got his hands slapped and got away with pleading 'no contest' out of the glare of public scrutiny. Hardly anyone knew 'the other O.J.' existed. Those who did weren't willing to admit it.

"Isn't it interesting? Even in that incident, Simpson eluded police for a time before his arrest. Old habits die hard with 'the other O.J.' But at least *then*—when faced with nothing more than a misdemeanor that could be paid for out of his pocket change—he admitted *in fact*, if not *in law*, that he was guilty of beating Nicole.

"Again, with the stakes so low, he didn't feel it necessary on that occasion to hide 'the other O.J.' behind some fanciful, concocted story about police misconduct. In any event, there would have been no more to it *then* than there is *now*. It's just that now the stakes are a lot higher, and it's any port in a storm. In 1989, it was 'the other O.J.,' not the police who brutally beat Nicole Simpson. In 1994, it was 'the other O.J.,' not the police, who brutally *killed* Nicole Simpson. Don't let 'the other O.J.' hide behind a smokescreen of some 'bad cop' nonsense. Just how cynical can the game of justice be? It was the men and women in blue who, time and again, were the only protection Nicole Simpson had from 'the other O.J.' Had it not been for the LAPD, 'the other O.J.' might well have been behind bars already for killing Nicole years ago.

"Of course, having been ordered by the court to do so, the O.J. *we* know went through a brief period of therapy in what now appears to have been a vain attempt at keeping 'the other O.J.' in a cage. Tragically, it didn't work. 'The other O.J.' kept escaping from the cage and threatening to kill Nicole.

"If you want to get to know 'the other O.J.' up close and personal, just play the 911 tapes over and over and over. That is what it was like for Nicole.

Threats and assaults—over, and over, and over. And on the night she was killed, the pattern was still the same. Only this time it was the vicious slashing of a knife—over, and over, and over. For reasons no one is likely to ever understand, 'the other O.J.' could just never stop.

"Ladies and gentlemen, it gives me no personal pleasure to prosecute O.J. Simpson for the crime of double murder. Nor, I suspect, will it be easy for you to return a verdict of murder against O.J. Simpson. But what you must keep in mind during your deliberations is that it is not [pointing to O.J.] *this* O.J. Simpson whom you are convicting, but 'the *other* O.J.'—the one whom you have never seen in this courtroom; the one who only rarely shows his face; and the one who, on the night of June 12, purposely put a knife in his gloved hand and went ballistic.

"*That*, ladies and gentlemen, is 'the other O.J. Simpson' who finally did what he had always threatened to do. *That*, ladies and gentlemen, is 'the other O.J. Simpson' who brutally murdered Nicole and her friend Ron Goldman. And *that*, ladies and gentlemen, is the other hidden, seething, violent O.J. Simpson who is guilty on both counts of murder-one.

"Ladies and gentlemen, whatever you may think of [pointing again] *this* O.J. Simpson, I submit that you have more than enough evidence to find 'the *other* O.J. Simpson' guilty of murder in the first degree!"

❧

Your Evaluation?

What did you think of Marcia Clark's closing?

....

....

....

....

Did she do a good job rebutting the defense's own argument?

....

....

....

....

Did anything Ms. Clark say in her closing persuade you on any particular point?

....

....

....

What strategy did you see at work in her argument?

....

....

....

....

....

Did Ms. Clark use any kind of a "hook"? If so, how effective was it?

....

....

....

....

....

Did you feel she was playing to your *mind*, or to your *heart*?

....

....

....

12

Here Comes the Law

✎

Judge's Instructions to the Jury

While the jury can contribute nothing of value so far as the law is concerned, it has infinite capacity for mischief, for twelve men can easily misunderstand more law in a minute than the judge can explain in an hour.

—Federal Judge Jerome Frank

With the close of counsel's arguments in the case, the time is drawing near for you and your fellow jurors to go to the jury room and deliberate on your verdict. But first, Judge Ito will instruct you as to the law which is applicable in the case. As you will know by now, counsel for both the prosecution and the defense have been arguing their understanding of the law from the moment you were questioned as potential jurors. However, it is only now, and only from Judge Ito, that you will be given the law *officially*. So now you must listen with every ounce of concentration you can muster.

As you will soon appreciate, jury instructions can be complicated, convoluted, and just plain confusing. (Hardly surprising; they were written by lawyers!) And even the way they are read can make a difference in your understanding. The good news is that you will have the judge's instructions in written form with you in the jury room. If you have any question about what was read, you may simply re-read the instructions for yourselves.

You, as jurors, are the ultimate finders of fact. If you make a mistake in your findings, there is no recourse by either side. By contrast, if Judge Ito should make a mistake in the process of giving you the correct law, then his error would be correctable on appeal. That is why you must take the law as he gives it to you at face value, even if you don't happen to agree with it. Where there is an error regarding the law, a conviction can be overturned.

The following paragraphs represent actual jury instructions which might be read to the jury in the O.J. Simpson case. These have been selected, based upon what can be known in advance about the legal issues which have been framed so far by both sides. Some instructions have been included on a contingency basis, just in case the defense changes in mid-trial what seems to be their posture prior to trial.

All of the instructions given below are standard jury instructions known to California lawyers and judges simply as CALJIC (California Jury Instructions, Criminal). The section numbers and headings which you see below are from CALJIC itself (reproduced by permission from West Publishing Co.).

It is standard practice for judges to read directly, word-for-word, from such uniform instructions, all of which have been carefully scrutinized by the highest courts in the jurisdiction, and revised when necessary to accurately reflect the current law. Listen now as Judge Ito begins to read you the following instructions (without referring to the CALJIC section numbers and headings).

As you hear these instructions being read, you might consider how valid it is for appellate courts to overturn convictions because of erroneous or conflicting instructions. Would any jurors, from simply hearing this much legalese being hurled at them in such a brief period of time, ever truly understand the law one way or the other? Even your having the opportunity to read them later in the jury room may leave you somewhat bewildered.

In any event, be alert, now. Judge Ito is about to speak.

※

CALJIC 1.00

RESPECTIVE DUTIES OF JUDGE AND JURY

Ladies and Gentlemen of the jury:

You have heard all the evidence and the arguments of the attorneys, and now it is my duty to instruct you on the law that applies to this case.

You will have these instructions in written form in the jury room to refer to during your deliberations.

You must base your decision on the facts and the law.

You have two duties to perform. First, you must determine the facts from the evidence received in the trial and not from any other sources. A "fact" is something provided directly or circumstantially by the evidence or by stipulation. A stipulation is an agreement between attorneys regarding the facts. Second, you must apply the law that I state to you, to the facts, as you determine them, and in this way arrive at your verdict.

You must accept and follow the law as I state it to you, whether or not you agree with the law. If anything concerning the law said by the attorneys in their arguments or at any other time during the trial conflicts with my instructions on the law, you must follow my instructions.

You must not be influenced by pity for a defendant or by prejudice against him. You must not be biased against the defendant because he has been arrested for this offense, charged with a crime, or brought to trial. None of these circumstances is evidence of guilt and you must not infer or assume from any or all of them that he is more likely to be guilty than innocent. You must not be influenced by mere sentiment, conjecture, sympathy, passion, prejudice, public opinion or public feeling. Both the People and the defendant have a right to expect that you will conscientiously consider and weigh the evidence, apply the law, and reach a just verdict regardless of the consequences.

CALJIC 1.01

INSTRUCTIONS TO BE CONSIDERED AS A WHOLE

If any rule, direction or idea is repeated or stated in different ways in these instructions, no emphasis is intended and you must not draw any inference because of its repetition. Do not single out any particular sentence or any individual point or instruction and ignore the others. Consider the instructions as a whole and each in light of all the others.

The order in which the instructions are given has no significance as to their relative importance.

CALJIC 1.02

STATEMENTS OF COUNSEL-EVIDENCE STRICKEN OUT-

INSINUATIONS OF QUESTION-STIPULATED FACTS

Statements made by the attorneys during the trial are not evidence, although if the attorneys have stipulated or agreed to a fact, you must regard that fact as conclusively proved as to the party or parties making the stipulation.

If an objection was sustained to a question, do not guess what the answer might have been. Do not speculate as to the reason for the objection.

Do not assume to be true any insinuation suggested by a question asked a witness. A question is not evidence and may be considered only as it enables you to understand the answer.

Do not consider for any purpose any offer of evidence that was rejected, or any evidence that was stricken by the court; treat it as though you had never heard it.

[COMMENT: It comes as a surprise to most people that what the lawyers say during opening statements, closing arguments and even their questions is not evidence. In high profile cases particularly, it is important to keep this in mind. None of the sound bites in the media or the rhetorical jabs in the courtroom are part of the *evidence*. The jurors, here, are being instructed to focus on the testimony that comes from the mouths of the sworn witnesses, and to any physical evidence Judge Ito allows in as evidence.]

CALJIC 1.03

JUROR FORBIDDEN TO MAKE ANY INDEPENDENT INVESTIGATION

You must decide all questions of fact in this case from the evidence received in this trial and not from any other source.

You must not make any independent investigation of the facts or the law or consider or discuss facts as to which there is no evidence. This means, for example, that you must not on your own visit the scene, conduct experiments, or consult reference works or persons for additional information.

You must not discuss this case with any other person except a fellow juror, and you must not discuss the case with a fellow juror until the case is submitted to you for your decision, and only when all jurors are present in the jury room.

CALJIC 2.00

DIRECT AND CIRCUMSTANTIAL EVIDENCE-INFERENCES

Evidence consists of testimony of witnesses, writings, material objects, or anything presented to the senses and offered to prove the existence or non-existence of a fact.

Evidence is either direct or circumstantial.

Direct evidence is evidence that directly proves a fact, without the necessity of an inference. It is evidence which by itself, if found to be true, established that fact.

Circumstantial evidence is evidence that, if found to be true, proves a fact from which an inference of the existence of another fact may be drawn.

An inference is a deduction of fact that may logically and reasonably be drawn from another fact or group of facts established by the evidence.

It is not necessary that facts be proved by direct evidence. They may be proved also by circumstantial evidence or by a combination of direct evidence and circumstantial evidence. Both direct evidence and circumstantial evidence are acceptable as a means of proof. Neither is entitled to any greater weight than the other.

CALJIC 2.01

SUFFICIENCY OF CIRCUMSTANTIAL EVIDENCE-GENERALLY

However, a finding of guilt as to any crime may not be based on circumstantial evidence unless the proved circumstances are not only (1) consistent with the theory that the defendant is guilty of the crime, but (2) cannot be reconciled with any other rational conclusion.

Further, each fact which is essential to complete a set of circumstances necessary to establish the defendant's guilt must be proved beyond a reasonable doubt. In other words, before an inference essential to establish guilt may be found to have been proved beyond a reasonable doubt, each fact or circumstance upon which such inference necessarily rests must be proved beyond a reasonable doubt.

Also, if the circumstantial evidence as to any particular count is susceptible of two reasonable interpretations, one of which points to the defendant's guilt and the other to his innocence, you must adopt that interpretation which points to the defendant's innocence, and reject that interpretation which points to his guilt.

[COMMENT: The last paragraph of this instruction is one of the most powerful allies the defense has. Read it again and think back on how the defense appealed to its logic in the closing argument.]

CALJIC 2.02

SUFFICIENCY OF CIRCUMSTANTIAL EVIDENCE TO PROVE

SPECIFIC INTENT OR MENTAL STATE

The specific intent or mental state with which an act is done may be shown by the circumstances surrounding the commission of the act. However, you may not find the defendant guilty of the crime of murder in the first or second degree or the crime of voluntary manslaughter which is a lesser crime, unless the proved circumstances are not only (1) consistent with the theory that the defendant had the required specific intent or mental state but (2) cannot be reconciled with any other rational conclusion.

Also, if the evidence as to such specific intent or mental state is susceptible of two reasonable interpretations, one of which points to the existence of the specific intent or mental state and the other to the absence of the specific intent or mental state, you must adopt that interpretation which points to the absence of the specific intent or mental state. If, on the other hand, one interpretation of the evidence as to such specific intent or mental state appears to you to be reasonable and the other interpretation to be unreasonable, you must accept the reasonable interpretation and reject the unreasonable.

CALJIC 2.03

CONSCIOUSNESS OF GUILT-FALSEHOOD

If you find that before this trial the defendant made a willfully false or deliberately misleading statement concerning the crimes for which he is now being tried, you may consider such statement as a circumstance tending to prove a consciousness of guilt. However, such conduct is not sufficient by itself to prove guilt, and its weight and significance, if any, are matters for your determination.

[COMMENT: If the defense strategy changes from an alibi defense (O.J. wasn't there) to a heat of passion defense (O.J. was there, but acted in the heat of passion) this instruction could be crucial. Keep in mind that Simpson offered an alibi at the time of his arrest; and therefore, if he should change his story, this instruction will be harmful to the defense.]

CALJIC 2.06

EFFORTS TO SUPPRESS EVIDENCE

If you find that a defendant attempted to suppress evidence against himself in any manner, such as by destroying evidence or by concealing evidence, such attempt may be considered by you as a circumstance tending to show a consciousness of guilt. However, such conduct is not sufficient by itself to prove guilt, and its weight and significance, if any, are matters for your consideration.

[COMMENT: We must take a wait-and-see approach with this instruction. However, if it develops that Simpson attempted to hide or conceal evidence, then this instruction would be appropriate.]

CALJIC 2.11

PRODUCTION OF ALL AVAILABLE EVIDENCE NOT REQUIRED

Neither side is required to call as witnesses all persons who may have been present at any of the events disclosed by the evidence or who may appear to have some knowledge of these events, or to produce all objects or documents mentioned or suggested by the evidence.

CALJIC 2.21.1

DISCREPANCIES IN TESTIMONY

Discrepancies in a witness' testimony or between his or her testimony and that of others, if there were any, do not necessarily mean that the witness should be discredited. Failure of recollection is a common experience; and innocent misrecollection is not uncommon. It is a fact, also, that two persons witnessing an incident or a transaction often will see or hear it differently. Whether a discrepancy pertains to a fact of importance or only to a trivial detail should be considered in weighing its significance.

CALJIC 2.21.2

WITNESS WILLFULLY FALSE

A witness, who is willfully false in one material part of his or her testimony, is to be distrusted in others. You may reject the whole testimony of a witness who willfully has testified falsely as to a material point, unless, from all the evidence, you believe the probability of truth favors his or her testimony in other particulars.

CALJIC 2.22

WEIGHING CONFLICTING TESTIMONY

You are not bound to decide an issue of fact in accordance with the testimony of a number of witnesses, which does not convince you, as against the testimony of a lesser number or other evidence, which appeals to your mind with more convincing force. You may not disregard the testimony of the greater number of witnesses merely from caprice, whim or prejudice, or from a desire to favor one side against the other. You must not decide an issue by the simple process of counting the number of witnesses who have testified on the opposing sides. The final test is not in the relative number of witnesses, but in the convincing force of the evidence.

CALJIC 2.40

TRAITS OF CHARACTER OF DEFENDANT

Evidence has been received which may tend to show the good character of the defendant for those traits ordinarily involved in the commission of a crime, such as that charged in this case.

If the defendant's character as to certain traits has not been discussed among those who know him, you may infer from the absence of such discussion that his character in those respects is good.

Good character for the traits involved in the commission of the crimes charged may be sufficient by itself to raise a reasonable doubt as to the guilt of a defendant. It may be reasoned that a person of good character as to such traits would not be likely to commit the crimes of which the defendant is charged.

However, evidence of good character for such traits may be refuted or rebutted by evidence of bad character for these traits.

Any conflict in the evidence of defendant's character and the weight to be given to such evidence is for the jury to determine.

CALJIC 2.42

CROSS-EXAMINATION OF A CHARACTER WITNESS

Where on cross-examination, a witness is asked if he has heard of reports of certain conduct of a defendant inconsistent with the traits of good character to which the witness has testified, such questions and the witness' answers thereto may be considered only for the purpose of determining the weight to be given to the opinion of the witness or to his testimony as to the good reputation of the defendant.

Such questions and answers are not evidence that the reports are true, and you must not assume from them that the defendant did in fact conduct himself inconsistently with such traits of character.

CALJIC 2.51

MOTIVE

Motive is not an element of the crime charged and need not be shown. However, you may consider motive or lack of motive as a circumstance in this case. Presence of motive may tend to establish guilt. Absence of motive may tend to establish innocence. You will therefore give its presence or absence, as the case may be, the weight to which you find it to be entitled.

[COMMENT: Judge Ito will instruct the jurors that motive is not an element of murder and that the prosecution need not show a motive. However, jurors may consider Simpson's motive or lack of motive as it may relate to the killings. Jealousy or rage at Nicole's involvement with other men may be offered to show motive. Clearly, the 911 tapes of Nicole calling to report O.J.'s harassment could bolster the prosecution's presentation of the motive issue.]

CALJIC 2.52

FLIGHT AFTER CRIME

The flight of a person immediately after the commission of a crime, or after he is accused of a crime, is not sufficient in itself to establish his guilt, but is a fact which, if proved, may be considered by you in the light of all other proved facts in deciding the question of his guilt or innocence. The weight to which such circumstance is entitled is a matter for the jury to determine.

[COMMENT: This instruction will become important in light of any testimony that came in regarding the low-speed freeway chase.]

CALJIC 2.60

DEFENDANT NOT TESTIFYING-NO INFERENCE OF GUILT MAY BE DRAWN

A defendant in a criminal trial has a constitutional right not to be compelled to testify. You must not draw any inference from the fact that a defendant does not testify. Further, you must neither discuss this matter nor permit it to enter into your deliberations in any way.

[COMMENT: If O.J. elects not to testify, this instruction becomes *very* important. However, should the defense shift from *alibi* to *heat of passion*, it would seem as if O.J. must testify. The defense decides whether this instruction will be given. Clearly every defendant has the right to not testify, and the jury is to draw no inference from that fact. However, having the Judge give this instruction may serve to highlight or remind the jurors of the defendant's absence from the stand. Therefore, many times the defendant will decide to forego this instruction.]

CALJIC 2.61

DEFENDANT MAY RELY ON STATE EVIDENCE

In deciding whether or not to testify, the defendant may choose to rely on the state of the evidence and upon the failure, if any, of the People to prove beyond a reasonable doubt every essential element of the charge against him. No lack of testimony on defendant's part will make up for a failure of proof by the People so as to support a finding against him on any such essential element.

[COMMENT: If the defense theory is that the case against Simpson is circumstantial evidence, some of which was "planted" by the police, then it may be that Simpson will not testify. The defense may content themselves with the belief that the prosecution's case is insufficient.]

∞✕∞

CALJIC 2.62

DEFENDANT TESTIFYING-WHEN ADVERSE INFERENCE MAY BE DRAWN

In this case defendant has testified to certain matters.

If you find that a defendant failed to explain or deny any evidence against him introduced by the prosecution which he can reasonably be expected to deny or explain because of facts within his knowledge, you may take that failure into consideration as tending to indicate the truth of such evidence and as indicating that, among the inferences that may reasonably be drawn therefrom, those unfavorable to the defendant are the more probable.

The failure of a defendant to deny or explain evidence against him does not, by itself, warrant an inference of guilt, nor does it relieve the prosection of its burden of proving every essential element of the crime and the guilt of the defendant beyond a reasonable doubt.

If a defendant does not have the knowledge that he would need to deny or to explain evidence against him, it would be unreasonable to draw an inference unfavorable to him because of his failure to deny or explain such evidence.

∞✕∞

CALJIC 2.71

ADMISSION-DEFINED

An admission is a statement made by the defendant other than at trial which does not by itself acknowledge guilt of the crime for which such defendant is on trial, but which statement tends to prove guilt when considered with the rest of the evidence.

You are the exclusive judges as to whether the defendant made an admission, and if so, whether such statement is true in whole or in part. If you should find that the defendant did not make the statement, you must reject it. If you find that it is true in whole or in part, you may consider that part which you find to be true.

[COMMENT: Was the statement written by O.J. and read by his lawyer on the day of his arrest an admission? Did that letter tend to prove his guilt when considered with the rest of the evidence? If the letter is introduced at trial, Judge Ito will probably give this instruction and let the jury decide the proper weight to be given the letter.]

CALJIC 2.80

EXPERT TESTIMONY

A person is qualified to testify as an expert if he has special knowledge, skill, experience, training, or education sufficient to qualify him as an expert on the subject to which his testimony relates.

A duly qualified expert may give an opinion on questions in controversy at a trial. To assist you in deciding such questions, you may consider the opinion with the reasons given for it, if any, by the expert who gives the opinion. You may also consider the qualifications and credibility of the expert.

You are not bound to accept an expert opinion as conclusive, but should give to it the weight to which you find it to be entitled. You may disregard any such opinion if you find it to be unreasonable.

[COMMENT: As you will be acutely aware by now, there has been significant expert testimony presented by both sides, especially on the issue of DNA testing.]

CALJIC 2.81 (1989 Revision)

OPINION TESTIMONY OF LAY WITNESS

In determining the weight to be given to an opinion expressed by any witness who did not testify as an expert witness, you should consider his credibility, the extent of his opportunity to perceive the matters upon which his opinion is based and the reasons, if any, given for it. You are not required to accept such an opinion but should give it the weight, if any, to which you find it entitled.

CALJIC 2.82

CONCERNING HYPOTHETICAL QUESTIONS

In examining an expert witness, counsel may propound to him a type of question known in the law as a hypothetical question. By such a question the witness is asked to assume to be true a set of facts, and to give an opinion based on that assumption.

In permitting such a question, the court does not rule, and does not necessarily find, that all the assumed facts have been proved. It only determines that those assumed facts are within the probable or possible range of the evidence. It is for you, the jury, to find from all the evidence whether or not the facts assumed in a hypothetical question have been proved. If you should find that any assumption in such a question has not been proved, you are to determine the effect of that failure of proof on the value and weight of the expert opinion based on the assumed facts.

[COMMENTS: The hypothetical question is an especially helpful vehicle by which counsel can present expert opinions framed around the facts of the particular case. You may have seen extensive use of hypothetical questions by both sides.]

CALJIC 2.83

RESOLUTION OF CONFLICTING EXPERT TESTIMONY

In resolving any conflict that may exist in the testimony of expert witnesses, you should weigh the opinion of one expert against that of another. In doing this, you should consider the relative qualifications and credibility of the expert witnesses, as well as the reasons for each opinion and the facts and other matters upon which it was based.

CALJIC 2.90

PRESUMPTION OF INNOCENCE-REASONABLE DOUBT-BURDEN OF PROOF

A defendant in a criminal action is presumed to be innocent until the contrary is proved, and in case of a reasonable doubt whether his guilt is satisfactorily shown, he is entitled to a verdict of not guilty. This presumption places upon the People the burden of proving him guilty beyond a reasonable doubt.

Reasonable doubt is defined as follows: It is not a mere possible doubt; because everything relating to human affairs, and depending on moral evidence, is open to some possible or imaginary doubt. It is that state of the case which, after the entire comparison and consideration of all the evidence, leaves the minds of the jurors in that condition that they cannot say they feel an abiding conviction, to a moral certainty, of the truth of the charge.

[COMMENT: This instruction is the defendant's greatest ally. Note the powerful phases such as "abiding conviction" and "moral certainty." To counteract this powerful defense tool, it is particularly important for the prosecution to point out that her burden is guilt beyond a *reasonable* doubt, not beyond *all* doubt or beyond a *shadow* of a doubt.]

CALJIC 2.91

BURDEN OF PROVING IDENTITY BASED SOLELY ON EYE WITNESSES

The burden is on the People to prove beyond a reasonable doubt that the defendant is the person who committed the crime with which he is charged.

If, after considering the circumstances of the identification and any other evidence in this case, you have a reasonable doubt whether defendant was the person who committed the crime, you must give the defendant the benefit of that doubt and find him not guilty.

CALJIC 4.50

ALIBI

The defendant in this case has introduced evidence for the purpose of showing that he was not present at the time and place of the commission of the alleged crime for which he is here on trial. If, after a consideration of all the evidence, you have a reasonable doubt that the defendant was present at the time the crime was committed, you must find him not guilty.

[COMMENT: This makes perfect sense. If O.J. was either at home, or already on his way to Chicago at the time of the killings, he could not have committed the murders.]

CALJIC 8.00

HOMICIDE-DEFINED

Homicide is the killing of one human being by another, either lawfully or unlawfully. Homicide includes murder and manslaughter, which are unlawful, and the acts of excusable and justifiable homicides, which are lawful.

CALJIC 8.10

MURDER-DEFINED (PENAL CODE 187)

Defendant is accused in Counts I and II of the Information of having committed the crimes of murder, a violation of Penal Code § 187.

Every person who unlawfully kills a human being with malice aforethought is guilty of the crime of murder in violation of Section 187 of the Penal Code.

In order to prove such crime, each of the following elements must be proved:

1.   A human being was killed,

2.   The killing was unlawful, and

3.   The killing was done with malice aforethought.

"Malice" may be either expressed or implied.

Malice is expressed when there is manifested an intention unlawfully to kill a human being.

Malice is implied when:

1.   The killing resulted from an intentional act,

2.   The natural consequences of the act are dangerous to human life,

and

3.   The act was deliberately performed with knowledge of the danger to, and with conscious disregard for, human life.

When it is shown that a killing resulted from the intentional doing of an act with express or implied malice, no other mental state need be shown to establish the mental state of malice aforethought.

The mental state constituting malice aforethought does not necessarily require any ill will or hatred of the person killed.

The word "aforethought" does not imply deliberation or the lapse of considerable time. It only means that the required mental state must precede rather than follow the act.

※

CALJIC 8.20

DELIBERATE AND PREMEDITATED MURDER

All murder which is perpetrated by any kind of willful, deliberate and premeditated killing with express malice aforethought is murder of the first degree.

The word "willful," as used in this instruction means intentional.

The word "deliberate" means formed or arrived at or determined upon as a result of careful thought and weighing of consideration for and against the proposed course of action. The word "premeditated" means considered beforehand.

If you find that the killing was preceded and accompanied by a clear, deliberate intent on the part of the defendant to kill, which was the result of deliberation and premeditation, so that it must have been formed upon pre-existing reflection and not under a sudden heat of passion or other condition precluding the idea of deliberation, it is murder of the first degree.

※

CALJIC 8.20

DELIBERATE AND PREMEDITATED MURDER

The law does not undertake to measure in units of time the length of the period during which the thought must be pondered before it can ripen into an intent to kill which is truly deliberate and premeditated. The time will vary with different individuals and under varying circumstances.

The true test is not the duration of time, but rather the extent of the reflection. A cold, calculated judgment and decision may be arrived at in a short period of time, but a mere unconsidered and rash impulse, even though it includes an intent to kill, is not such deliberation and premeditation as will fix an unlawful killing as murder of the first degree.

To constitute a deliberate and premeditated killing, the slayer must weigh and consider the question of killing and the reasons for and against such a choice and, having in mind the consequences, he decides to and does kill.

❧

CALJIC 8.25 (1989 Revision)

MURDER BY MEANS OF LYING IN WAIT (PENAL CODE § 189)

Murder which is immediately preceded by lying in wait is murder of the first degree.

The term "lying in wait" is defined as a waiting and watching for an opportune time to act, together with a concealment by ambush or by some other secret design to take the other person by surprise. The lying in wait need not continue for any particular period of time provided that its duration is such as to show a state of mind equivalent to premeditation or deliberation.

[COMMENT: We will not know if this instruction is appropriate until and if such evidence develops at trial.]

❧

CALJIC 8.30

UNPREMEDITATED MURDER OF THE SECOND DEGREE

Murder of the second degree is also the unlawful killing of a human being with malice aforethought when there is manifested an intention unlawfully to kill a human being, but the evidence is insufficient to establish deliberation and premeditation.

[COMMENT: This is more or less a simplified restatement of CALJIC 8.20. If the defendant had the intent to kill, and he reflected on that fact, then he is guilty of first degree murder. If, on the other hand, he had the intent to kill but there is insufficient proof that he reflected on the killing, it is murder in the second degree.]

❧

CALJIC 8.37

MANSLAUGHTER-DEFINED (PENAL CODE § 192)

The crime of manslaughter is the unlawful killing of a human being without malice aforethought. It is not divided into degrees but is of two kinds, namely, voluntary manslaughter and involuntary manslaughter.

CALJIC 8.42 (1991 Revision)

SUDDEN QUARREL OR HEAT OF PASSION AND PROVOCATION EXPLAINED

To reduce an intentional felonious homicide from the offense of murder to manslaughter upon the ground of sudden quarrel or heat of passion, the provocation must be of such character and degree as naturally would excite and arouse such passion, and the assailant must act under the influence of that sudden quarrel or heat of passion.

The heat of passion which will reduce a homicide to manslaughter must be such a passion as naturally would be aroused in the mind of an ordinarily reasonable person in the same circumstances. A defendant is not permitted to set up his own standard of conduct and to justify or excuse himself because his passions were aroused unless the circumstances in which the defendant was placed and the facts that confronted him were such as also would have aroused the passion of the ordinarily reasonable person faced with the same situation. Legally adequate provocation may occur in a short, or over a considerable, period of time.

The question to be answered is whether or not, at the time of the killing, the reason of the accused was obscured or disturbed by passion to such an extent as would cause the ordinarily reasonable person of average disposition to act rashly and without deliberation and reflection, and from such passion rather than from judgment.

If there was provocation, whether of short or long duration, but of a nature not normally sufficient to arouse passion, or if sufficient time elapsed between the provocation and the fatal blow for passion to subside and the reason to return, and if an unlawful killing of a human being followed such provocation and had all the elements of murder, as I have defined it, the mere fact of slight or remote provocation will not reduce the offense to manslaughter.

[COMMENT: The voluntary manslaughter instruction has been included in the event the defense team decides to change from the pre-trial strategy that says O.J. was in no way involved, to an alternative strategy that admits O.J. was responsible for the deaths, but that the killing was done in the heat of passion. This, of course, would be a radical departure from the pre-trial posturing, but in view of what may be overwhelming physical evidence linking O.J. with the killings, this may be the only remaining course of action.

Voluntary manslaughter is not a complete defense. Rather, it is the mitigation of a killing which otherwise would have been murder.

In order for the jury to find that these killings were voluntary manslaughter rather than murder they must be convinced of two things. First, that the killer acted while under an overriding emotional explosion. This is the classic heat-of-passion scenario. Second, the jury must find that the average reasonable person acting under the same circumstances as the defendant would have been provoked to do the act. In other words, would an average reasonable person in the shoes of the killer and seeing and hearing what the killer saw and heard, have been sufficiently provoked to commit the acts resulting in the killing? This provocation element clearly would be a very difficult hurdle for the defense in this case.]

❧

CALJIC 8.43

MURDER OR MANSLAUGHTER-COOLING PERIOD

To reduce a killing upon a sudden quarrel or heat of passion from murder to manslaughter the killing must have occurred while the slayer was acting under the direct and immediate influence of such quarrel or heat of passion. Where the influence of the sudden quarrel or heat of passion has ceased to obscure the mind of the accused and sufficient time has elapsed for angry passion to end and for reason to control his conduct, it will no longer reduce an intentional killing to manslaughter. The question as to whether the cooling period has elapsed and reason had returned is not measured by the standard of the accused, but the duration of the cooling period is the time it would take the average or ordinarily reasonable person to have cooled such passion and for that person's reason to have returned.

❧

CALJIC 8.50

MURDER AND MANSLAUGHTER DISTINGUISHED

The distinction between murder and manslaughter is that murder requires malice while manslaughter does not.

When the act causing the death, though unlawful, is done in the heat of passion or is excited by a sudden quarrel such as amounts to adequate provocation, the offense is manslaughter. In such a case, even if an intent to kill exists, the law is that malice, which is an essential element of murder, is absent.

To establish that a killing is murder and not manslaughter, the burden is on the People to prove beyond a reasonable doubt each of the elements of murder and that the act which caused the death was not done in the heat of passion or upon a sudden quarrel.

⌘

CALJIC 8.70

DUTY OF JURY AS TO DEGREE OF MURDER

Murder is classified into two degrees, and if you should find the defendant guilty of murder, you must determine and state in your verdict whether you find the murder to be of the first or second degree.

⌘

CALJIC 8.71

DOUBT WHETHER FIRST OR SECOND DEGREE MURDER

If you are convinced beyond a reasonable doubt that the crime of murder has been committed by a defendant, but you have a reasonable doubt whether such murder was of the first or the second degree, you must give the defendant the benefit of that doubt and return a verdict fixing the murder as of the second degree.

⌘

CALJIC 8.72

DOUBT WHETHER MURDER OR MANSLAUGHTER

If you are satisfied beyond a reasonable doubt that the killing was unlawful, but have a reasonable doubt whether the crime is murder or manslaughter, you must give the defendant the benefit of such doubt and find it to be manslaughter rather than murder.

⌘

CALJIC 8.73 (1992 Revision)

EVIDENCE OF PROVOCATION MAY BE CONSIDERED IN

DETERMINING DEGREE OF MURDER

If the evidence establishes that there was provocation which played a part in inducing an unlawful killing of a human being, but the provocation was not sufficient to reduce the homicide to manslaughter, you should consider the provocation for such bearing as it may have on whether the defendant killed with or without deliberation and premeditation.

CALJIC 8.74

UNANIMOUS AGREEMENT AS TO OFFENSE-FIRST OR SECOND

DEGREE MURDER OR MANSLAUGHTER

Before you may return a verdict in this case, you must agree unanimously not only as to whether the defendant is guilty or not guilty, but also, if you should find him guilty of an unlawful killing, you must agree unanimously as to whether he is guilty of murder of the first degree or murder of the second degree or voluntary manslaughter.

[COMMENT: It is essential to emphasize that the jurors must unanimously agree on the *particular* crime. It is insufficient if the jurors all agree the defendant was guilty of *some* crime but cannot agree on the *particular* crime. This would result in a hung jury.]

CALJIC 8.75 (1989 Revision)

JURY MAY RETURN PARTIAL VERDICT-HOMICIDE

If you are not satisfied beyond a reasonable doubt that the defendant is guilty of the crime of first degree murder as charged in Count I [or Count II], and you unanimously so find, you may convict him of any lesser crime provided you are satisfied beyond a reasonable doubt that he is guilty of such crime.

You will be provided with guilty and not guilty verdict forms as to Count I [and Count II] for the crime of murder in the first degree and lesser crimes thereto. Murder in the second degree is a lesser crime to that of murder in the first degree. Voluntary manslaughter is lesser to that of murder in the second degree.

Thus, you are to determine whether the defendant is guilty or not guilty of murder in the first degree or of any lesser crime thereto. In doing so, you have discretion to choose the order in which you evaluate each crime and consider the evidence pertaining to it. You may find it to be productive to consider and reach tentative conclusions on all charged and lesser crimes before reaching any final verdicts.

Before you return any final or formal verdicts, you must be guided by the following:

1. If you unanimously find the defendant guilty of first degree murder as to Count I [or Count II], your foreperson should sign and date the corresponding guilty verdict form. All other verdict forms as to Count I [or Count II] should be left unsigned.

2. If you are unable to reach a unanimous verdict as to the charge in Count I [or Count II] of first degree murder, do not sign any verdict forms as to that Count, and report your disagreement to the court.

3. The court cannot accept a verdict of guilty of second degree murder as to Count I [or Count II] unless the jury also unanimously finds and returns a signed verdict form of not guilty as to murder of the first degree in the same Count.

4. If you find the defendant not guilty of murder in the first degree as to Count I [or Count II] but cannot reach a unanimous agreement as to murder of the second degree, your foreperson should sign and date the not guilty of murder in the first degree form, and should report your disagreement to the court. Do not sign any other verdict form.

5. If you unanimously find a defendant not guilty of first degree murder, but guilty of second degree murder, your foreperson should sign and date the corresponding verdict forms. Do not sign any other verdict forms as to that Count.

6. The court cannot accept a verdict of guilty of voluntary manslaughter unless the jury also unanimously finds and returns a signed not guilty verdict form as to both murder of the first degree and murder of the second degree.

7. If you unanimously find a defendant not guilty of murder in the first degree, and not guilty of, murder in the second degree, but are unable to unanimously agree as to the crime of voluntary manslaughter, your foreperson should sign and date the not guilty verdict form for first and second degree murder, and you should report you disagreement to the court.

[COMMENT: The instruction will be repeated, this time with specific reference to Count II. Remember, Count I refers to the murder of Nicole Brown Simpson, and Count II refers to the murder of Ronald Lyle Goldman.]

CALJIC 17.02

SEVERAL COUNTS-DIFFERENT OCCURRENCES-JURY MUST FIND ON EACH

Each count charges a distinct crime. You must decide each count separately. The defendant may be found guilty or not guilty of either or both of the crimes charged. Your finding as to each count must be stated in a separate verdict.

CALJIC 17.16

PERSONAL USE OF DANGEROUS/DEADLY WEAPON (PENAL CODE § 12022(B))

It is alleged in Count I [and Count II] that in the commission of the crime charged, the defendant personally used a deadly or dangerous weapon.

If you find such defendant guilty of the crime thus charged or lesser included crime, you must determine whether or not such defendant personally used a deadly or dangerous weapon in the commission of such crime.

A deadly or dangerous weapon means any weapon, instrument or object that is capable of being used to inflict great bodily injury or death.

The term "used as a deadly or dangerous weapon," as used in this instruction, means to display such a weapon in a menacing manner or intentionally to strike or hit a human being with it.

The People have the burden of proving the truth of this allegation. If you have a reasonable doubt that it is true, you must find it to be not true.

You will include a special finding on that question in your verdict.

[COMMENT: Allegations such as this, and for infliction of great bodily injury, if found true, add to the sentence of the defendant if he is convicted on Counts I or II (something which the real jury will not be told.) Clearly if the jury convicts O.J. of the murders, they will find the allegations to be true.]

CALJIC 17.20 (1992 Revision)

INTENTIONAL INFLICTION OF GREAT BODILY HARM

(PENAL CODE § 667.5(C)(8) AND 12022.7)

It is alleged in Count I [and Count II] that in the commission of the crime therein described the defendant, with the specific intent to inflict such injury, personally inflicted great bodily injury on Nicole Brown Simpson [and Ronald Lyle Goldman].

If you find the defendant guilty of Count I [or Count II] or a lesser included offense, you must determine whether or not such a defendant, with the specific intent to inflict such injury, did personally inflict great bodily injury, on Nicole Brown Simpson [or Ronald Lyle Goldman] in the commission of Count I [or Count II].

"Great bodily injury" as used in this instruction means a significant or substantial physical injury. Minor, trivial or moderate injuries do not constitute great bodily injury.

The People have the burden of proving the truth of this allegation. If you have a reasonable doubt that it is true, you must find it to be not true.

You will include a special finding on that question in your verdict.

CALJIC 17.30

JURY NOT TO TAKE CUE FROM THE JUDGE

I have not intended by anything I have said or done, or by any question that I may have asked, or by any ruling I may have made, to intimate or suggest what you should find to be the facts, or that I believe or disbelieve any witness.

If anything I have done or said has seemed to so indicate, you will disregard it and form your own conclusion.

CALJIC 17.31

ALL INSTRUCTIONS NOT NECESSARILY APPLICABLE

The purpose of the court's instructions is to provide you with the applicable law so that you may arrive at a just and lawful verdict. Whether some instructions apply will depend upon what you find to be the facts. Disregard any instruction which applies to facts determined by you not to exist. Do not conclude that because an instruction has been given that I am expressing an opinion as to the facts.

CALJIC 17.40

INDIVIDUAL OPINION REQUIRED-DUTY TO DELIBERATE

The People and the defendant are entitled to the individual opinion of each juror.

Each of you must consider the evidence for the purpose of reaching a verdict if you can do so. Each of you must decide the case for yourself, but should do so only after discussing the evidence and instructions with the other jurors.

Do not hesitate to change an opinion if you are convinced it is wrong. However, do not decide any question in a particular way because a majority of the jurors, or any of them, favor such a decision.

Do not decide any issue in this case by chance, such as the drawing of lots or by any other chance determination.

CALJIC 17.41 (1989 Revision)

HOW JURORS SHOULD APPROACH THEIR TASK

The attitude and conduct of jurors at all times are very important. It is rarely helpful for a juror at the beginning of deliberations to express an emphatic opinion on the case or to announce a determination to stand for a certain verdict. When one does that at the outset, a sense of pride may be aroused, and one may hesitate to change a position even if shown it is wrong. Remember that you are not partisans or advocates in this matter. You are impartial judges of the facts.

CALJIC 17.42

JURY MUST NOT CONSIDER PENALTY-NONCAPITAL CASE

In your deliberations do not discuss or consider the subject of penalty or punishment. That subject must not in any way affect your verdict.

CALJIC 17.43 (1993 new)

JURY DELIBERATIONS

During deliberations, any question or request the jury may have should be addressed to the Court. Please understand that counsel must first be contacted before a response can be formulated. If a readback of testimony is requested, the reporter will delete objections, rulings, and sidebar conferences so that you will hear only the evidence that was actually presented. Please understand that it may take time to provide a response. Continue deliberating until you are called back into the courtroom.

CALJIC 17.47 (1993 Revision)

ADMONITION AGAINST DISCLOSURE OF JURY BALLOTING

Do not discuss to anyone outside the jury, not even to me or any member of my staff, either orally or in writing, how you may be divided numerically in your balloting as to any issue, unless I specifically direct otherwise.

[COMMENT: At the conclusion of the trial the judge will tell the jurors that they are free to discuss the case at their discretion.]

CALJIC 17.49

USE OF MULTIPLE VERDICT FORMS

In this case there are three possible verdicts as to each count. These various possible verdicts are set forth in the forms of verdict which you will receive. Only one of the possible verdicts may be returned by you as to any particular count. If you all have agreed upon one verdict as to a particular count, the corresponding form is the only verdict form to be signed, as to that count. The other forms are to be left unsigned.

CALJIC 17.50

CONCLUDING INSTRUCTION

You shall now retire and select one of your number to act as foreperson. He or she will preside over your deliberations. In order to reach verdicts, all twelve jurors must agree to the decision and to any finding you have been instructed to include in your verdict. As soon as all of you have agreed upon verdicts, so that when polled, each may state truthfully that the verdicts express his or her vote, have them dated and signed by your foreperson and then return with them to this courtroom. Return any unsigned verdict forms.

Time For Reflection

Do you think you understood the judge's instructions fairly well?

....

....

Are there any specific questions you might have about the instructions?

....

....

....

....

....

....

....

After months of testimony, lawyer wrangling, and judge's rulings, the case is finally in your hands. Did you ever think it would get to this point? And are you psychologically ready for the task ahead? You are about to embark upon what may be one of the most crucial decisions you will ever make. And the whole world waits.

13

The Moment of Truth Has Arrived

❦

Jury Deliberation and Verdict

*A jury too frequently has at least one member
more ready to hang the panel than to hang the traitor.*

—Abraham Lincoln

You step inside the jury room and notice for the first time the cold draft of an air-conditioner. Or perhaps a shaft of light you hadn't seen before. You and your fellow jurors have assembled in this room many times before, but today will be different. For weeks and months you have engaged in idle chit-chat just to pass the time. You've been specifically and repeatedly instructed not to discuss the case with anyone, not even among yourselves. Today, that will change. Today, you have been specifically instructed to talk about the case. To deliberate. To reach a verdict.

So, now, what do we do? The first order of business is to select a foreperson. By this time, after weeks of close confinement, it may be that one of the twelve has almost naturally stood out as a leader. If you are lucky, the choice of foreperson will resolve itself simply by someone pointing to this natural leader and everyone else nodding in agreement. That is, if you're lucky. If not, there may need to be a ballot between two or more of the twelve.

Once the foreperson is determined, he or she will probably want to inquire as to how the rest of the jury wants to organize their discussion. Do you want to spend a day going back over the evidence and trying to identify the points most starkly in issue? Do you want to read the verdict forms to remind yourselves of the ultimate goal toward which you are working? Would it be good to think again about the specific theory of the case that each side was presenting?

As the discussion settles into some fairly comfortable format, it will be interesting to discover whether there are individual jurors whose personality or temperament promises to make deliberations unnecessarily difficult. It wouldn't be the first time that some cantankerous juror threatened to derail what otherwise could be a reasonable search for truth. Hopefully, the foreperson, backed by the rest of you, can rein in the obstinate one and get on with the seriousness of your mission.

More troublesome than any one individual is the growing awareness that there is a significant difference of opinion on one issue or another. Half the jurors believe the defense's charge that the police bungled the investigation; the other half think the police did a good job. Part of the jury is convinced that the "window of opportunity" would have permitted O.J. to be at the murder scene when the homicides occurred; part of the jury remains unconvinced. Most of the jurors are comfortable with the bloody glove found at O.J.'s residence, but a couple of jurors are adamant in their belief that it could have been "planted."

What to do? How are you going to resolve those crucial differences? Will it be possible to change anyone's mind? If so, how will that happen, and what will it take?

More important, how do you yourself react to these differences? Are *you* willing to change if someone brings up a compelling point? Is your pride going to stand in the way of changing your mind? This is a good time to find out something you've always wanted to know about yourself: just how open-minded are you?

If the foreperson is wise, there will not be an early vote. That tends to entrench jurors into positions which they feel bound to defend, whatever other good points might be brought out by others. But the initial vote inevitably must come. And there is not likely to be unanimous agreement on the first ballot—or perhaps the second, or even the third.

In fact, it is possible in a case of this nature that you appear to be immovably deadlocked on one issue or another. Perhaps there is a question of law which you need clarified by the judge. You send out a note and the judge's explanation is returned. But the confusion remains; or at least the jurors' positions remain fixed. What to do now? It's been days and the jury is still mired in conflict.

What you could find yourselves facing is what is known as "an Allen charge" (so named because of the case in which it was first approved). The judge, having been made aware of your deadlock, is going to do whatever he can to get you off dead-center. Maybe all you need is for the judge to light some dynamite under you and get you moving in a different direction. He will remind you that another jury is not going to be any more learned or skilled at finding the facts. In many cases, that is all it takes to breathe new life into a jury's deliberations.

So you're off and running again, but at the end of the week it is clear that the jury is split at the extremes. About half of the jurors are pretty sure O.J. is guilty of murder in the first degree. They are convinced that he carefully planned the killing, right down to the knife, the gloves, and what he knew would be a very tight "window of opportunity" in which he would have the best chance for an alibi.

The other half feel just as strongly that O.J. could not possibly have committed the crime. There is no way he could have calmly had a Quarter Pounder with Kaelin, called his girlfriend at 10:05 (and asked her to return his call), and arrived back at the house in his Bronco, with his headlights unnoticed by the limo driver as he drove up. Besides, there is simply no way he could have killed both Nicole and Ron by himself, so maybe the defense is right in suggesting that a couple of hoodlums did the killing.

On the first ballot, then, the vote is evenly split: six for murder-one; six for not guilty. That won't do. So the discussion resumes and you see a couple of jurors at each extreme peel off from their fellow jurors. They want to move things along, regardless of the technical definitions of the crimes. Two move from murder-one down to murder two; two move from not guilty up to assault with great bodily injury (G.B.I. assault). The first two are chided for giving up on premeditation. If O.J. did it at all, he must have planned it! Maybe not, they counter. Maybe the others are right about how cool he was at McDonald's. Surely, if he was about to kill Nicole he would have been acting sullen or nervous. The two manage to convince a third.

The other two (who have moved away from "not guilty") are attacked for wanting to find O.J. guilty of G.B.I. assault. "How in the world can you think he assaulted them, when on the first ballot you thought he was not guilty?" someone presses. "If he was at the scene for the purpose of assaulting them, then he was at the scene and was their killer!" The two are not put off. One of them explains that he feels O.J. may even have had something to do with their deaths, but the way the police handled the investigation leaves just enough doubt that there shouldn't be a murder conviction. Maybe G.B.I. assault, but not murder! Surprisingly enough, that fairly convoluted reasoning hooks yet another juror.

After further discussion, you take a vote and the result is three for murder-one; three for murder-two; three for G.B.I. assault; and three for not guilty.

The discussion continues, and so does attrition. It seems everyone is anxious to do whatever it takes to reach a verdict. Looming over every discussion is an awareness that the verdict must be unanimous. How can two so divergently-split sides ever reach a common point of agreement? If anything, it seems that both sides have reasonable doubts. Those on the guilty end are well aware that not all the pieces fit as well as they would like for them to fit. There is no doubt in their minds that O.J. did the killings, but it sure would be nice to know all the details. ("Why didn't the stupid coroner keep Nicole's stomach contents so that we could settle our minds on the nagging detail of timing?" one juror grumbles.)

But the others, who think there is good reason to doubt that O.J. is guilty, have their own doubts about even that. The DNA results *were* awfully convincing. And, it's not as if this would have been the first time that O.J. had assaulted Nicole. And, let's face it, the semi-suicidal low-speed chase in the white Bronco didn't exactly reflect the reactions of someone who has been falsely accused of murder.

So on the next ballot there is yet more movement: six for murder-two; six for G.B.I. assault. Well, at least that is progress. Or is it?

Sorting Out Confusing Verdict Forms

One of the jurors seems a bit distracted. He's been reading the verdict forms over and over, and scratching his head. Finally, he raises his hand and says, "You know, I've been perplexed from the first time I laid my eyes on these verdict forms. Some of you want to find Simpson guilty of assault with great bodily injury, but from what I can tell, we can't render a verdict on assault as a separate crime. It looks like just a finding we are to make as part of our verdict on one of the *other* crimes."

To that, another juror says, "Yeah, it's like the deadly-weapon finding. If we decide that he's guilty of murder-one, or murder-two, or voluntary manslaughter, we then have to indicate to the Court whether he did it with a deadly weapon."

"That finding makes sense," says someone else, "but what sense would it make to find him guilty of killing them and then have to indicate further that—oh, by the way—he also assaulted them with great bodily injury! Surely, it must be telling us that we can find assault as a separate crime."

Unable to resolve their misunderstanding, they send a note out to Judge Ito. His response is firm that assault is *not* a separate crime which they can find in lieu of the other crimes charged. But he still doesn't clarify to their liking why they are asked to make a G.B.I. assault finding along with some other guilty verdict.

What Judge Ito cannot tell the jurors is that the law in this area is somewhat confusing. The two special findings are intended as part of the sentencing process—especially when capital punishment is a possibility. Since the prosecution has already decided not to ask for the death penalty should Simpson be convicted of murder-one, and since the jury is not to consider potential punishment in any event, their special findings will make little sense to them. This is particularly true (as they have already recognized) when they are asked to make a special finding regarding G.B.I. assault.

Moving Toward Compromise

With that detour out of the way, can the jury continue to work toward some middle ground? Until now, hardly anyone has mentioned the possibility of voluntary manslaughter. But finally someone says, "Look, we've been at loggerheads for over a week now. If we've been able to move away from murder-one and not guilty, surely we are close enough to compromise on voluntary manslaughter. It finds O.J. guilty of committing the homicides, which ought to satisfy those of you who are sure he did it, and may even have planned it. And it doesn't go too far up the ladder for those of you who have already moved from not guilty to G.B.I. assault. After all, if O.J. did, in fact, *assault* them, he also *killed* them! So, what do you say?"

The five o'clock hour is drawing near and everyone is anxious to go home. A voluntary manslaughter verdict is looking better and better by the minute. "What do you think?" asks the foreperson. "Can we conscientiously settle on voluntary manslaughter and get this thing over with?" Heads are nodded in agreement.

But suddenly something inside you stirs, and you hear yourself saying to the rest of them, "Could we just read the voluntary manslaughter instructions one more time before we vote—just to make sure?" Reluctantly, the foreperson reads again about the need for a heat-of-passion killing and everyone agrees that, if O.J. did the killing, they can envision that he did it in the heat of passion.

Once again you draw some icy stares when you remind them that the instruction says there can be no voluntary manslaughter unless there was some provocation that would have caused reason to be dethroned in the average person. "What would that have been?" you ask tentatively. You know there is no evidence suggesting anything happened that night which would have provoked such passion. Even supposing that O.J. had gone by Nicole's and Ron had suddenly appeared, there isn't anything in that alone which should cause a reasonable person to fly off the handle and kill someone.

With that, someone else chimes in, "That's why it's *murder!* That's why we ought to be talking murder-one instead of some namby-pamby compromise verdict. Listen, if O.J. *did* kill Nicole and Ron in cold blood, then he deserves what he gets. And what he ought to get is murder-one!"

Not unexpectedly, that brings one of the original "not guilty" jurors to his feet. "You're right. We ought not to be compromising. It's a matter of justice. And we all know we have doubts in this case. If there is guilt beyond a reasonable doubt, then why has it taken us over a week to decide this case? That of itself speaks volumes. And where there is reasonable doubt, we are supposed to return a verdict of not guilty! I'm going back to my original position."

Whew! Just when it seemed to be at an end, the deal fell apart and the jury is now back to square one. Is there any way that you can all get together again? Will there be a hopeless impasse—a hung jury? That possibility is not lost on the foreperson. You are reminded that months and months of investigation, preparation, and trial have led up to this moment. The world is watching and desperately wants a verdict. Is there no way you can back off and reconsider afresh the facts in the case and what those facts translate into in terms of a just verdict? Will you give it one more try? Are you willing to go to extraordinary lengths to render a verdict in the trial of the century?

One by one around the table, that question is answered in the affirmative. And in that common commitment alone shines a ray of hope that the jury in the trial of the century can do its duty and win a victory for justice.

⌘

Have You Overlooked Other Possibilities?

In the spirit of renewed cooperation, one of the quieter jurors finally speaks up and suggests that you may have been overlooking, not only a possible avenue of compromise, but a correct verdict as well. "For over a week now, we've been assuming that if Simpson is guilty of killing Nicole and Ron, he is guilty of the same crime for both. That is, either he is guilty of murder-one for both, or murder-two for both. But what if that is not true?

"Remember when Ms. Clark presented her theory of how the homicides occurred? She said Simpson had the gloves and knife in the car just waiting for the right moment to kill Nicole. So, O.K., if Simpson did the killing, that's murder-one. But Clark's theory about Goldman is slightly different. If Clark is right about it, Goldman pops on the scene *after* Nicole is killed and never was in Simpson's game book. So, if we decide that Simpson did the killings, he wouldn't be guilty of murder-one in Goldman's death, but only murder-two. Goldman's murder wouldn't have been premeditated.

"And what I'm thinking is that maybe that's our compromise. We don't find him guilty of murder-one for both victims—only for Nicole."

The other jurors sit quietly, mulling over that possibility. "But that assumes we are all convinced beyond a reasonable doubt that Simpson did, in fact, do the killings!" someone says, breaking the silence.

"I tell you," someone else pipes up, "this is sounding to me more and more like the jury in the Menendez case. Did you read about them? Most people think they hung up over whether the brothers were guilty or not guilty. But what they got hung up over was only the *degree* of guilt. Some wanted murder-one, some murder-two, and some voluntary manslaughter. And, believe it or not, despite the fact that all twelve jurors agreed that the two brothers had killed their parents, they hung up over degrees!"

"Well, sure," came the response, "but in the Menendez case they *admitted* to killing their parents. So the issue there was never anything *but* degrees! In this case, Simpson isn't admitting anything."

"I appreciate that distinction," said the first juror, "but still it would be a shame if we all really do think Simpson did the killing, but we're just too stubborn to come to a unanimous agreement on whether it's murder-one, murder-two, or voluntary manslaughter."

More than one juror still wasn't convinced about Simpson's guilt. "Talk to me again about the odds of Simpson dropping one glove at Nicole's condo and the other glove as he supposedly walked into his house," says one. "Are you trying to tell me that O.J. would even have taken the time to put on gloves if he was so mad at Nicole?" another offers. "Don't forget that O.J. had a gun to his head during the low-speed chase," yet another chimes in. "If he had access to a *gun*, why wouldn't he have used *it* instead of a knife? I would have!"

And the clock on the wall moved ever so slowly....

༂

The Moment of Truth—Time to Decide

Two days of intense debate have passed since that discussion. In the meantime, the jury has agonizingly reviewed all of the evidence one more time, and once again you have heard the impassioned arguments presented by your fellow jurors. Sensing that the time is ripe, the foreperson asks that each of you write on a slip of paper the verdict which you think would be just in this case. It is the final moment of truth. You must decide. What will your verdict be?

For purposes of this exercise, your personal verdict will be considered that of the entire jury. (That, ever so conveniently, will make the verdict unanimous!) So, instead of writing your verdict on a simple ballot, go ahead and fill in the appropriate verdict forms provided. Remember, there are two counts to decide; and don't forget to also indicate your special findings regarding use of a deadly weapon and assault with great bodily injury. When you have completed the verdict forms, alert the Court that you are ready to return.

IN THE SUPERIOR COURT OF THE STATE OF CALIFORNIA
IN AND FOR THE COUNTY OF LOS ANGELES

THE PEOPLE OF THE STATE OF CALIFORNIA,   )
)
                 Plaintiff,   ) Department 103
) No. BA097211
   V.   )
)
Orenthal James Simpson   )
)
          Defendant,   )
)

VERDICT

We, the jury in the above entitled case, find the defendant, Orenthal James Simpson (guilty/not guilty) of the crime of first degree murder of Nicole Brown Simpson, in violation of Penal Code Section 187, as charged in Count I of the Information.

And we further find defendant (did/did not) use a deadly weapon, to wit, a knife in the commission of the above crime.

And we further find that in the commission and attempted commission of the above offense the defendant, Orenthal James Simpson, (did/did not) personally inflict great bodily injury upon Nicole Brown Simpson, not an accomplice to the above offense, within the meaning of Penal Code Section 12022.7.

Dated: _____, 199__   _____

                                         FOREPERSON

IN THE SUPERIOR COURT OF THE STATE OF CALIFORNIA
IN AND FOR THE COUNTY OF LOS ANGELES

THE PEOPLE OF THE STATE OF CALIFORNIA,   )
)
                    Plaintiff,   ) Department 103
) No. BA097211
    V.   )
)
Orenthal James Simpson   )
)
               Defendant,   )
)

_____

VERDICT

We, the jury in the above entitled case, find the defendant, Orenthal James Simpson (guilty/not guilty) of the crime of second degree murder of Nicole Brown Simpson, in violation of Penal Code Section 187, as charged in Count I of the Information.

And we further find defendant (did/did not) use a deadly weapon, to wit, a knife in the commission of the above crime.

And we further find that in the commission and attempted commission of the above offense the defendant, Orenthal James Simpson, (did/did not) personally inflict great bodily injury upon Nicole Brown Simpson, not an accomplice to the above offense, within the meaning of Penal Code Section 12022.7.

Dated: _____, 199__   _____

                                         FOREPERSON

IN THE SUPERIOR COURT OF THE STATE OF CALIFORNIA
IN AND FOR THE COUNTY OF LOS ANGELES

THE PEOPLE OF THE STATE OF CALIFORNIA,	)
	)
Plaintiff,	) Department 103
	) No. BA097211
V.	)
	)
Orenthal James Simpson	)
	)
Defendant,	)
	)

VERDICT

We, the jury in the above entitled case, find the defendant, Orenthal James Simpson (guilty/not guilty) of the crime of voluntary manslaughter of Nicole Brown Simpson, a lesser included offense of murder, as charged in Count I of the Information.

And we further find defendant (did/did not) use a deadly weapon, to wit, a knife in the commission of the above crime.

And we further find that in the commission and attempted commission of the above offense the defendant, Orenthal James Simpson, (did/did not) personally inflict great bodily injury upon Nicole Brown Simpson, not an accomplice to the above offense, within the meaning of Penal Code Section 12022.7.

Dated: _____, 199__   _____

FOREPERSON

IN THE SUPERIOR COURT OF THE STATE OF CALIFORNIA
IN AND FOR THE COUNTY OF LOS ANGELES

THE PEOPLE OF THE STATE OF CALIFORNIA,　　　)
　　　　　　　　　　　　　　　　　　　　　　)
　　　　　　　　　　　　　　Plaintiff,　　　) Department 103
　　　　　　　　　　　　　　　　　　　　　　) No. BA097211
　　　V.　　　　　　　　　　　　　　　　　　)
　　　　　　　　　　　　　　　　　　　　　　)
Orenthal James Simpson　　　　　　　　　　　)
　　　　　　　　　　　　　　　　　　　　　　)
　　　　　　　　　　　　　Defendant,　　　　)
　　　　　　　　　　　　　　　　　　　　　　)
_____

VERDICT

We, the jury in the above entitled case, find the defendant, Orenthal James Simpson (guilty/not guilty) of the crime of first degree murder of Ronald Lyle Goldman, in violation of Penal Code Section 187, as charged in Count II of the Information.

And we further find defendant (did/did not) use a deadly weapon, to wit, a knife in the commission of the above crime.

And we further find that in the commission and attempted commission of the above offense the defendant, Orenthal James Simpson, (did/did not) personally inflict great bodily injury upon Ronald Lyle Goldman, not an accomplice to the above offense, within the meaning of Penal Code Section 12022.7.

Dated: _____, 199__　　　　　　_____

　　　　　　　　　　　　　　　　　　　　　FOREPERSON

IN THE SUPERIOR COURT OF THE STATE OF CALIFORNIA
IN AND FOR THE COUNTY OF LOS ANGELES

THE PEOPLE OF THE STATE OF CALIFORNIA,	)
	)
Plaintiff,	) Department 103
	) No. BA097211
V.	)
	)
Orenthal James Simpson	)
	)
Defendant,	)
	)

VERDICT

We, the jury in the above entitled case, find the defendant, Orenthal James Simpson (guilty/not guilty) of the crime of second degree murder of Ronald Lyle Goldman, in violation of Penal Code Section 187, as charged in Count II of the Information.

And we further find defendant (did/did not) use a deadly weapon, to wit, a knife in the commission of the above crime.

And we further find that in the commission and attempted commission of the above offense the defendant, Orenthal James Simpson, (did/did not) personally inflict great bodily injury upon Ronald Lyle Goldman, not an accomplice to the above offense, within the meaning of Penal Code Section 12022.7.

Dated: _____, 199__   _____

                                                    FOREPERSON

IN THE SUPERIOR COURT OF THE STATE OF CALIFORNIA
IN AND FOR THE COUNTY OF LOS ANGELES

THE PEOPLE OF THE STATE OF CALIFORNIA,   )
)

                    Plaintiff,   ) Department 103
) No. BA097211
    V.   )

)
Orenthal James Simpson   )

)
                    Defendant,   )
)

_____

VERDICT

We, the jury in the above entitled case, find the defendant, Orenthal James Simpson (guilty/not guilty) of the crime of voluntary manslaughter of Ronald Lyle Goldman, a lesser included offense of murder, as charged in Count II of the Information.

And we further find defendant (did/did not) use a deadly weapon, to wit, a knife in the commission of the above crime.

And we further find that in the commission and attempted commission of the above offense the defendant, Orenthal James Simpson, (did/did not) personally inflict great bodily injury upon Ronald Lyle Goldman, not an accomplice to the above offense, within the meaning of Penal Code Section 12022.7.

Dated: _____, 199__   _____

                                                      FOREPERSON

The Tension Mounts

As you return to the courtroom for the last time, you avert your eyes. No one on the jury wants to give anything away by his or her body language. If ever there was a time, now is the time to be poker-faced.

"Mr. (or Madame) Foreperson, have you reached a verdict?" Judge Ito will ask.

"Yes, we have, Your Honor," the foreperson will reply, as the verdict forms are handed to the bailiff, who hands them, in turn, to the Judge.

Judge Ito, himself placid, will read over the verdicts to be certain that they have been completed correctly. Assured that everything is in order, the Judge will hand the signed verdict forms to the clerk of the court, whose job it will be to read aloud the long-awaited outcome of this celebrated trial.

As the clerk briefly scans the verdicts, you dare to take a quick glimpse at O.J. His head is bowed in anticipation. His body is taut. The silence and tension around the room is stifling. Your heart races; your breath shortens. And, with that, you hear the clerk read, almost hesitantly, the fate of O.J. Simpson.

The Aftermath

Without knowing your verdict in advance, it is not possible to comment on what might erupt in the courtroom the moment the verdicts are read. But just when you are breathing a sigh of relief and think that your job is over, it could well be that lawyers for the losing side will want to go through a formality to which they are entitled: the polling of the jury. In this procedure, the judge will go down the row and ask each of you, "Is this verdict well and truly yours?" One by one, you will all answer, simply, "Yes." At that, the verdict is formally proclaimed to be final.

And now it's time for the accolades. Judge Ito will thank you profusely for a job well done. And no one but yourselves will ever know what a difficult and arduous task it has been. Nor will anyone ever quite appreciate how it will have changed your lives to have been a juror in the O.J. case.

As you are dismissed and leave the courtroom, your head will be filled with a thousand memories. And new expectations. There will be the challenge of going back to a normal life with your family and job. Also, the trauma of being hounded by the media. Perhaps, too, the lingering second-thoughts, "Did we really do the right thing?"

It will never really be life as usual again—not for you. For, whether you

215

wish it or not, you have been inextricably linked by destiny with one Orenthal James Simpson. And you can take pride in knowing that it was not simply the O.J. trial in which you served. It was the trial of the century.

Appendix A

Rules of Evidence

In order to help you understand the various legal objections which you might hear during the trial of the century, the following crash course in Evidence is now in session. After you have studied these commonly-used rules of evidence, listen carefully, not only to any objections which might be made, but also to the reasons given. If the wrong reason is given despite a timely objection, Judge Ito might well overrule the objection.

❧

Objections and Objection Strategy at Voir Dire

1. ARGUING THE LAW OR FACTS, OR ATTEMPTING TO INDOCTRINATE THE JURORS ON THE LAW

Objection, Your Honor. The purpose of counsel's question is to argue his case or to pre-instruct the jury on the law.

Purpose. It is improper for lawyers to instruct the jury on details of law or fact during voir dire questioning. The purpose of this rule is to ensure that the jurors will try the case on the basis of all the evidence presented during the trial, and not prejudge the case on the basis of limited or slanted comments made by counsel during jury selection.

2. ASKING THE JURY TO PREJUDGE THE EVIDENCE

Objection, Your Honor. The question asks the jury to prejudge the evidence.

Purpose. Voir dire questions are improper if they call for a promise from the jurors to vote a particular way if certain specific facts are proven at trial. For example, it is objectionable for the defense to say, "If I prove that the defendant couldn't have been at the crime site, would you promise to acquit him?" This is improper because a juror's mind becomes closed to other possibilities when he commits himself to a verdict. The case is virtually tried before all the evidence has been presented.

3. ASKING A QUESTION WHICH INTRODUCES PREJUDICIAL OR INFLAMMATORY EVIDENCE

Objection, Your Honor. The question introduces inadmissible prejudicial evidence.

Purpose. It is not permissible to ask a prospective juror a question that suggests anything which would unduly prejudice or inflame the jury. For example, use of voir dire questions to create the impression that the defendant has a prior criminal record constitutes misconduct.

4. ASKING A QUESTION WHICH IS NOT RELATED TO AN INTELLIGENT EXERCISE OF A PEREMPTORY CHALLENGE OR CHALLENGE FOR CAUSE

Objection, Your Honor. The question is not related to an intelligent exercise of a peremptory challenge or challenge for cause.

Purpose. Questions during voir dire must be "reasonably designed to assist in the intelligent exercise of peremptory challenges whether or not such questions are also likely to uncover grounds sufficient to sustain a challenge for cause."

❧

Objections and Objection Strategy During Opening Statement

1. ARGUING THE CASE

Objection, Your Honor. Counsel is arguing his case.

Purpose. Opening statements are meant to inform the jury of what the attorney hopes to prove, not to argue or prove the case. In other words, counsel should state his version of the facts but not what conclusion can be drawn from them. Nevertheless, this rule is not followed strictly, and counsel is generally allowed some leeway.

2. FACTS STATED WILL NOT BE PROVEN

Objection, Your Honor. Facts stated will not be proven by evidence adduced at trial.

Purpose. It is improper even to allude to evidence which, though true, is incapable of being proven at trial. Evidence falling into this area is either evidence that went beyond the allowable boundaries set by a pretrial ruling or evidence generally considered inadmissible.

3. PERSONAL OPINIONS BY OPPOSING COUNSEL

Objection, Your Honor. Opposing counsel is giving his personal opinion.

Purpose. An attorney may not disclose to the jury his personal opinion about the opposing counsel, defendant, witnesses, or any evidentiary matter before the court. While it is proper to attack the testimony or credibility of a witness or defendant, this attack should never become a personal one. Personal opinions are not permitted because they directly insert the integrity of the trial lawyer into the trial. Accordingly, a statement based on a counsel's personal belief that something is or is not true is strictly forbidden.

Objections and Objection Strategy During Direct Examination and Cross-Examination

1. LEADING

Objection, Your Honor. The question is leading. Or, Objection—Leading!

Definition and Purpose. A leading question is one which suggests to the witness the answer the questioner expects to hear. (e.g., "You were at the victim's home that night, weren't you?") Leading questions are permissible under certain circumstances. For example, they may be used in cross-examination or in preliminary questions on direct examination; or when questioning an expert witness, or a child, or a person who is mentally retarded, or an elderly witness who has poor independent recall; and also with any hostile, evasive, or adverse witness. In all other circumstances, particularly in direct examination, a leading question is objectionable

The rationale is that the witness should be the one to testify. Otherwise, the lawyer who asks a leading question is actually doing the testifying by giving the information to the jury himself.

2. ASKED AND ANSWERED

Objection, Your Honor. The question has already been asked and answered. Or, Objection—Asked and answered!

Definition and Purpose. Attorneys will frequently emphasize a point by repeating a question that has elicited a crucial answer. This practice is prohibited for two reasons. First, having the question and answer repeated wastes time. Second, it places undue emphasis on that question and answer. Courts normally allow limited repetition, especially during cross-examination, but will sustain an objection if the question has been asked two or three times.

3. RELEVANCE

Objection, Your Honor. The question calls for an irrelevant answer. Or, Objection—Irrelevant!

Definition and Purpose. An answer is irrelevant if it does not serve to logically, naturally, or by reasonable inference establish an issue of fact. The court is motivated by judicial efficiency and has an interest in preventing the jury from becoming distracted by extraneous issues that do not have a relationship to the trial.

4. NARRATIVE CALLED FOR

Objection, Your Honor, counsel's question calls for a narrative. Objection, Your Honor, the witness is giving a narrative answer.

Definition and Purpose. Narrative testimony occurs when a witness runs away with his story outside of the question-and-answer format. Such testimony is potentially dangerous because inadmissible evidence could come pouring out before counsel has a chance to make an objection. Once the information has been heard by the jury, it is difficult to "un-ring the bell." In addition, some witnesses tell a more compelling story when they are not confined by questions.

For these reasons, it is wise for counsel to object as soon as he suspects that a witness is about to enter into narrative testimony. His objection will force opposing counsel to ask specific questions, and insist that the witness give succinct answers.

5. HEARSAY

Objection, Your Honor, the question calls for hearsay. Or, Objection—Hearsay!

Definition and Purpose. Hearsay is a statement that is made by someone other than by the witness while testifying and is offered to prove its own truth. Hearsay is excluded because the statements are unreliable. They cannot be tested by cross-examination and the jury has no opportunity to measure the speaker's sincerity, perception, memory, and intention, or to resolve ambiguities in the declarant's statement.

6. CUMULATIVE

Objection, Your Honor, this evidence is cumulative.

Definitions and Purpose. Cumulative evidence merely repeats evidence already introduced, and may be excluded at the judge's discretion. In other words, the judge may stop the production of the same evidence by one witness after another, or the introduction of similar exhibits if no new information is being offered.

7.   CALLS FOR CONCLUSION

Objection, Your Honor, counsel's question calls for a conclusion.

Definition and Purpose. A conclusion is the end result of reasoning which flows from a fact or series of facts. Generally, conclusions based on facts are left to the jury. Normally, the witness shouldn't draw conclusions, but rather only present facts.

However, a lay witness is permitted to testify and give his opinion about inferences and deductions drawn from facts when it will assist the jury in interpreting the facts. For example, if the witness says, "The car was traveling very fast," he is interpreting a fact. If he says, "The car was traveling *too* fast," he is probably drawing a conclusion. It is within the discretion of the judge to decide whether or not to allow a witness to testify as to conclusions and inferences drawn from perceived facts.

8.   OPINION BY AN UNQUALIFIED WITNESS

Objection, Your Honor. Counsel's question calls for an improper opinion. Or, Objection, Your Honor. The witness hasn't been sufficiently qualified as an expert. Or, Objection, Your Honor. Insufficient foundation.

Definition and Purpose. Opinion testimony is similar to the testimony of a lay witness' conclusion. Opinion testimony is generally proper only in areas in which the specialized knowledge of a qualified expert witness will assist the trier of fact. Lay witnesses may give opinions and inferences only where the witness' perception is helpful to the jury in understanding the facts (e.g., time, distance, speed, and sobriety).

9.   ARGUMENTATIVE

Objection, Your Honor. The question is argumentative.

Definition and Purpose. An "argumentative question" is one in which opposing counsel states a conclusion and then asks the witness to argue with it. The attorney usually engages in this kind of questioning in order to prompt the witness into changing his mind. An argumentative question is not permitted, however, because it is essentially an argument to the jury, and does not bring forth any new information. In sum, opposing counsel is not permitted to argue with, or badger the witness.

10.   AMBIGUOUS, CONFUSING, MISLEADING, VAGUE, UNINTEL-
      LIGIBLE

Objection, Your Honor. The question is (confusing) (ambiguous) (vague) (unintelligible) (misleading).

Definition and Purpose. A question must be posed in a clear and precise manner so that the witness can know with certainty what information the examiner is seeking.

11.   ASSUMES FACTS NOT IN EVIDENCE

Objection, Your Honor. The question assumes facts not in evidence.

Definition and Purpose. This objection is used when the introductory part of a question assumes the truth of a material fact that is in dispute and is not in evidence. There are two problems with this type of question.

(1)   The jury may wrongly believe the presumed fact is true.

(2)   The jury may believe the witness adopted the assumption in his answer.

Questions that assume facts are permitted, however, when they are used in cross-examination to impeach the witness' credibility.

12.   CALLS FOR SPECULATION

Objection, Your Honor, calls for speculation.

Definition and Purpose. Any question that invites a witness to speculate or guess is objectionable. The rationale behind this objection is that cases should be determined by the *facts*. Speculation as to what *possibly* could have happened is of little probative value. Nevertheless, witnesses are generally allowed to give estimates and approximations of time, speed, distance, and age. Greater freedom is allowed during the examination of expert witnesses, so that questions which are primarily speculative in nature will sometimes be permitted.

13.   COMPOUND QUESTION

Objection, Your Honor. Compound question.

Definition and Purpose. A compound question asks two or more separate questions within the framework of a single question. It is objectionable because it confuses the witness, the jury, and the court. A witness may answer a two-part question with "No." This answer is confusing since it is not clear which part of the question was being answered.

14. IMPROPER IMPEACHMENT

Objection, Your Honor. Improper Impeachment!

Definition and Purpose. Impeaching a witness means attacking his credibility to discredit him. An attorney may impeach any witness, sometimes including his own. Impeachment is carried out by showing a witness': 1) bias or prejudice; 2) prior inconsistent statement; 3) lack of ability to observe, remember, or recount; 4) poor character for honesty or veracity; or 5) contradictory evidence.

If the witness denies ever making the statement, then other evidence of the prior inconsistent statement may be introduced. Any important variance between the testimony and the prior statement is sufficient to constitute grounds for impeachment. (e.g., Witness said that he worked the day of the burglary, and in a prior statement he stated he had the day off.)

15. BEYOND THE SCOPE

Objection, Your Honor, this is beyond the scope of the direct.

Definition and Purpose. California restricts cross-examination to the subject matter testified about during direct examination. However, due to the vital importance of determining whether a witness is being truthful, judges do permit unrestricted questions that pertain to witness credibility.

Note that the re-direct examination cannot go beyond the scope of the cross-examination testimony; re-cross cannot go beyond the scope of the re-direct testimony; and so on. The reason for scope restrictions is to maintain focus and structure in the trial.

16. BEST EVIDENCE RULE

Objection, Your Honor. Offered exhibit fails to meet the best evidence rule.

Definition and Purpose. This objection applies only to writings, and only when a party seeks to prove the truth of the contents of the writing itself (e.g., a will). To prove the terms of a writing, the attorney must produce the *original* writing—that is, the "best evidence." The purpose of requiring the original document is to insure that the contents have not been altered in some way.

17. NON-RESPONSIVE ANSWER

Objection, Your Honor. Non-responsive!

Definition and Purpose. A non-responsive answer is one which does not directly answer the question. If the response goes beyond that called for in the question, the excess is objectionable.

Objections and Objection Strategy at Closing Argument

1.   MISSTATING THE EVIDENCE

Objection, Your Honor. Opposing counsel is misstating the evidence offered at trial.

Definition and Purpose. While opposing counsel may draw any reasonable inference or deduction from the evidence, it is always objectionable if the evidence is misstated or the testimony is misquoted. It is important to raise the objection when the objectionable remarks are made in order to preserve grounds for appeal. In California, counsel must additionally show that the outcome of the trial was prejudiced by the misstatements.

2.   MISSTATING THE LAW AND QUOTING INSTRUCTION

Objection, Your Honor. Opposing counsel is (misstating the law) and/or (quoting instructions).

Definition and Purpose. It is improper for counsel to misstate the law in his closing argument. In some courts it is also inappropriate to recite the jury instructions verbatim during closing argument. The reason is that some judges feel that jury instructions lie within their purview and do not want the attorney taking over the job. Others are afraid that an attorney might put a twist in the instruction that shouldn't be there. However, a majority of courts do permit attorneys to paraphrase the jury instructions, so long as they do it fairly and accurately.

3.   PERSONAL ATTACKS ON COUNSEL, DEFENDANT OR WITNESS

Objection, Your Honor. Opposing counsel is personally attacking (me)(defendant)(a witness).

Definition and Purpose. It is proper to attack the testimony or credibility of a witness or defendant, but it is improper to engage in personal attacks on opposing counsel or other parties at trial. If the attack becomes personal, the attorney jeopardizes all of his carefully constructed logic just to indulge in a fit of ineffective emotions. A jury never likes a bully and may side with the underdog where there has been a personal attack.

4.   FAILURE OF DEFENDANT TO TESTIFY

Objection, Your Honor. Counsel is commenting on the defendant's failure to testify.

Definition and Purpose. This objection is unique in that it is available only to the defendant's attorney. Although you may comment on an opponent's failure to call a defendant in a civil case, it is strictly forbidden in a criminal case. This rule is grounded in the Fifth Amendment of the United States Constitution which states that no man "shall be compelled in any criminal case to be a witness against himself." [Note, however, that if the defendant does testify, the Fifth Amendment is waived as to related areas].

5.   GIVING PERSONAL OPINIONS

Objection, Your Honor. Counsel is stating his own personal belief.

Definition and Purpose. An attorney is an advocate. What he personally believes is not relevant. Counsel may comment on the credibility of a witness, he may discuss the weight particular testimony should be given, and may argue about the evidence. But it is improper for him to suggest that something is true or false on the basis of his own personal beliefs.

6.   PREJUDICIAL OR INFLAMMATORY ARGUMENTS

Objection, Your Honor. Counsel's argument is solely designed to prejudice the jury.

Definition and Purpose. Arguments are improper if they have little to do with the evidence and are devised to appeal to the jury's sympathies, passions, or prejudice. For example, in a criminal case it is improper for the prosecutor to argue that the jury has a moral obligation to protect society from the defendant; or that if the defendant is released he will commit more crimes; or that the defendant might decide to strike back personally against the jury. Equally objectionable is for the defense to remind the jury of the defendant's young family, sobbing mother, or bright future. These comments are only proper at sentencing.

Are You Ready to Make Your Own Objections?

As a juror, of course, you would not have the right to make any of the above objections. But as you watch the trial, you may wish to make your own mental objections as you listen to the testimony. What may surprise you is that counsel will oftentimes not make objections to which they are legally entitled. Sometimes it may be sheer ignorance or oversight. More often, it will be because little damage is done and raising an objection would only serve either to further highlight a witness' testimony, or to make the jury upset with counsel for not being able to hear a witness' answer.

One of the most fascinating aspects of objections comes when the judge sustains an objection. He may turn to the jury and say, "Ladies and gentlemen, you are instructed to ignore the testimony which you have just heard." Ironically, many jurors—whose minds may have been wandering ever so slightly at the time of the question—find themselves thinking, "What testimony? Oh, you mean *that* testimony! The answer given by the witness must be pretty important, otherwise counsel wouldn't have made such a fuss over it!" It's like telling someone, "Don't think about pink elephants," a sure invitation for them to think so much about pink elephants that they can't get them off their minds.

On that strange note, Evidence Class is dismissed.

Appendix B

Glossary of Legal Terms

Admissible Evidence - Evidence (something that furnishes proof) which may be received by the trial court and presented to the jury to ascertain the truth of a matter. Each state has its own rules on what can be used. Sometimes a judge will not allow evidence if there are other reasons not to, such as undue prejudice, excessive consumption of time (e.g., travel to visit a scene), or a tendency to mislead the jury.

Admission - The voluntary acknowledgement of a party to the case that certain factors exist or are true. An admission is a hearsay statement that comes within the hearsay rule exception and is therefore admissible. See *Hearsay Rule.*

Adversary Proceeding - A legal controversy where two or more opposing parties contest the issues in a court of law.

Aggravated Assault - An attempt or threat to inflict serious bodily injury on another. Weapons are commonly associated with an aggravated assault.

Aid and Abet - To intentionally or purposefully assist another individual to commit or attempt to commit a crime.

Alibi - An account, excuse, or description of where an individual was at the time of the commission of a crime. Tends to establish that the accused could not possibly by placed at the scene of the crime.

Allegation - Assertion of fact or statement which a party is prepared to prove. Allegations can be charged in the information or indictment and if the jury finds them to be true, they will enhance the punishment of the accused. For instance, an allegation of inflicting great bodily injury can increase the punishment by two years.

Allen Charge - In a criminal case, a potential jury instruction usually given during the deliberations. The judge encourages the jury to make a renewed effort to come to a decision. Reminds them that another jury is not going to be any more learned or skilled at finding the facts.

Alternate Juror - An extra trial juror who is selected to attend the trial and be ready to substitute for any member of the jury panel who becomes unable to serve during the trial or deliberations for health or other reasons. In a case that is expected to take months, it is not unusual to select several alternate jurors. [Eight alternate jurors will be utilized in the Simpson case.]

Amend - To alter or make an addition to a pleading or legal document.

Appeal - A petition to a higher court to review a lower court's decision. Usually this is a consolidation of all disputed rulings made by the lower court.

Appellant - The party who appeals the decision ("the loser" in the trial).

Appellee - The party opposing the appeal ("the winner" in the trial).

Appellate Court - A court that has the power to review a lower court decision. It does not decide the facts in a case, but rather the legal precedent and whether the lower court used the correct law.

Arraignment - An initial step in the criminal process where the accused is formally charged with an offense, informed of his Constitutional rights, and enters his plea.

Arrest - To deprive a person of his liberty because of a belief that the person has committed some criminal activity.

Attorney-Client Privilege - A rule of evidence that allows an attorney to keep confidential all communications between the attorney and his client during the course of their professional relationship. The client owns the privilege and only the client may waive it. The purpose of the attorney-client privilege is to encourage full communications between the attorney and the client. The privilege protects past crimes but does not usually include proposed future crimes. The privilege can be destroyed if other persons, not a part of the attorney's staff, are present. The privilege continues after the legal representation ceases. See *Privileged Communication*.

Autorad - Autoradiograph, which is a sheet of X-ray film used in DNA testing. The DNA fragments are placed in a gel which is subjected to an electric current. The gel is then put into a radioactive solution which binds the radioactive material to the DNA. Then the DNA is placed onto the autorad. The radioactive material leaves traces on the X-ray film called bands. The differences in the band lengths allow trained experts to identify and match particular DNA samples. See also the case material on DNA set forth in the Appendix.

Bail - Cash or other form of acceptable security that is given to insure the defendant's appearance at court when the defendant is free pending his criminal trial. The money is security for the possible costs of securing the accused's appearance in court and cannot be "excessive."

Battery- The unlawful use of force to or on another person without his consent.

Bench Warrant - A court order allowing legal authorities to seize a person and compel their attendance before a court.

Beyond a Reasonable Doubt - Burden of proof which the State must meet in a criminal case. The prosecution must prove the defendant is guilty beyond any reasonable argument or condition. This is a high standard of proof and in practice requires that the proof of the crime must be overwhelming. However, even the slightest doubt must be reasonable. Reasonable doubt is a doubt for which one could give a reason.

Blood Sample - A sample of blood that can be used for blood grouping and possible DNA testing. Blood is identified by certain "factors". The basic blood groups are called the A B O blood groups. Each person belongs to either AB, O, A, or B blood group. Complete blood typing, using sub-groups, may not show that a particular person did an act; however, it can serve to eliminate a person from consideration.

Burden of Proof - The requirement that a party substantiate an allegation to the extent that the trier of fact (judge or jury) accepts that the party is correct and should prevail at a trial. In criminal cases the burden on the prosecution is "beyond a reasonable doubt."

Burglary - The breaking and entry into a structure with the intent to commit a felony or theft within the structure.

Cadaver - The body of a dead or deceased person.

Capacity - The mental ability of a person to make a rational or serious decision.

Capital Offense - A criminal offense that can be punished with a death sentence.

Capital Punishment - The death penalty.

Certiorari - Latin "to be informed of." A Writ of Certiorari issued by an upper court commands the lower court to produce the records so that the higher court can review it for irregularities.

Chain of Possession - Traces the various persons or entities that have possession of an item. Also referred to as Chain of Custody.

Challenge for Cause - Request made to the trial judge to excuse a juror from being selected because of some bias. This challenge suggests that the person's bias renders him unfit or not qualified to sit on the jury panel. For example, a challenge for cause will be granted if a prospective juror is related to a party to the action, or is a convicted felon, or cannot hear, etc. There is no preset limit on the number of challenges for cause each side may make.

Change of Venue - To move the trial of a case from one county or judicial district to a different county or district. Such a change is usually brought about because the defendant's ability to receive a fair trial is compromised by excessive publicity.

Charge - The underlying crime to which the defendant must answer. The charge or charges are listed in an indictment, complaint, or information. Charge also refers to the lengthy instructions which a judge gives the jury advising them of the rules of law in the case prior to their deliberations.

Clemency - Forgiving a person for a criminal act. The chief executive (the President or Governor) usually has such power.

Closing Statement - This is the summation made to the jury by the attorneys representing each side. The closing argument sums up the evidence and attempts to sway the jury to accept a particular version or interpretation of the evidence. The party bearing the burden of proof (prosecution in criminal cases) offers closing argument first. The defense's closing argument is next, followed by the prosecution rebuttal. See *Rebuttal.*

Confession - An incriminating statement made by the accused. A confession must be voluntary and in compliance with *Miranda* to be admissible. A confession is not admissible unless the prosecution can first prove corpus delicti. See *Miranda, Corpus Delicti.*

Confidential Communication - Information transmitted between a client and his lawyer in the course of that relationship is confidential. Except under very limited circumstances, confidential communications are protected and the client and his lawyer have a privilege to refuse to disclose. See *Attorney-Client Privilege.*

Conspiracy - A group of two or more persons who agree to commit a criminal or unlawful act.

Contempt of Court - Any act or statement that interrupts the peaceful and orderly functions of the court. Contempt may by punished by a fine or imprisonment.

Convict - A person who has been declared guilty of a crime.

Conviction - The legal act of declaring a person a convict and which is the basis for pronouncing a sentence.

Coroner - A public official who investigates the causes and reasons for death.

Corpus Delicti - Latin expression for "body of the crime." It is proof that a crime was committed. It is composed of two parts: first, the fact that harm has occurred; and, second, that the harm came about by an act of criminal agency. Note that it is a part of every crime and not just a murder case.

Corroborating Evidence - Additional evidence that strengthens the evidence that is already present.

Credibility - Any matter that has a tendency in reason to prove or disprove the witness's truthfulness including the following:

1. His demeanor while testifying.

2. The character of his testimony.

3. The extent of his capacity to perceive, to recollect, or to communicate any matter about which he testifies.

4. The extent of his opportunity to perceive any matter about which he testifies.

5. His character for honesty or veracity, or vice versa.

6. The existence or nonexistence of a bias, interest, or other motive.

7. A statement previously made by him that is consistent or inconsistent with his testimony.

8. The existence or nonexistence of any fact testified to by him.

9. His attitude toward the action in which he testifies or toward the giving testimony.

10. His admission of untruthfulness.

Crime of Passion - A crime committed under an extremely powerful or compelling emotion or feeling. Typically used in criminal cases to describe violent anger preceding a homicide. It is one of the critical component parts of voluntary manslaughter. See *Voluntary Manslaughter.*

Cross Examination - Questioning of a witness by the lawyer representing the adverse side. Questioner tries to discredit testimony or present additional facts to make the situation more favorable to his client than first described.

Culpable Mental State - State of mind required to commit a crime. Different states of mind or culpability are set forth in various laws.

Curative - An instruction given to correct a legal error.

D.A. - Abbreviation for District Attorney. He is the chief legal authority in a specific area such as a county. The district attorney is the hub of the criminal justice system. It is the district attorney and his deputies who decide who is to be charged and what crimes they will be charged with.

Deadly Weapon - Any weapon, device, or tool that is capable of producing death or serious bodily injury.

Death Penalty - Ultimate penalty imposed for murder or other capital offense. After a death sentence has been imposed, a court usually holds a separate hearing to consider aggravating and mitigating circumstances. Certain persons, such as minor children and the insane, are often excluded from being given this ultimate penalty.

Declaration Against Interest - A statement against the speaker's interest (e.g., where some loss of reputation or money would result) is admissible as an exception to the hearsay rule. See *Hearsay Rule.*

De Facto - Latin term "As a matter of practice" or conduct, but without lawful authority.

Deliberate (verb) - To consider the evidence and arguments presented.

Deponent - A person who testifies under oath at a deposition.

Deposition - A pre-trial discovery procedure where a witness answers questions under oath. This is recorded and transcribed and can be used at trial.

Direct Evidence - Evidence that directly proves a fact, without an inference or presumption, and which if true, conclusively establishes that fact. The direct evidence of one trustworthy witness is sufficient for proof of any fact.

Direct Examination - Questioning by the party calling a witness as its own. No leading questions are permitted on direct examination except where questions are foundational or asked of an expert or one with some disability, such as age.

DNA Testing - A new bodily fluids testing method. Deoxyribonucleic acid provides a distinct pattern that is identified with a particular person. Except for identical twins, it is believed each human has unique and different DNA.

Due Process of Law - Constitutional guaranty that no person shall be deprived of life, liberty, or property without due process of law. Due process is often invoked when seeking basic fairness and equity.

Eighth Amendment- Part of original Bill of Rights (1791) which prohibits cruel and unusual punishment and excessive bail.

Exclusionary Rule - Evidence seized by the police in violation of the Fourth Amendment is typically excluded from the trial.

Exculpatory - Evidence and statements that tend to exonerate or excuse a defendant from alleged guilt or fault.

Executive Clemency - The power of the President or a Governor to pardon, reduce, or commute a criminal sentence.

Expert Witness - Witness who has special knowledge beyond that which is normally possessed by an average person. Each court has its own standards relative to special knowledge, training, skill, and experience.

Exigent Circumstances - Excuses the police from the search warrant requirement in an emergency. However, once the police determine the emergency is over the warrant requirement reemerges. See *Fourth Amendment.*

Evidence - The way in which a factual matter can be established or disproved. Testimony, documents, or physical objects can be evidence. The law of evidence is a group of specific rules that determine what can be admitted and the weight to be given each item. See *Relevant Evidence.*

Felony - Generic term for serious crime punished by imprisonment or death.

Forensic Medicine - Branch of medicine which uses medical technology to help in solving legal issues and problems.

Fourth Amendment - Guarantees the rights of persons to be secure in their homes and property. It prohibits unreasonable searches and seizures and requires that a magistrate issue a search warrant only upon an oath or affirmation based upon probable cause. If the police seize items in violation of the Fourth Amendment, the court will exclude that evidence from trial. See *Exigent Circumstances; Exclusionary Rule.*

Fruit of the Poisonous Tree - Refers to illegally seized evidence and prohibits use of this evidence. The poisonous tree is the illegal search; the fruit are the items taken as a result of the illegal search. See *Exclusionary Rule.*

Frye Test - The case setting forth the standard for the admissibility of scientific evidence. For such evidence to be admissible, an expert in the field under question must testify that the scientific procedure is generally accepted within that scientific community. See *Kelly-Frye Hearing.*

Grand Jury - Body of people selected from community who determine whether sufficient evidence exists to hold a person for trial. This is an alternative to having a defendant being charged in a complaint and being bound over after a preliminary examination. The district attorney has the option of proceeding via the grand jury or the preliminary examination. See *Preliminary Hearing.*

Great Bodily injury - Refers to the infliction of serious injury. This can be charged as an additional allegation and, if found true, can add two years to the sentence.

Guilty - Determination that a person has committed the crime charged or a lesser included crime.

Habeas Corpus - Latin "you have the body." Procedure to determine if individual is legally retained in custody. Generally an appellate procedure permitting a convicted individual the opportunity to go beyond the trial record in establishing his innocence.

Hearsay Rule - An out-of-court statement offered to show its own truth. Hearsay evidence is inadmissible unless it comes within one of the hearsay exceptions. See, e.g., *Inconsistent Statement, Spontaneous Declaration.*

Hung Jury - A jury that is unable to reach a unanimous verdict. If there are degrees of a crime or lesser crimes, the jurors must all agree on the same crime.

Impaneling - Process used to select jurors.

Inconsistent Statement - An out-of-court statement inconsistent with a witness's testimony at trial is admissible. This is an exception to the hearsay rule. See *Hearsay Rule.*

Indictment - Formal written accusation of a specific crime. This is the charging document from the grand jury. See *Grand Jury.*

Inference - A deduction of fact that may logically or reasonably be drawn from another fact or group of facts found in the action.

Information - Formal written accusation of a specific crime. There are two ways a case can proceed to trial. One is the indictment issued from the grand jury and the other is the information issued by the district attorney following a preliminary examination. See *Indictment, Grand Jury, and Preliminary Hearing.*

In Limine - Latin phrase "at the threshold" or place of beginning, often associated with pre-trial motions.

Insanity - Not mentally responsible. In criminal law this defense relieves a person from responsibility. There are two main tests in use by different state courts: *M'Naghten* Rule holds that a person is not responsible if he did not understand that what he did was wrong; the Model Penal Code holds a person not responsible for criminal conduct if it results from mental disease or defect or that the accused does not have capacity to appreciate the wrongfulness of the conduct. An insanity finding results in an acquittal.

Intent - State of mind that indicates if a person wants and understands consequences of his action. Criminal intent at the time of the crime is required for conviction.

Interrogation - Questioning. This form of intense custodial questioning proceeds after a "Miranda" warning relative to self-incrimination. See *Miranda.*

Involuntary Manslaughter - A person may be held criminally culpable for the death of another if his conduct grossly deviated from a reasonable standard of care.

Jeopardy - In danger of conviction for a crime. Under the Fifth Amendment, no person shall be placed in jeopardy twice for the same offense ("Double Jeopardy").

Judge-made Law - This is a common law tradition (that means stemming from our English origins) that allows judges to rule based upon prior decisions rendered by other judges in similar matters. Also called "precedent."

Judicial Discretion - Power of a judge to rule on certain concepts as part of their official capacity. If power is exceeded it is "an abuse of discretion." To be considered an abuse, the judge must go beyond the bounds of what is considered reasonable and act with bias, prejudice, or with lack of good judgment.

Judicial Immunity - A judge is immune from a civil suit for acts made in judge's official capacity. This protects the independence of the judiciary so that disagreement with a decision or ruling made in good faith is not actionable.

Judicial Notice - Rule allowing judge to recognize certain well known facts without the need for specific proof. Only facts that are so well known as to be without dispute can be the subject of Judicial Notice. For example, a judge might take judicial notice that January 1 is New Year's Day.

Judicial Review - Procedure allowing higher court to review the acts of a lower court or other branch of government. Power to review acts of other branches of government.

Jurisdiction - Power of a particular court to hear a specific case. Personal jurisdiction is where the parties have a connection to the place where the court sits.

Juror - A person who is sworn in as a member of a jury.

Jury Instruction - Directions to the jury before they deliberate. These instructions inform the jury what the law to be applied is and generally guide the jury in the process of reaching a verdict. See *Charge.*

Jury Nullification - The right of a jury to disregard the judge's instructions and rule on a case based upon the jury's belief as to what is just. Usually this occurs without the jury being told that they have this inherent power.

Jury Selection - The act of selecting the jurors who will hear and decide the case. The jury panel will be subjected to questions from the judge and then the attorneys representing the state and the defendant. Some will be excused "for cause" inasmuch as their answers reveal that they cannot be impartial or for some other reason (example, a belief that the death penalty is sinful) or by the use of a peremptory challenge by either side (this is an automatic removal without any explanation). See *Challenge For Cause*. See also *Peremptory Challenge*.

Jury Trial - A trial before a jury of one's peers. The Sixth Amendment guarantees all criminal defendants the right to a jury trial. A jury must be impartial and selecting an impartial jury may be difficult where there is extensive pre-trial publicity. The standard of guilt is "beyond a reasonable doubt."

Kelly-Frye Hearing - The hearing at which the trial judge determines the admissibility of scientific evidence. This is typically an In Limine motion. See *Frye Test; In Limine Motion*.

Leading Case - A court decision that is repeatedly used as legal precedent for a particular area of law. For example Frye is the leading case setting forth the standard for the admission of scientific evidence.

Leading Question - A question which suggests a particular answer to the witness. Leading questions are allowed in cross examination (where witness presumably isn't friendly) but not in direct examination of a witness unless witness is hostile. See *Direct Examination*.

Lie Detector Test - A polygraph, which is an electromechanical device which measures and records changes in the body functions. The premise is that a body undergoes involuntary changes when a person attempts to deceive. Many jurists believe this technique is not reliable, particularly for criminal cases. Any reference to an offer to take, failure to take, or taking of a polygraph examination, shall not be admitted into evidence in any criminal procedures. See *Polygraph*.

Limiting Instruction - Some evidence may be admitted for a limited purpose, but may not be considered for any other purpose.

Malum In Se - Latin term for "evil in itself."

Manslaughter - Unlawful killing of another. An alternative to murder and does not require specific intent. Usually charged when there are no witnesses (automobile wreck) or when there are other reasons (lack of intent) which might cause an ordinary person to lose control (including heat of passion). See *Voluntary Manslaughter, Involuntary Manslaughter*.

Mens rea - Latin for "Guilty mind." A mental state that must occur in order to find a person guilty of a deliberate crime.

Miranda Rights - This is the requirement that a person be informed of his rights before police can question the individual while in their custody. Responses to custodial interrogations are generally inadmissible unless preceded by a waiver of the Miranda rights.

Misdemeanor - A lesser class of criminal offense. The punishment for a misdemeanor may not include a state prison sentence. The maximum punishment is up to one year in local jail.

Mistrial - Trial that is terminated by a judge before the trial concludes because prejudicial error has occurred which cannot be corrected. A mistrial has the same effect as no trial at all. Thus, there is no violation of the Fifth Amendment prohibition against Double Jeopardy and another trial on the same charges can be instituted with a new jury panel. See *Double Jeopardy.*

M'Naghten Rule - See *Insanity.*

Modus Operandi - Latin term for "manner of operation." The term is used to describe the way [pattern] in which crime was accomplished.

Motion - A formal request that the court act or rule in a particular manner.

Murder - A common law offense for the unlawful killing of another with malice. Murder may be divided into degrees which reflect the culpability of the accused. First Degree Murder is the deliberate and premeditated killing of another person.

Nolle Prosequi - Latin term for "unwilling to prosecute." This term is used when a prosecutor abandons a claim, charge or count. This is typically done because the prosecution in its discretion believes there is insufficient evidence to proceed.

Nolo Contendere - Latin term for "I do not wish to contend or challenge" a charge. A person can be found guilty without an admission of guilt or the expense of a trial. The advantage of this plea is that it cannot later be used in a civil lawsuit.

Non Compos Mentis - Latin "no control over the mind." Same as insanity.

Non Sequitur - Latin term for "does not follow." Illogical.

Not Guilty - Plea in criminal case that requires prosecutor to prove every essential element of the criminal charge beyond a reasonable doubt. The burden of going forward and proving the crime is on the prosecutor. The defendant does not have to prove anything. Strictly speaking, a not guilty verdict does not mean that the defendant is necessarily innocent. It means that the prosecutor did not prove that the defendant was guilty beyond a reasonable doubt.

Objection - A procedure that allows a party or counsel to protest against a witness's statement, the admission of a particular piece of evidence or other matter that the party or attorney feels is improperly before the court. In order to appeal on an evidentiary issue, the attorney must make a timely objection to the evidence or statement and provide an explanation or "record" of the reason for the objection. It is not necessary to state the reason at the same instant that the attorney says, "Objection!"

On the Record - The matter must be presented or stated in court and before a court reporter so that a written record is available for review.

Opening Statement - In a trial each party has the opportunity to address the jury before any evidence is presented. The opening statement sets the stage for the jury to understand the charges, the theory of the case, and previews the evidence which will be presented. In most criminal cases the defense has the option to reserve their opening statement until the state has completed their presentation of evidence and testimony.

Order - Ruling by a court or judge on a matter that directs some legal step be taken in a legal proceeding.

Pardon - To relieve a person from any further punishment. The chief executive officer (President or Governor) has the power to grant a pardon.

Parole - A conditional release from prison. Parole allows a prisoner to serve the remainder of the prison sentence outside the prison walls. The person is still subject to certain restrictions imposed.

Penal Code - The codification of the criminal law.

Penitentiary - Prison.

Peremptory Challenge - Allows counsel to exclude up to a certain number of potential jurors without giving any specific reason. However, the challenges cannot be made on the basis of ethnicity or gender. (In the Simpson case, each side will be given twenty peremptory challenges.)

Perjury - A false statement under oath.

Petit Jury - Ordinary trial jury which is entrusted to determine facts of the case. Traditionally, twelve jurors from the community comprise the jury "of peers." The jury listens to testimony, examines evidence, and resolves conflicts in the presentation of the prosecution and defense cases. The judge instructs on the law, and the jury applies the law to the facts of the case as they have found them. From this process a decision or verdict is obtained.

Plain View - An exception to the general rule requiring a search warrant before a search of a home. If the items are not hidden there is no requirement for a warrant so long as the law officer can see, hear, or smell seizable evidence. The courts will then declare the item admissible as it was "in plain view." See *Search Warrant, Fourth Amendment.*

Plea - The answer to a criminal charge. The accused can plead guilty, not guilty, or no contest.

Plea Bargain - An agreement in which the prosecutor and defendant (defense counsel) negotiate a disposition of a case. The prosecutor usually offers a reduced charge and a recommended reduced sentence. The defendant agrees to plead guilty to the lesser charge, if the Court agrees, in order to receive a guaranteed sentence. Plea bargaining is a final disposition of a case without a time consuming and expensive trial. It must be finalized in open court. In the U.S., well over ninety percent of all criminal charges are disposed of in this fashion.

Polling the Jury - A courtroom practice that allows a criminal defendant to challenge a jury verdict of guilty. Each juror is asked, one at a time, whether the verdict which was reached is his or her voluntary decision on the case.

Polygraph - See *Lie Detector.*

Post Conviction Relief - A court procedure that allows a criminal defendant to challenge the conviction for a number of reasons including a change in the law or newly discovered evidence.

Post Mortem - Latin term "after death." The term is usually used to refer to an examination of the body of a person after death to determine the cause of death.

Precedent - A previously decided law case which is used for guidance or as an authority in a current dispute, trial, or supplemental proceeding.

Preliminary Hearing - A hearing to determine whether there is "probable cause" to accuse a person of a crime. The hearing determines that there is a reasonable basis for believing that a crime was committed and that the defendant committed the crime. If the magistrate at this hearing determines that probable cause exists, the option returns to the district attorney to file an information. See *Information.*

Premeditation - Forethought; giving thought to a matter. Premeditation does not necessarily mean advance planning and may be formulated during a short period of time. Generally contemplates a weighing of the consequences of engaging in the act.

Presentence Report - A report, and attachments, typically prepared by the probation department to assist the trial judge in fixing an appropriate sentence after a defendant has been convicted. Report usually includes family factors, prior convictions, prior arrests, employment history, and defendant's educational and social background.

Presumption - An assumption of fact that the law requires to be made from another fact. A presumption is not evidence.

Presumption of Innocence - This rule of law states that a person is not guilty of any crime until and unless proven guilty beyond a reasonable doubt. The defendant does not have to prove anything and may sit silent. The burden rests solely on the prosecution to prove guilt beyond a reasonable doubt.

Privileged Communications - The defendant has a right to keep secret his conversations with his defense counsel. Other communications are also protected in our society (patient and doctor, husband and wife, priest-penitent, journalist-source, to name a few). The effect of a privileged communication is to prevent it from being forced out into the open. See *Attorney-Client Privilege, Confidential Communication.*

Probable Cause - This is a requirement for a valid arrest or search. Facts and circumstances must be present which indicate that a reasonable person would believe that a crime has been committed or that specific property is connected with a crime is actually in the stated place. Probable cause must be based on actual facts and not hunches or conclusions. If the information comes from an informant the judge must determine that the informant is credible and reliable.

Probation - A procedure which allows a person found to be guilty of a crime to be released without imprisonment subject to conditions which the court may impose. The defendant will remain under the supervision of a probation officer. If the defendant violates any condition of probation, the defendant can be incarcerated in jail or prison to serve out the remaining time on the sentence.

Probative - Tending to prove a particular fact or allegation.

Prosecutor - The person who presents the criminal case on behalf of the state and seeks to obtain justice (and not just a conviction). This person often uses the phrase "The People will show..." to remind the jury that they are representing society as a whole. See *District Attorney.*

Question of Fact - A disputed factual contention which the jury must decide.

Question of Law - This is a disputed legal contention which the judge must decide based upon precedent and codification.

Reasonable Doubt - Refers to the amount of certainty that is needed for a criminal conviction. The proof must be so established and conclusive that ordinary people would not have any reasonable doubts as to the certainty that the person did the acts alleged. Reasonable doubt does not mean any doubt whatsoever. However, it does require a very high degree of proof. See *Beyond A Reasonable Doubt*.

Rebuttal - Refers to the prosecutor's opportunity to make the final remarks to the jury following the defendant's closing argument.

Recross-Examination - An examination of a witness by a cross-examiner subsequent to a redirect examination of the witness.

Redirect Examination - An examination of a witness by the direct examiner subsequent to the cross examination of the witness.

Relevant Evidence - Evidence relevant to the credibility of a witness or evidence having any tendency in reason to prove or disprove any disputed fact that is of consequence to the determination of the action. The judge may exclude evidence if its probative value is substantially outweighed by its prejudicial effect.

Remand - To send back for further deliberation or consideration.

Res Judicata - Latin term "the thing has been decided." This is a policy of finality which means that the decision concludes the litigation for the parties.

Search and Seizure - Practice which allows the police to search an area and seize described evidence. A search warrant is normally needed before the police can perform a search and seizure. The search must be reasonable and be based on the existence of probable cause to search and the limitations of the Fourth Amendment.

Search Warrant - A document prepared by a police officer setting forth probable cause to believe that specific property is connected with a crime and is located at a particular place. If, after judicial review, the judge concurs as to probable cause, the search warrant is signed and ready for the police to execute. See *Probable Cause*.

Self-Incrimination - A person has a privilege to refuse to disclose any matter that may tend to incriminate him. A defendant in a criminal case has a privilege not to be called as a witness and not to testify.

Sequester - To separate from or hold apart. Occasionally, in high-profile cases, the jury is ordered sequestered to prevent the jurors from being subjected to outside information concerning the trial. The jury can either be sequestered only for deliberation or in an extreme case during the entire trial including deliberations.

Spontaneous Declaration - A statement describing an act or event made while the speaker was under the stress of excitement caused by the event. This is an exception to the hearsay rule. See *Hearsay Rule.*

Stare Decisis - Latin term "to stand by a prior decision."

Stay - Judicial order whereby an action is held in abeyance or prevented until some event occurs or the judge "lifts" the order.

Subpoena Duces Tecum - An order by the court compelling the production of physical materials.

Suppress - To prevent or restrain. Typically as regarding potential evidence. See *Exclusionary Rule.*

Suppression of Evidence - To refuse to allow evidence to be introduced in court. Most commonly, evidence is suppressed because it was illegally seized and, therefore, violated a defendant's rights under the Fourth Amendment. See *Fourth Amendment, Exclusionary Rule, Fruit of Poisonous Tree.*

Trier of Fact - See *Jury.*

Verdict - The finding of a fact question by a jury during a jury trial. Also the finding of a fact question by a judge during a trial to a judge without a jury. The verdict is used to form a judgment.

Voir Dire - French term for "to speak the truth." The questioning of a prospective juror before he is impaneled or selected to serve as juror in a case. The questions are asked by a judge or attorney to insure that the juror has no bias or prejudice against any party and to determine whether there are any grounds to challenge a particular juror. The court or an attorney may also "voir dire" a prospective expert witness to establish whether or not they are qualified.

Voluntary Manslaughter - A killing that ordinarily qualifies for murder, except that the defendant acted while in the heat of passion, which passion is prompted by a kind of provocation which would temporarily dethrone the reason of the average reasonable person.

Waiver - An intentional and voluntary giving up of a right.

Warrant - A written order made by a government official which directs that someone do a particular act. See also *Search Warrant.*

Witness - A person who gives evidence during a trial.

Writ - General term for any number of appellate remedies. If trial counsel is dissatisfied with the trial judge decision, he can apply for a writ to obtain quick resolution of the matter in order that the trial may proceed.

Appendix C

Cases on Admissibility of DNA Analysis

In courtrooms across the nation, the twentieth century's rapid technological growth has presented state and federal courts with the difficult task of deciding when to allow juries to hear testimony regarding new and complex forms of scientific evidence. The Simpson trial is no exception. In the Simpson case, there is no known witness to the killing of Nicole Brown Simpson and Ronald Lyle Goldman. Instead, police and prosecutors are relying on sophisticated DNA laboratory tests of blood and hair samples retrieved from the crime scene to prove Simpson's identity.

Because DNA evidence can be used so effectively to build a case against the accused, defense attorneys wisely chose to focus their efforts on preventing the Simpson jury from ever hearing such testimony. History demonstrates that a jury might overlook other exonerating evidence when an expert convincingly assesses the possibility that the blood in question belonged to someone other than the defendant at odds such as one in a million. The method for challenging the validity of scientific evidence for use in the courtroom, however, varies from jurisdiction to jurisdiction.

In the early 1920's a "conservative" test for the admissibility of scientific evidence evolved from the landmark decision of *Frye v. United States*, and this test quickly emerged as the standard for deciding the admissibility of scientific evidence in nearly all American courts. The basic premise of *Frye* was that the reliability of scientific evidence needed to be demonstrated by expert testimony before it could be heard in court. Under this approach, evidence is deemed reliable once it can be shown that the scientific technique has gained "general acceptance" in its particular scientific field.

The *Frye* doctrine emerged from a period in American legal history in which the courts looked with skepticism on the accuracy of scientific evidence. It sought to prevent unreliable evidence from entering into the trial arena. The *Frye* court emphasized the difficult nature of identifying exactly when a scientific discovery should be thought of as an established and reliable form of evidence and not merely an experimental one. Therefore, the "general acceptance" standard advanced by *Frye* ensured that qualified individuals possessing sufficient education and experience in a given scientific field would make the final determination.

Proponents of *Frye* argue that the conservative test is both fair and efficient. Those advocating the rule believe that it reduces the likelihood of a lay jury assigning undue weight to expert testimony based upon questionable scientific theory. Additionally, the rule is thought to promote uniformity in the court system and ensure that numerous experts who endorse the technique will be available to testify at trial.

The major criticism of those dissatisfied with the *Frye* standard is that it unduly obstructs the consideration of reliable evidence during the lengthy period of time necessary for a technique to gain "general acceptance" in the scientific community. In the 1978 case of *United States v. Williams*, Chief Judge Markey of the Second Circuit stated, "A determination of reliability cannot rest solely on a process of counting scientific noses." Courts have experienced frustration with the lack of consensus that sometimes exists in the scientific community and the corresponding slowness by which a majority coalition is built.

In 1993, despite the seventy-year dominance of the *Frye* test, the United States Supreme Court eliminated use of the *Frye* test among the federal courts. This was done in the landmark case of *Daubert v. Merell Dow Pharmaceutical. Daubert* stated that once Congress enacted the Federal Rules of Evidence in 1975, all judicially created law involving the admissibility of scientific evidence was no longer valid in the federal courts.

In contrast to the conservative nature of *Frye*, the Federal Rules of Evidence embody a liberal scheme for introducing evidence at trial. Under the federal rules, evidence may be heard in court as long as it is "relevant" and does not unduly waste time or confuse, mislead, or prejudice the jury. In practical effect, a trial judge may allow evidence to be heard once he determines that a particular scientific technique will be "helpful" to the jury. Therefore, under *Dauber*, a controversial or even a novel scientific technique has a greater possibility of finding its way into the courtroom since a trial judge no longer has to wait for it to gain "general acceptance" in the appropriate scientific community.

In *Daubert*, the Supreme Court stated that although the liberal Federal Rules of Evidence supersede *Frye* in federal courts, safeguards still exist to ensure that unreliable evidence is screened. The trial judge is essentially charged with the task of functioning as a "gatekeeper." First, the judge must evaluate whether a technique is based on a testable scientific theory. The second pertinent question is whether the technique has been subjected to peer review and publication.

Third, the court should consider the potential rate of error of a given scientific method. Finally, the court may actually utilize the *Frye* "general acceptance" test as a method of inquiry.

Critics of *Dauber* assert that the decision will improperly permit "junk science" to enter into the courtroom. The fear is that trial court judges differ greatly in their ability to screen highly technical information and should not be forced into the role of "amateur scientist." The possibility exists that the same scientific evidence might receive different treatment in neighboring courts on the same day.

It is unclear how the many state courts that have adopted *Frye's* "general acceptance" test over the years will treat the new *Daubert* decision. In 1976, California adopted the *Frye* test in the case of *People v. Kelly.* The California Supreme Court recently considered arguments that it should adopt the *Daubert* decision and strike down the state's *Kelly-Frye* standard. The California court justifiably refused to strike down *Kelly-Frye*, however, since the *Daubert* decision was based on an interpretation of the Federal Rules of Evidence and not the United States Constitution. Therefore, like California, other state courts may freely choose to accept or reject its reasoning. Since the *Daubert* decision was handed down, only five of seventeen state courts considering the issue have decided to abandon *Frye* in favor of the new federal test.

The standard used to evaluate scientific evidence in California will have a dramatic impact on the Simpson murder trial since the heart of the prosecution's case centers around sophisticated DNA evidence. Since most jurisdictions applying even the conservative *Frye* test allow DNA evidence to be admitted at trial, California's recent ruling may not be a serious barrier to the prosecution's case.

DNA fingerprinting involves the identification of an individual's unique genetic characteristics. The method is based on the notion that, with the exception of identical twins, no two human beings possess the same genetic code. In a three-step inquiry, investigators first analyze the genetic characteristics of a defendant's DNA code and the evidence found at a crime scene. Next, the genetic information is compared. Finally, experts calculate the statistical probability of the DNA evidence sample matching someone in society other than the accused.

It is the final step of attaching a statistical probability to DNA results that has drawn criticism in California and other jurisdictions. In 1991, an article in *Science* magazine written by two Harvard geneticists argued that statistical formulas used by the major DNA laboratories might be grossly inaccurate. Based on that 1991 publication, California's first appellate district found that the method used for calculating DNA statistical probabilities was not generally accepted in the community of population geneticists for the purposes of *Kelly-Frye*.

The 1991 article effectively called into question broad generalizations made by the laboratories regarding the genetic characteristics of certain racial groups. Some population geneticists believed that by dividing racial groups only into the broad categories of white, black, and Hispanic, for example, statistical error would be made by overlooking unique sub-populations within each of the categories.

The concern, however, has been largely abated due to a more conservative method of calculation presented in 1992 by the prestigious National Research Council. As a result, even though the California Supreme Court refused to strike down *Frye*, current statistical formulas for calculating DNA probabilities have already achieved "general acceptance" under the conservative approach. Thus, the Simpson defense team will have a difficult time keeping the prosecution's DNA evidence from the jury.

What remains for the defense and prosecution to argue to the jury are the precise odds that should be attached to any finding. That remains an area of DNA testing which is wide open for differences of agreement. You can be sure that those differences of agreement will be exploited to the maximum by both sides in the case. The greater the odds, the better for the prosecution. (There is only one chance in tens of millions that the blood in question could have been anyone's other than Simpson's.) The lesser the odds, the better for the defense. (The chance that it was O.J.'s blood is only something like one in 250,000.)

Of those kinds of differences great trials are made!

Appendix D

Suppression Motion

Suppression Motion of the Blood on the Driveway
and the Bloody Glove

At the preliminary examination, the defense attempted to suppress the evidence found at the Simpson estate by bringing a suppression hearing under California Penal Code §1538.5. The defense in their written motion described the police entry of the estate as follows:

On Monday, June 13, 1994, at approximately 5:00 a.m., four detectives of the Los Angeles Police Department came to the residence of the defendant at 360 North Rockingham Avenue, West Los Angeles, California to notify him of his former wife's death. The residence is fully enclosed by walls and fences, and is entered through two electronically controlled gates. After ringing a button at the intercom system adjacent to one of the gates and, receiving no response, they contacted the private security company which protects the premises. They were given the telephone number of the residence, called, and reached an answering machine with recorded instructions from the defendant to leave messages. Rather than leave a message, one of the detectives climbed over the five-foot wall protecting the defendant's residence, opened the gate, and admitted the remaining detectives. They proceeded to the front door and attempted to rouse someone. They then assumed control of the premises, entered the pool area in the rear of the premises, roused the defendant's daughter and another guest in separate quarters adjacent to the pool, searched the quarters of the guest, and engaged in general inspection of the premises, including a gated narrow passageway behind the guest quarters. They also engaged in an intense inspection of the driveway pavement behind the entry gates. At approximately 7:30 a.m., they informed the defendant's daughter she would have to leave her home so they could search the premises. The other guest was detained and removed from the premises. Based on their observations in the course of these warrantless observations and searches, they obtained a search warrant at 10:45 a.m., nearly six hours after they had seized the premises, and three hours after they evicted the lawful occupants. In addition to the unlawfully obtained observations within the premises, the affidavit for the search warrant misrepresented the nature of the defendant's absence by stating the defendant "had left on an unexpected flight to Chicago during the early morning hours of June 13, 1994." when they were fully aware that the defendant was on a planned business trip, they had telephonically spoken to him in a call arranged by his daughter, and that he was fully cooperative and indicated his intention to immediately return to Los Angeles on the next available flight.

After the issuance of the search warrant, which only commanded them to search the residence at "360 Rockingham Avenue, West Los Angeles, California," they proceeded to complete general search of both the residence and a Ford Bronco automobile parked in front of the residence, seizing numerous items that were not described in the search warrant.

Even though the defense's view of the events of that morning is crafted in a light most favorable to their position, this scenario presented serious Fourth Amendment problems for the prosecution.

The Fourth Amendment to the United States Constitution prohibits unreasonable searches and seizures. Generally speaking, searches of an individual's property should be conducted with a search warrant and, as such, are presumed reasonable. A search warrant interposes a neutral judge into the picture, and that judge makes his determination as to whether it is reasonable for the police to search.

There are, of course, exceptions to the search warrant requirement. Perhaps the most notable is the "exigency exception." Under exigent or emergency circumstances, such as the belief that there is a threat to human life, the police may enter someone's residence, and any evidence that comes to light may properly be seized. However, once the exigency has ended, the search warrant requirement reemerges. If the police persist in their search after the point at which the exigency no longer exists, then all evidence gathered from that point forward would be the product of an unreasonable search and, therefore, inadmissible at trial.

Against this background, Municipal Court Judge Kathleen Kennedy-Powell heard the defense's motion to exclude from evidence blood drops on the driveway and a bloody glove on a pathway inside the Simpson compound. The entry by the police was obviously warrantless, and, therefore, the prosecution had to argue exigent circumstances. As alleged by the police, the special exigent circumstances in this case involved the possibility of an assassin on the premises (if he killed Nicole, he might also be after Simpson), or, perhaps, other injured persons at the Simpson compound in the wake of finding the bodies of Nicole Simpson and Ron Goldman.

The defense maintained that even if the original police entry was justified by exigent circumstances, the search that located the blood and the glove was conducted after the police had determined that there was no longer an exigency. If that were the case, the blood and the glove were found unlawfully and should be excluded from trial.

Assuming the legitimate exigent nature of the original entry, the question for Judge Kennedy-Powell was whether the police exceeded their power under the exigency exception and continued to search once they were convinced no exigency existed. After listening to days of testimony, Judge Kennedy-Powell found that the police were still properly investigating the emergency and, therefore, still properly on the premises during the discovery of both items. The result of the judge's controversial ruling is that the evidence was not excluded and is usable by the prosecution at trial.

Once Judge Kennedy-Powell made her ruling, the matter could not be reopened unless new evidence that was not available at the time of the first hearing somehow came to light.

Not surprisingly, defense attorney, Gerald Uelmen, sought to bring out new evidence concerning that police conduct during the early morning hours of June 13. The defense sought to show that the police had not done everything they claimed to have done before they entered the compound. Judge Ito was not persuaded by the defense's claim and would not allow the defense to reopen the matter, or, in effect, to take a second bite at the apple.